A History of
The Hampshire &
Isle of Wight Constabulary
1839-1966

Original County Headquarters situated next door to the Winchester County Gaol on West Hill, built in 1847.

A History of
The Hampshire &
Isle of Wight Constabulary
1839-1966

Compiled by Ian A. Watt

Phillimore

2006

Published by
PHILLIMORE & CO. LTD
Shopwyke Manor Barn, Chichester, West Sussex, England
www.phillimore.co.uk

First edition published by
Hampshire and the Isle of Wight Constabulary, 1967

© Hampshire Constabulary History Society, 2006

ISBN 1-86077-383-4
ISBN 13 978-1-86077-383-9

Printed and bound in Great Britain by
THE CROMWELL PRESS LTD
Trowbridge, Wiltshire

Contents

List of Illustrations

The photograph on the back cover of the dust jacket shows P.C. 415 W.A. Playdon at Mr Hedges' farm, Chandler's Ford, in 1947 (not P.C. Hellard).

List of Subscribers, 2006

Harry John Ancill
Alan G.R. Barnard
David G. Basson QPM
D. Borrett
Richard A. Boryer
P.C. 221 David G. Brown 1966-1996
Bob Cameron
Colin Campbell
A. Clack
Assistant Chief Constable Simon Cole
Cllr. Adrian Collett, Hampshire Police
  Authority
The Curtis Museum, Alton
Robert Dawson
Brian Dixon
Dr Roger Donaldson
Steve Dumper
Pete Forster
John Griffith
Michael Haunschild, Hannover,
  Germany
John K. Head
Inspector Glynis Hopgood
Inspector Peter Hughes
J.D.G. Isherwood
Maurice Jackson
P.C. 3075 Del Jones, New Milton
Captain Mark Jones
Peggy Jones
J. Philip Judson
Paul Robert Kernaghan CBE QPM
Norman G. Langdon
Martin Laux

John R. Lee
Jack Lucas
Patricia McCardle
Rodney I.J. McCarthy
John Moore
Becky Morgan
Sylvia Morgan
R.M. Morris
Joanne Nelson
S.O. 9943 Richard Owen (Havant)
Stewart Packham SC.
Bob Parkhouse
Ron Payne
Colin Peake
Bill Playdon
Jim Reed
Matt Richards VOSA
DC 1708 Setford
Kelvin V. Shipp
Trevor Sloan Retired P.C. RUC
Phil Smith
Peter Southey
J.E.H. Spaul
Martin Stallion
Paul Stickler
P.C. 2976 Simon Stocker
Peter Stoddard
William Robert Thomas 1969-1998
Darryl F. White
Clifford Williams BA MPhil. PhD
Eric B. Woodsford Chief Inspector
  (RTD)
Lt Col M.G.A. Young

Introductory Note

This history of the Hampshire and Isle of Wight Constabulary could not have been written without the abundance of detailed personal reminiscence contributed by former officers of the force and members of their families. Inevitably much has had to be omitted, but one cannot read through the wealth of anecdotes and memoirs without being deeply moved by the quiet dignity and good humour of the individuals concerned, and by their just pride in their profession. Fortunate indeed is the service which has been able to imbue such fine individuals with so strong and persistent a loyalty. The author is very grateful to them.

The author similarly wishes to thank all those officers now serving for the mass of information which they furnished concerning every branch and activity of the force. An especial tribute is due to Inspector J. Head for all his preparatory work at the inception of this book, and for his continual, cheerful and indispensable assistance. Finally, the author is most grateful to Mr A.J. Broomfield for his kindness, his forbearance, and his constant help.

The publication of this edition has been possible through the work of members of the Hampshire Constabulary History Society, and in particular, Paul Stickler, Clifford Williams and Colin Peake.

Apart from some formatting and styling, the text in this edition remains unchanged from the original 1967 version.

Preface

The roots of English police are local. Unlike many of the great continental states, there has never been in England anything like a national police force. Even today, suggestions for such a body provoke deep and far-ranging controversy. Broad sections of the English people still think essentially in terms of their own locality, of their borough or county. This attitude is reflected in the firm attachment on the part of many to the historic traditions of their own small part of the world. Certainly Hampshire and the Isle of Wight command the pride of their inhabitants. The Hampshire and Isle of Wight Constabulary fully deserve to share in this pride. It is one of the oldest county forces in the country, one of the most successful, and one of the fastest growing. With the shift and development of population, Hampshire is destined to become increasingly popular, and increasingly prosperous. This will bring at once more problems and opportunity for the police. As our society becomes even more dependent on technology and ever more subtly varied, so does it become more complex, more delicate, and more vulnerable; and so does the function of the police become more difficult, more fascinating, more comprehensive, and more vital.

The prime cause of the creation of the various British police forces, metropolitan, borough, and county, in the course of the 19th century, is to be found in the consequences of the Industrial Revolution. That great process meant, among all its other manifold consequences, the growth of towns, the development of new modes of transport and communication, and the inevitable ever-widening scope of government, both central and local. Society was becoming more complex, unprecedented problems were revealing themselves, and new and more efficient means of law enforcement became essential. For the most part Hampshire last century was not an industrial area; but no more than the rest of England could Hampshire escape the tide of change. And the Hampshire force, formed in 1839, is, with that of Essex, the oldest county constabulary in the country.

Before this, police arrangements in Hampshire were characteristically loose and rural. They were based on the parish. The only police officers were parish constables, of whom there were one or more per parish. In emergencies, justices might swear in extra constables. But not until 1831 did an Act lay down the procedure to be followed, and regularise the practice. In the earlier part of the century the duties of the justices were wide, the problems of law enforcement grave, and punishments harsh. At Easter 1800, one John Green, who had been convicted of a felony, was sentenced to be imprisoned in the Bridewell, at Winchester, for 12 weeks, and on the last day of that time to be taken to Basingstoke and 'there publickly whipped for the space of 100 yards, and then discharged'. In the previous year one Martha Grover was convicted of obtaining goods under false pretences, and transported for seven years. To deal with public disorder on a larger scale, recourse was inevitably had to the military. In September 1800 the justices placed on record their thanks to 'the officers, gentlemen, and soldiers' of the Flintshire Militia, the Royal Cornish Minors and Fawley Light Dragoons, and the Bramdean Yeomanry Cavalry, 'for their prompt and cheerful assistance to the civil power' on the occasion of an unlawful and tumultuous assembly at Alresford. That the 'hundred' constable was regarded as little more than the general factotum of the justices is shown by the speed with which individuals were replaced if found unsatisfactory. Within a month of George Ellis of Froyle being appointed Constable of the Hundred of Alton 'in the Room of William Ross Esquire', he was replaced by Henry Digweed of Chawton. The problem of payment for police work was vexing to all concerned, then as now, though certainly at that time there was no notion of any regular remuneration. To offset the expenses of conveying 'rogues and vagabonds' to gaol on foot, petty constables and tythingmen were in 1818 allowed 2s. a day: but the justices were empowered to check on their accounts. In 1820 those who acted as constables at two fairs in that year did better: they were given the princely sum of 5s. a day. While in 1822 an order went out that 'the Treasurer do pay unto William Lavington, William Thomas, William Hale, James Middleton, David Patterson, and Richard Barham, the sum of 15s. each for attending as special constables at Magdalen Hill Fair'. It is clear that fairs then as now attracted all sorts of undesirables, and lent themselves to the easy commission of petty larceny, and to disorderly incidents. Throughout the 1820s discontent simmered and flared throughout the country. The socially disruptive effects of the Industrial Revolution were becoming steadily more apparent. Thousands of unemployed and despairing men wandered over the face of the land. Among the well-to-do classes there were very real fears of revolution. The red horizon of the French Revolution and of Napoleonic tyranny was still plainly in view. Thus the justices were much concerned with the danger to life and property posed by the ominous movements of 'rogues, vagabonds, and other wandering idle and disorderly persons'. Most individual crime was still concerned with agricultural and rural matters – poaching and the like. But the authorities were frightened of more formidable upheavals and thus the habitual harshness of judgments was reinforced by fear. Moreover, difficulty was experienced by the authorities in gaining trustworthy instruments. In 1828 one of the turnkeys in the County Bridewell was guilty of fraud and it was ordered that 'no part of the profits arising from the prisoners' labour be paid to the officers of the said prison until the county shall have been indemnified for the loss it has sustained'.

It was against this background of growing disorder, social change, and brooding uncertainty, that the modern English police emerged.

BOOK 1
1839-1865

After 1829, by virtue of the Metropolitan Police Act, the whole of London, apart from the city, was brought under one authority. The Municipal Corporations Act of 1835 *required* each of 178 boroughs to appoint a Watch Committee, which in turn would appoint a sufficient number of constables, who would have power in the borough concerned and in the surrounding area. The cost was to be entirely on the rates and each corporation had complete control. So successful were these new police forces that the deep-rooted fears of the very notion of 'police' as the evil harbinger of inevitable tyranny began rapidly to fade. What had proved an advantageous system for the boroughs could surely now be adapted to the equivalent needs of the counties. In 1836, a Royal Commission of three, including the great reformer Edwin Chadwick, sat to consider the best means of establishing a rural constabulary. Its various suggestions met with misunderstanding and opposition. Finally, the County Police Act of 1839 enabled justices, if they so wished, to maintain a paid police force either for the whole county or any part of it. The number of policemen in any such county force was not to exceed one for every thousand inhabitants and the cost was to be borne by the general county rates. It was as a result of this permissive Act that the Hampshire Constabulary was formed in December 1839. At a meeting held at the Grand Jury Chamber in Winchester it was resolved that the county should adopt the provisions of the Act and that the constabulary force should consist of:

1 chief constable at a salary of £300 a year with an allowance for the purchase and forage of two horses of £100.

2 superintendents. One for the Isle of Wight and one for Headquarters at Winchester at £120 a year each.

12 superintendents for the remaining divisions at £75 a year each. 14 constables first class at 21s. per week each.

28 constables second class at 19s. per week each.

49 constables third class at 18s. per week each.

The above rates of pay may well seem not inadequate, taking into consideration the circumstances and prices of the day. Station houses were to be provided as required, a horse was to be available for each superintendent and constables were to be clothed in conformity with Her Majesty's regulations. However, it was also gloomily recorded that all pay was to be subject to such deductions 'as may be thought proper to defray the expense of lodgings, medical advice, etc.'.

At the very end of the year, the method of appointment of the chief constable by the justices was also determined. The names of all candidates were to be put up at once and 'if neither of them should have a majority of the whole number of justices present', then 'the name of such candidate as shall have the smallest number of votes shall be withdrawn until such time as one of the candidates should have a majority of the whole number Present'. As a result of this procedure, Captain George Robbins of Hythe was appointed chief constable of the embryo force. Captain Robbins was a regular army officer who had had a very creditable military career and he set to work vigorously to form the new constabulary. The first members were sworn in in January 1840. John Callingham, Robert Messenger, Samuel Whitehouse and John Wigmore were the first four men of the Hants Constabulary. They were strangely assorted in background, character, and destiny. Callingham had served in both the Royal Navy and the Metropolitan Police, Messenger had been a shoemaker, Whitehouse a soldier, and Wigmore a labourer. Callingham served until April 1862, when he was discharged with a pension of £69 and a good character. Messenger died in Andover in 1841, just 18 months later. Whitehouse rose rapidly to reach the rank of superintendent in 1842, but only the following year was allowed to resign for neglect of duty. Wigmore oscillated rapidly between the ranks of constable second and first class and even reached the dizzy height of sergeant. Indeed, this impression of uncertainty, of restlessness, of the authorities struggling desperately to make an efficient force out of not altogether satisfactory material, is characteristic of those early days of the force. Many constables apparently soon found the discipline irksome or the material rewards insufficient and resigned at their own request. Some were disobedient and insolent to their superiors, some were neglectful of duty and all too many made a habit of being drunk and incapable. Between 1840 and 1860 General Orders record constantly the disgraceful drunkenness of police officers. On 20 May 1840, the chief constable announced that he wished it 'to be fully understood by the men belonging to the force that drunkenness will never be overlooked but any case coming to his knowledge of a constable being in that state either on duty or off duty will be invariably followed by dismissal and forfeiture of all pay then due to him added to any punishment the magistrates may think fit to order'. On another occasion that year the superintendents were directed to be very particular in looking after the men on pay days immediately after they had received their money; and any of whom they had the slightest suspicion were to be ordered to be at certain places at fixed hours in order that their superintendents might see if they were perfectly regular and sober. On 24 September 1859, Third-Class Constable H. Joint was dismissed the service with one week's pay for absenting himself from his beat in Andover and being found concealed in a cupboard in a public house, while in the next year Third-

Class Constable W. Tegarty had perhaps cause to reflect sadly on the old saw about giving a dog a bad name. He was called on to resign because 'the chief constable feels certain from the reports against him that it is impossible for Christmas Day and pay day to pass without his disgracing himself'.

Other faults besides drunkenness were not lacking. Constables were enjoined, whilst on duty at fairs or any places of public amusement, to keep continually on the alert and not to cluster together, laughing and joking among themselves. They were reminded sternly that they were not to smoke on duty. They had to keep in mind that on being moved from one station to another, or being employed on duty at fairs or on any other special service, they had on no account to get into debt to any person. Miscreants would be fined double the debt and be under stoppages till debt and fine were paid. Any constable who left or was dismissed from the force while still owing money, was not to receive any testimonial of character until he should have cleared the debt. Superintendents of police were reminded that they must discourage any attempt at intimacy with them on the part of lower ranks and must exact salutes from their men. Too much familiarity was apt to exist between the superintendents and those placed under their command and without the exaction of proper respect both from the constables and 'from the lower orders in whose company they may be thrown', they would lessen themselves both in the estimation of their men and of the public generally. Police officers were forbidden to act as agents (in briefing counsel) for attorneys who did not themselves attend court and warned of the odium which such a practice brought upon the service. Only repeated instructions on this point seem to have had any effect. Meantime, throughout these early years, many men continued to leave the force for a variety of reasons, some of them very curious. Edward Heath joined on 14 March 1840, and the following month was allowed to resign 'on account of his not liking the division in which he was stationed". David Farmer likewise had a short and inglorious police career. He joined in April 1840 and was dismissed in May, with pay forfeited, for not assisting a colleague in the execution of his duty. With some others, he ran away when his comrade was assaulted by a mob outside a public house. Another man, Charles Rowden, experienced a police career that was brief indeed. Appointed on 2 May 1840, he resigned one week later because he feared the duty would injure his health and constitution. Michael Dore, who joined about the same time, lasted some months longer, but in 1841 was allowed to resign 'being nearsighted and hard of hearing'. Evidently his constitution had already been impaired! A more sombre fate was that of Joel Bath, who in 1845 committed suicide by throwing himself under a train on the South Western Railway. The most frequent cause of dismissal, however, was drunkenness of every degree and variety.

Nevertheless, it would be wrong to conclude that the authorities issued none but negative and admonitory orders and that their task was only a despairing struggle to keep in the service the few good men, while wearily getting rid of the unsatisfactory majority. From the foundation of the force there was a steady stream of positive instructions, designed to mould the Hants Constabulary into an effective body. The first General Orders issued were much concerned with basic matters of duty, organisation, and pay. The newly-appointed superintendents were adjured to report themselves to the magistrates in their divisions on arrival at their destinations and to attend punctually at Petty Sessions thereafter, wearing their dress coats. No superintendent was to be allowed to purchase the slightest article for the use of the force without written permission from the chief constable. Nor were superintendents ever to allow their horses to be ridden by a constable – even without a saddle – without making a special report of the circumstances under which it was allowed. All prisoners were to be brought into headquarters by the superintendents themselves and care was to be taken that in the cart the prisoners were properly secured. Furthermore, officers of all ranks were forbidden to ride or drive faster than seven miles per hour, without giving a substantial reason! Whenever a superintendent was absent with his horse for some length of time, a conveyance was to be hired to convey any prisoner to Winchester if the distance was too great to be walked and a written report made of the circumstances. Arrangements were made too for the rapid circulation of information relating to crime. In this and other connections the chief constable drew the attention of all officers to the necessity of improving themselves as much as possible in their writing and composition, 'as in the event of any vacancy occurring it will invariably be filled by the most deserving and best qualified man in the force'. Other qualifications for high rank entailed, it was urged, unremitting exertion in patrolling to remote villages and farmhouses, in order to ascertain that subordinates were fully active and attentive in the execution of their duty.

Especial emphasis was put on the need for smartness of appearance. Uniform coats were to be kept buttoned, clean white gloves of regulation patterns were invariably to be worn on duty and above all no shirt collars were to be allowed to appear. From time to time individuals were singled out for censure. One man was denounced for 'lounging along like any old cadger with his greatcoat thrown over his shoulders like a blanket or a woman's shawl, as if drill and discipline, greatcoat straps and the use of them, orders and instructions regarding dress and general appearance were unknown in Hampshire'. While another constable was described as carrying his cape under his arm like an umbrella, in place of having it slung to his waist belt in proper style. Superintendents were repeatedly urged to inspect their men's clothing more carefully, and to ensure that, apart altogether from uniform, each constable was possessed of a respectable suit of plain clothes. To an uninvolved eye, much of the concern constantly expressed in General Orders with details of uniform might seem at first glance pettifogging and even comic. To remind members of the force that their greatcoats were to be carried folded at all parades, fairs, races and on the road to headquarters unless the weather should be wet, when the coats were to be worn, might well appear to be a mere glimpse of the blindingly obvious, so pedantic as to be risible. Such a view would be wrong. For it is on such minor details of dress and uniformity that the discipline and efficiency of any service largely depend. The early chief constables of Hampshire were not hide-bound Victorian pedants. They were engaged in making and perfecting a disciplined body of law-enforcement officers.

Captain Robbins resigned in 1842 and was succeeded in 1843 by another army man, Captain William Charles Harris. Captain Harris had served in the 68th Regiment of Light Infantry, and during his service had for four years commanded a detachment employed in aid of the police in Ireland. Apart from his time as Chief Constable of Hampshire, Captain Harris is notable in the general history of the police service because of the evidence he gave before the Select Committee of the House of Commons on Police in 1853. He resigned in 1856, with the intention of taking up an appointment as Assistant Commissioner of the Metropolitan Police and in leaving thanked the magistrates of the county for their 'uniform kindness and consideration'. He also paid tribute to the members of the force he had had the honour to command. As he said, 'Their duties are arduous and demand qualities of a high order and they have been performed entirely to my satisfaction.' At a later meeting of the Quarter Sessions a vote of thanks to Captain Harris was passed and particular mention was made of his work in improving the organisation of the force, reducing crime and successfully building upon the foundations created by Captain Robbins out of the early years of chaos. The third chief constable was Captain John Henry Forrest, who was to hold office from 1856 until 1891. He had before this commanded the Nottingham Police and came to Hampshire with the reputation of a martinet. Certainly his influence on the Hampshire Constabulary was to be profound.

Throughout these early years the organisation of the force grew and became more elaborate. A uniform system of beat working was introduced in 1844, and thereafter amendments and improvements were made as circumstances dictated. On night patrol emphasis was given to the need for surveying the sides of roads, for speaking in low tones, and for stopping frequently to listen and, presumably, to learn. The most common offences dealt with were larceny, damage to property and desertion from the armed forces. In 1855 the value of property stolen was £1,172, of which £572 was recovered. Two thousand one hundred and thirty-two arrests were made and, of those convicted, three were sentenced to transportation for 14 years, three were transported for life and one was sentenced to death for murder. However, the straightforward fight against crime was far from being the only preoccupation of the police. In 1856 the superintendents of Hampshire Constabulary were appointed Inspectors of Hawkers Licences and the chief constable pointed out that by 'an active performance of these duties much benefit will arise to the public revenue of the county' in that when penalties were inflicted on unlicensed hawkers one moiety would be paid 'to the

Constabulary Superannuation Fund, thus increasing the fund for the pensioning of old and deserving constables and members of the force who may be disabled in the service of the county'. Another activity was that of attempting to obtain volunteers for the Hampshire regiments of militia to try to bring them up to strength. For every volunteer who was approved 5s. was to be paid to the police constable who brought him forward. Bills publicising service with the militia were circulated and it is significant that the chief constable recommended that some should be affixed to the blacksmiths' shops. Rural life was still largely centred on horse transport and advertisements at the blacksmiths were likely to be as effective as those at service stations today.

In 1846 the force was increased from its original strength of 106 to 165, which comprised fifteen superintendents, one inspector, thirteen sergeants, and 136 constables of various grades. Changes in pay also took place and remuneration now ranged from £95 per annum for the senior superintendents to 15s. per week for the junior constables. From 1845 the constables were paid monthly and ten years later were granted three days' leave of absence in the course of the year without stoppage of pay. In 1855 it was determined that the force should be further augmented to reach a total of 235 of all ranks. From 1851 there had been a scale of stoppages from the pay of the various ranks in the force in order to form a Superannuation Fund. In 1853 the annual salary of superintendents crept up again by £10, but the pay of constables remained at 21s., 19s., and 17s. per week, according to the class of the man concerned. In 1862 a further 17 constables were authorised, but not without a good deal of discussion as to whether such increase was really necessary and whether or not a better return on existing numbers might not be obtained by a more judicious disposition of police about the county. More than one member of the governing body felt that his own quiet area was inclined to be over-policed. Reasons adduced for this enlargement included the increase of the county population by 76,000 and in particular the influx of persons attendant upon the formation and enlargement of camps and garrisons, which sort of people specially required the control of an effective police: also, increased vigilance was necessitated by the process whereby such rural districts as lay near Bournemouth were gradually absorbed into the town. It was pointed out that in the Isle of Wight the proportion of undetected crime had risen to no less than 40 per cent of the county total. Even with the proposed increase in the force, the Hampshire Constabulary would still be weaker in proportion to the population than had earlier seemed desirable. Each police officer would still have to be responsible for 1,200 or 1,300 inhabitants of the county.

The Hampshire Constabulary was growing in numbers and also in the area it was concerned with. In 1846 Andover Borough joined the county and in 1852 Lymington followed suit. In 1865 Romsey's police were to be incorporated into the county force, to the mutual satisfaction of both parties. The historic city of

Winchester, the ancient capital of Saxon England, however, remained aloof. The citizens of Winchester, indeed, may be justly proud of the fact that an organised police force was established in Winchester before the Hampshire Constabulary itself came into existence. For on 24 May 1832, only three years after the Metropolitan Police had been formed, a general meeting of the inhabitants of Winchester was held at the Guildhall for the purpose of forming an efficient police establishment to suppress, in the first place, vagrancy in the city. A committee was formed, charged with the task of obtaining subscriptions from the various parishes of the city to defray the expenses involved. At a meeting of this committee on 28 July 1832, it was decided to appoint one Robert Buchanan as inspector of the new force at a weekly salary of £1. Buchanan had been recommended by the Commissioners of the Metropolitan Police as competent. At the same time seven constables were appointed, namely James Finch, Thomas Ellery, William Shedman, William Masters, William Scorey, Thomas Leach and John Browning. Winchester evidently had no greater success with their choice of police officers than had Hampshire. Drunkenness was the principal cause of the rapid turnover of constables. Little more than a year after the little force had been formed only three of the original eight members remained in office, the rest having resigned or been dismissed. Mr Buchanan himself resigned in 1833 and was replaced by William Shepherd, late of the Metropolitan Police, who now took over with the rank of superintendent. In those early days crime was rife, punishments were as harsh as elsewhere and the unsettled conditions of the Winchester force reflected the unsettled nature of society everywhere.

After the passing of the Municipal Corporations Act in 1835, Winchester appointed a Watch Committee. One of the first acts of this body was to invite tenders for the supply of uniform. This was probably the first time that uniform was supplied to the city force – before this, presumably, the constables had performed their duty in civilian clothing and had been marked off from their fellow citizens only by some token or badge of office. The Watch Committee also drew up regulations to govern the conduct and working of their tiny force, from which it is clear that all except one officer performed night duty from 9 p.m. until 6 a.m., the day duty being carried out by the remaining officer and the beadle. In February 1836 the Committee asserted its sense of local pride by directing that – 'the police staffs be painted with a royal crown surmounted by the city arms with the letters W.R. and W.P., and that the procession staffs be repaired all of which to be done at a cost of 5s.'

The establishment of a permanent police headquarters in Winchester was the early concern of the Watch Committee. In December 1836 directions were given to the city surveyor to prepare plans and estimates for the conversion of the city Bridewell into a police station and engine house (i.e. fire station). Convicted prisoners were thereafter to be detained in the county gaol. This underlines the fact that, naturally, close co-operation existed between Winchester and Hampshire from the start. The city was determined to maintain its independence in police matters but was certainly not bent on a policy of isolation. Thus the old Bridewell, dating from 1800, was transformed into a police station and engine house at a cost, respectively, of £51 8s. and £58 10s. Here Winchester Police Headquarters remained until 1873, when the new Guildhall, incorporating a police station, was constructed. The fact that the police station and fire station were kept together draws attention to the responsibility of the police at that time of protecting the public and its property from fire as well as from crime. In 1838 the Watch Committee recommended to the council that, in order to render the fire engine which had been procured fully beneficial to both police and public, an engineer 'being a mechanic conversant with machinery' be appointed to take care of engine and hose, to grease and air dry the same when exercised. Two shillings per annum were to be allowed to the engineer for the purpose of greasing, oiling and keeping the engine in repair. It was also suggested that the names of householders with their places of residence be entered at 'Station House', so that once a quarter they might turn out and exercise the machine and attend all fires, each householder being allowed 2s. 6d. It was the responsibility of the police, apparently, to call out the voluntary firemen. Shortly after this a separate Director of the Fire Brigade, a Mr Arrowsmith, was appointed to superintend the two dozen volunteer firemen. Nevertheless, the police were not completely divested of their responsibility and authority in connection with fires; for in 1841 the council recommended that the bell at the police station be sold and another provided with a louder sound. It is reasonable to suppose that the function of this bell was to act as a fire alarm, the fire station being next door. In 1849 the superintendent of police was supplied with a key to enable him to ring the bell at the Guildhall in case of fire.

In 1840, the Winchester force had the opportunity to show the newly-formed Hampshire Constabulary just what it could do. The county magistrates sought the assistance of some of the city force to apprehend several railway workers at Warren Farm and with this help the miscreants were duly secured and brought to the borough Station House. In May of that year, in consequence of the strength of the force being depleted by two, day duty was suspended. The same month the police officers applied to the Watch Committee for 'an increase in salary on account of the dearness of bread and provisions'. In the upshot it was recommended that a superintendent be paid 2s. more per week, and other officers who had served two years or more, 1s. a week. In February 1843 a Mr Courtney, who had earlier supplied uniforms to the force, was again commissioned to supply a hat, a frock-coat, two pairs of trousers and two pairs of boots to the superintendent, for a total price of £7 12s. 6d. The Watch Committee that year was in generous mood. It allowed to the superintendent an additional body-coat in consideration of his long services but cautiously announced that such allowance is not to be considered a precedent. Perhaps the members of the committee had reason later to consider that they had done well to keep their enthusiasm within bounds, for on inspection of the police station in September it was found that the station was in an unsatisfactory state as to cleanliness and that pig styes had been erected in the rear of the building causing an accumulation of soil. Perhaps in those hungry forties the pig styes had been erected by the police in an effort to overcome the high cost of living and the inadequacy of their salaries.

The duties attaching to the ancient office of the beadle were combined with those of a police officer in November 1847, when the incumbent was sworn in as a constable at the instigation of the mayor and magistrates. Until then, it must be remembered, the beadle with one constable had been the sole law enforcement officers available during the daytime. The beadle was one George Dumper and after being appointed constable he often performed duty as temporary sergeant. He died in 1853 and the committee thereupon resolved that no new beadle should be appointed to replace him and that an extra constable be appointed. The name of Dumper, however, was to be heard of again in the police history of Winchester.

In 1850, Sergeant Masters, one of the original seven constables, retired on account of ill-health occasioned to some extent at least by injuries he had received on duty. In the absence of an effective pension scheme he petitioned the committee, which recommended the award of a gratuity of £7 for his service during the preceding 18 years. This was perhaps not quite such a miserly sum as might first appear, being the equivalent then of two months' pay, but even so it underlines the insecurity of employment in the police service in those early days. Officers were appointed and dismissed with monotonous regularity and often were appointed only for a limited period. In November 1853 John Gale and James Stratton were appointed as policemen during the winter months, on the express understanding that at the expiration of that time the more efficient would be elected as a permanent policeman; and if in the meantime either should wish to leave the force before the expiry of his temporary appointment, one month's notice would be required of him. By this time, too, a change of command had taken place. Superintendent Sheppard resigned in July 1851 and was replaced by Mr Henry Hubbersly, who had been highly recommended by Mr Mayne, one of the commissioners of Metropolitan Police, and had in addition produced most satisfactory testimonials as to ability and character.

Winchester's force was to remain a separate entity until 1942, but suggestions of amalgamation with the county were put forward on several occasions earlier in the 19th century. In 1854 a bill was laid before the House of Commons by Lord Palmerston with the intention of consolidating borough and county forces, reducing the number of separate and independent constabularies, and encouraging greater efficiency in the whole police service. This bill, which on its enactment was to become the County and Borough Police Act of 1856, aroused strident opposition from many local authorities. It was held to be inimical to the principle of municipal self-government and in some quarters was seen as a sinister step in the direction of the worst type of continental despotism. The Mayor and Corporation of Winchester were stoutly opposed to any threat of amalgamation with the county and sent off a petition of protest to the House of Commons. This proclaimed

> That your petitioners have seen with the greatest regret a bill brought into your honourable house, entitled a bill to render more effectual the police in counties and boroughs in England and Wales. That the bill in question as affecting cities and boroughs is based on evidence wholly of an *ex parte* character given before a Select Committee of your honourable house, by interested chief constables of counties, county magistrates, or persons favourable to their particular views on the question on which enquiry none of the cities or boroughs so largely affected by such evidence were heard.
>
> That your petitioners regard the bill in question as an unconstitutional interference with the privileges of boroughs and subversive of the independence and right of self-government secured to them by the Municipal Corporations Reform Act, as it will practically place the entire control of the whole police of the kingdom in the hands of Her Majesty's Home Secretary.
>
> Your Petitioners therefore humbly pray that your honourable house will refuse to sanction any measure which shall interfere with the jurisdiction of municipal corporations in reference to the appointment, management and control of their police as now established by law.
>
> And your petitioners as in duty bound will ever pray, etc.
>
> Given under the common seal of the said city this fourteenth day June, one thousand eight hundred and fifty-four.
>
> Chas. R. Rogers, Mayor.

The fact that Captain Harris, the Chief Constable of Hampshire, had been a witness before the Select Committee of the House in June 1853, which had culminated in the presentation of the bill in question, must have been especially annoying to the petitioners. No doubt the reference in the petition to interested chief constables of counties was a thrust aimed at Captain Harris. In any case the efforts of the Winchester authorities and those of many similar bodies were rewarded. For when the County and Borough Police Act appeared in 1856, it made provision for the amalgamation of borough and county forces by mutual agreement and not by compulsion. Another consequence of the Act was the abolition of all fees and emoluments hitherto received by police constables. In Winchester this meant that the system whereby constables previously had received Christmas boxes was discontinued. To compensate them for the loss their wages were increased so that they might 'more nearly assimilate with the wages of the police in neighbouring towns'. The Watch Committee therefore recommended that the following sums be paid to the police:

Superintendents - £2.
Sergeants - £1 2s.
First-Class Constables - £1.
Second-Class Constables - 17s. rising later to 18s. per week.

As we saw, by the same period the Hampshire force had further advanced in numbers, pay and organisation. By 1859 it consisted of a chief constable, 16 superintendents, one inspector, 24 sergeants and 256 constables. The headquarters were at West Hill, Winchester and there Mr J.C. Wheeler was chief clerk. The superintendents and their divisions were as follows: J. Martin, Alton; C. Wedge, Andover; T. Drew, Basingstoke; C. Dorse, Droxford; David Harvey, Fareham; C. Grant, Alverstoke; Edmund Horan, Kingsclere; E. Pilbeam, New Forest and Lyndhurst; J. Callingham, Odiham; W. Howard, Aldershot Camp; Thomas Fey, Petersfield; W. Sparshott, Romsey; Harrison Stannard, Ringwood; Oliver Longland, Southampton; Samuel Everitt, Winchester; and Thomas Campbell, Isle of Wight. Apart from the Winchester city force other independent groups were at Newport in the Isle of Wight, Basingstoke and Romsey. The last-named was to merge with the county in 1865, as mentioned earlier. As the combined police strength at Newport and Basingstoke consisted of nine men the non-integration of these places was no great diminution of the county's strength.

Meantime the steady routine of police work went on; as always, progress in the efficiency of law-enforcement brought its consequence in the shape of unpopularity. Policemen were still sufficient of a novelty to be resented, resisted and even physically attacked. An order of 1843 assured officers that whenever assaults took place upon a police constable the superintendents would enquire into the circumstances and report the particulars immediately to the chief constable who would attend, if possible, before the magistrates when the case was heard. A foreshadowing of more recent controversies is perhaps to be discerned in the suggestion that 'The constables will understand that their interests and safety are best consulted by refraining from unnecessary or vexatious proceedings while they will at all times be efficiently protected by every legal means in cases that require prosecution.' Assaults upon constables were likely to take place in consequence of their efforts to remove intoxicated persons from beer houses. Thus in 1845 it was laid down that constables were no longer to enter beer and other liquor houses solely for the purpose of clearing these premises, but only to keep the peace in cases of assault or where the landlord required protection while he himself removed persons he had allowed to become disorderly. By such conduct on the part of the constables, it was hoped, it would become the interest of the owners of such ale-houses to prevent disorder by refusing liquor to those who were becoming intoxicated as they would not then be able to count upon the aid of the constables in ridding them of the nuisance and those cases of violence would be prevented which otherwise would inevitably arise from 'the attempt on the part of the constables to turn intoxicated and infuriated men into the streets'. Graver disorders on a larger scale were contemplated when the chief constable published to the force an extract from a letter from an Under Secretary of State, Sir George Grey. Sir George conceded that it was right and proper for the police to apply for military aid in the event of a 'protracted tumult for the suppression of which the civil power is insufficient'. But he emphasised that in any resort to the military, it was essential to seek the direction and authority of the nearest magistrate. The law had made a special provision for the suppression of riots by subjecting all persons engaged in them to extraordinary penal consequences, after due warning had been given: but such warning could only be by the mouth of the magistrate and in language of the Act of Parliament. Consequently the police should always bear in mind the importance of reporting without delay the existence of a tumult which they were unable to repress. The necessity of this reminder both throws some light on the unsettled conditions of the time and calls attention to one of the perpetual problems of those trying to maintain order in a libertarian society. In the democracy we live in today mass demonstrations have become familiar and have grown in scale; but at the same time they have become better organised and disciplined. Nevertheless the latent threat of violence is always present and it becomes a nice problem to strike a balance between the free expression of opinion and the maintenance of the Queen's peace. As much as any part of the kingdom in the 19th century Hampshire had its share of rowdyism and of mass outbreaks of lawlessness; for on the coast was the great naval base of Portsmouth and at the other extremity of the county was the new military centre at Aldershot. Servicemen have a reputation as disturbers of the peace and the Hampshire police had to take account of this, as well as the more commonplace manifestations of social discontent. Early in the 20th century, Winchester was to be the scene of a notable riot.

One activity that county police had to undertake last century was the detecting and preventing of prize fights, usually organised by a sponsoring ring in London. To succeed in any such preventive operation called for effective intelligence of the time and place of the proposed match. In the spring of 1860 the Hampshire police seem to have plucked failure from the jaws of success on one such occasion. An officer sent to London to find out details of a forthcoming prize fight succeeded very well. Unfortunately the vital information was sent, not by telegraph, but as a parcel on a train which left Waterloo an hour *after* that on which the pugilistic miscreants themselves were travelling. The latter train stopped at the very place indicated in the tardy parcel, but no constable was there on the lookout. Afterwards, the chief constable, Captain Forrest, waxed indignant over the fact that 'no more measures were taken to ensure its speedy delivery than if it had contained waste paper' and even more over the very 'extraordinary oversight that this information was never forwarded to him at all'. A crowning affliction was that the officer in London at the last moment sent information to the chief constable that the fight would probably take place in quite another part of the county so that not only was Captain Forrest left without the latest and most correct information but he was put completely on the wrong scent. Reproofs were bestowed on all concerned by the chief constable and hopes expressed that never again would careful planning be marred and the credit of the constabulary compromised in such a way.

If the chief constable was annoyed with this particular fiasco, he was far more enraged by the laxity he considered to prevail in the Isle of Wight Division. In March 1862 he issued a broadside of denunciation of the inefficiency of the island's police. For a full month he had examined the journals of the superintendent and the sergeants to ascertain what supervision had been exercised over the constables on night duty, particularly after midnight and during the early hours in the morning when, as was known to most police officers, crimes were most frequently committed. The superintendent at his headquarters at Newport, and the four sergeants stationed at West Cowes, Ventnor, Yarmouth and Ryde respectively, were all condemned as being extremely remiss in supervising their constables at night. The latter were rarely visited after midnight, or 1.30 a.m. at the latest, and no adequate check had been exercised to prevent constables 'from leaving their beats before the hour appointed for them to come off duty or to prevent them from passing their time in public houses when they should have been on patrol, or to prevent them from booking one another at the different conference points without patrolling to them'. Captain Forrest went on to state that it was no wonder that under such circumstances the division exhibited so high a percentage of undetected offences and that 'lead pumps are stolen and carried away with the same impunity as a few apples might be'. Excuses proffered by the officers concerned were brushed aside as of no merit and severe admonishments were distributed. All officers were reminded with all the weight of the chief constable's authority 'that between twelve o'clock and daylight are the hours during which constables who would evade night patrol are most likely to do so. That prevention of crime is better than detection. That to prevent crime is essential. That to perform night duty and prevent crime is less troublesome than to evade night duty and therefore to be engaged for days in endeavouring to detect some offence that has been committed in consequence.'

As mentioned earlier, Captain Forrest had the reputation of being a strict disciplinarian. Often during his long period in office he was at the centre of controversy and the target of criticism. Both magistrates and public were at different times annoyed by what seemed to be his harsh treatment of men under his command. One such instance was the affair of Superintendent Dore. Charles Dore had entered the Hampshire Constabulary in 1840, and had advanced to the rank of superintendent. He had performed his duty worthily, no complaint had ever been made against him and throughout his service he had contributed to the police superannuation fund. Early in 1859 it became necessary to reduce one superintendent in the county force, since the government no longer required a police officer of that rank to be stationed at Aldershot (and was no longer prepared to continue the allowance for the maintenance of additional police in that neighbourhood). Acting within his powers, Captain Forrest had dismissed

1 J.H. Forrest, Chief Constable of Hampshire, 1856-91.

Dore, who was then only 45 years of age, and apparently in good health. Later, certainly, he had recommended that Dore be awarded a gratuity of £300 from the superannuation fund, a proceeding of doubtful legality. In the meantime the chief constable had maintained another officer, Martin, in the rank of superintendent, who was far junior to Dore. Martin, however, stood well with his chief constable, having previously served under him in Nottingham and returned to Hampshire at his behest. Dore, in consequence of the blow to his career, had been reduced to a state of great distress. A doctor opined that there was no energy or capability of exertion left in Dore, he had not slept properly for three months and that the whole affair would likely be the death of him. As a result of the kindly intervention and recommendation of Captain Harris an appointment in the Devon force as superintendent had been secured for Dore: but he did not feel in his place there, and felt that the station and authority of superintendents in Devon by no means compared with those attaching to the same rank in Hampshire. Dore remained a miserable man, broken in health, uprooted and concerned (as many of those who spoke on his behalf were) with the future upkeep of his nine children. A motion to set up a select committee to investigate the whole business was defeated. Everyone agreed that the chief constable had acted technically within his rights and so the affair passed over. But the feeling that Captain Forrest was inclined to be too autocratic persisted, reinforced by this instance.

Another incident which seemed to demonstrate the despotic disposition of Captain Forrest occurred four years later. The chief constable issued an order deploring the rarity with which sergeants and constables were to be seen on duty near established churches in those divisions, the superintendents of which were dissenters; the consequence of this was that churchgoers were liable to be annoyed by idle men and boys, who congregated in the paths leading to the churches, laughing and jeering. He went on to remark that he disapproved entirely of encouragement being given to constables to attend chapel in place of church. 'The chief constable would not force a police constable to attend a church if he is a dissenter, but he considers it far better that constables should be churchmen than chapelgoers and that those who have no decided inclination for chapel should be encouraged by the superintendent to attend church. He is further of opinion that the superintendents who are dissenters would exercise a wise discretion if they went occasionally to the parish church.' To a present-day observer this seems high-handed indeed. It is also a reflection of the much stronger sectarian feeling which prevailed in England a hundred years ago. To many worthy citizens then, dissent was still something faintly disreputable. It is not always easy to recall that Roman Catholics had been emancipated from their civil disabilities only in 1829, and that the historic universities of Oxford and Cambridge were to remain closed to all but Anglicans until 1870. Nevertheless, the voices of those vaunting their devotion to the ideals of liberty were to make themselves heard. The editor of the *Hampshire Independent*, referring to the chief constable's order, opined that 'it was with some thoroughly assured that we are living in what is popularly believed to be free England, because the instructions for the guidance of the police are much more suited to the atmosphere of Spain or Russia than to that of one of the leading counties of the most liberty-loving nation on the face of the earth'. A correspondent darkly suggested that 'the consequence of such instructions is just this, that the best men leave the force and the chief constable may find the same thing happen in the Hampshire police which occurred in Nottingham when he superintended the force of that county'. Other self-styled 'enemies of tyranny' filled the local press with their lamentations. Perhaps they did protest too much. For a lighter note was struck by a correspondent who wrote to complain of what he termed a '*barberous*' order. Amongst the number of the police, he said, there were many who did not care overmuch about church or chapel, but *were* proud of their personal appearance, and in particular of their whiskers, which served to keep their owners warm as well as comely! Thus they resented an order of the chief constable's which directed superintendents to take note each pay day of any constable who had his hair longer than the regulation length, to send such individuals to the barber and deduct the cost of the hair-cutting from his pay. Another earlier order which doubtless caused discontent was one denouncing 'the dirty habit' of smoking. So offensive from the smell of stale smoke were certain papers and reports submitted for Captain Forrest's perusal that he could not keep them in his office. And smoking at night would infallibly betray any constable's proximity to the idle and disorderly.

Behind all this bickering serious police work went on unimpaired. In 1862 brutal murders at Waterloo, near Bournemouth and at Fordingbridge had to be dealt with. Both outrages resulted in the death of young women, the one having her throat cut by her demented husband, while the other was found strangled, the victim of a lustful attack. The same year saw the successful investigation of a complicated case of forgery of bank notes which involved the stealing of special paper from Laverstoke Mills and much coming and going between London and Hampshire. In 1863 a £100 reward was offered for information and evidence leading to the discovery and conviction of the murderer or murderers of one Henry Holton, who had been found dead in a canal at Aldershot. Alongside such spectacular crimes there ran a steady tide of theft and drunkenness, pothouse brawling and domestic quarrels. Little wonder if at times Captain Forrest appeared somewhat harsh in his efforts to maintain the discipline and efficiency of his force and testy in his attitude towards local authorities. The mayor and councillors of Newport felt aggrieved that the chief constable had declined to send men to keep order at elections in the town and were inclined to suspect that his motive stemmed from jealousy of the council's earlier desire to keep their police under their own control; however, wiser moods prevailed and it was decided that Captain Forrest had not sent any men on that particular occasion because he had none to spare. As always, efficient policing was intimately associated with a sufficiency of finance. By 1865, the annual cost of the county police was £21,486. Of this sum, one-quarter was borne by the government, while the remainder was contributed by the county rate-payers. Furthermore, as the *Hampshire Independent* pointed out dolefully, 'This great and increasing expense is borne by the rural part of the county – the boroughs of Portsmouth, Winchester, Southampton, and other large towns, having their own police, and each of them bearing the chief cost of its own force.' However, from 1856 the national exchequer contributed to the cost of provincial forces and was to do so on an increasing scale as the century advanced. In 1874, the Police (Expenses) Act did away with the maximum limit on the police grant of one-quarter of the total expenditure; the exchequer contribution was increased to half the cost of pay and clothing. By 1890, by which time many of the smaller forces had disappeared, swallowed up in larger units, every force in the country except the City of London was in receipt of exchequer grant. English policing was still essentially local in structure and character; but already the central government was establishing a substantial measure of financial control.

BOOK 2
1865-1890

Throughout the latter part of the 19th century the military establishment at Aldershot grew in size and complexity. As already mentioned, this reservoir of soldiery presented peculiar problems to the Hampshire police. For several years correspondence went on between the War Office and the county authorities with regard to the police barrack at Aldershot and early in 1867 the War Office took possession of the building so that the divisional headquarters were moved to Odiham. Only a sergeant and two constables were left in Aldershot, the government relying for its own law-enforcement purposes on members of the Metropolitan Police as was already the practice in such places as Portsmouth and Chatham. The inhabitants of Aldershot, however, who enjoyed no direct protection from these Metropolitan officers, became alarmed and made application to the magistrates for the appointment of six special constables. This was done, under the authority of an Act passed early in the reign of William IV, years before the county police came into existence. As was remarked, this proceeding was hardly complimentary to the regular Hampshire force. Thus the magistrates considered that the sooner the county police were back in Aldershot in effective numbers, the better, even if it meant an increase in the rates. A three-farthing rate in the pound for constabulary purposes was consequently agreed to and Captain Forrest requested that measures be taken, with as little delay as possible, to provide a police station at Aldershot. The building should have a magistrates' room attached, should contain accommodation for no fewer than four married constables and no fewer than six cells for prisoners. This last provision was of the first importance. As Captain Forrest said, 'one cell there would be more security than half-a-dozen police constables'.

Security was far from total in other parts of the county. At this time there was a great number of daring burglaries in the New Forest area and many worthy persons were put in a state of trepidation. Complaints were made of the laxity and slowness of the police in pursuit of these malefactors, one of whom was apparently bold enough to operate in a van with the legend 'furniture removed' emblazoned on it. Some individuals had had recourse to hiring private watchmen or constables, though with only indifferent advantage to themselves, for one such guardian, employed at Minstead, was found at a moment of crisis locked in the ample arms of his employer's cook. To all these complaints, Captain

Forrest replied with the potent argument that he was 15 men short in the force and he could not see how he could possibly send an increased force where it was required. He believed that the burglaries which had been committed were very largely the work of one gang of criminals and that the police knew pretty well who they were. Characteristically, he also said that if only the Lymington magistrates had granted a warrant when applied for several of the attempts at burglary since made would have been prevented. It must be remembered that all police work then was dependent upon communications far slower and less comprehensive than at the present day. It is true that by this time Hampshire was well served with railways. As early as 1840 the London and South Western Railway was opened to Southampton and later it was extended further west. This line entered Hampshire at Farnborough and undulated through the County via such places as Basingstoke and Winchester. Branch lines reached to Portsmouth and Gosport, to Andover, to Romsey and Salisbury, to Alton and from Basingstoke to Reading in Berkshire. The London, Brighton and South Coast Railway extended into Hampshire from Chichester to Portsmouth. A branch of the South Eastern Railway had stations at Farnborough and Blackwater. Along all the main lines, and many of the branches, telegraph wires afforded far speedier communication of information at least. However, the day of the telephone, of radio and of the motor car was yet to come. Society was still knit very much more loosely than was to be the case in the 20th century. It was all very well for local dignitaries to urge that all suspected parties be kept under observation all day. The strain on police resources and techniques would soon have proved intolerable.

At the Easter Sessions in 1866 a Select Committee had been appointed to consider a letter from the Home Secretary recommending an increase in the pay of the county constabulary; and further to enquire generally into the circumstances and conditions of the said constabulary. In March 1867 the committee presented its final report, which gives an interesting picture of the state of the force at that time. Two recommendations regarding the discipline and general arrangements of the force were made, in the following terms:

> It has been the practice in this county, as in others, when the removal of a police constable from one station to another has, in the opinion of the chief constable, become necessary on account of misbehaviour not so great as to require his dismissal from the force, to throw on him the expense of such removal by way of punishment, and this practice is sustained by the approbation of Her Majesty's Inspector of the District.
>
> Your committee are nevertheless of opinion that, inasmuch as it is unequal in its operation and sometimes involves punishment unnecessarily heavy, it should be discontinued.
>
> It also appears to have been the custom from the beginning of the police force, with one intermission for a time, and with some variation in extent, to employ police constables otherwise than strictly in the public service, viz., in the stable of the chief constable.
>
> Your committee are of opinion that no such employment ought to be sanctioned for the future.

Recommendations were also made to increase the pay and allowances of the chief constable, in order to bring his remuneration to a level commensurate with that of chief officers of forces of similar size, dealing with areas roughly equivalent to Hampshire. Also noted were the increased labour and responsibility of the chief constable by the augmentation of his force from 165 to 265 men. And mournful sympathy from the 20th century will be elicited by a reference to 'the advance within the same period of the prices which govern the expense of living, keeping horses, etc.'. Consequently the chief constable was no longer to be charged £50 rent for his house and moreover £50 was to be added to his allowance of £100 per annum. This meant that his salary was now £400 and his allowance £150. The pay and rent charges of all other ranks were also adjusted, so that every man was materially better off. The cost of all this meant a net increase on the police rate of barely £730 – not quite equal to one-eighth of a penny in the year.

The organisation and structure of the force continued to change over the next quarter century. In 1869 Ryde became possessed of a borough force of its own and the county constabulary was decreased by three men. In 1874 came the beginning of a C.I.D., when approval was given to the chief constable sending the officers selected for the Detective Department to be attached to the Metropolitan Police for instruction. At the end of 1875 the Earl of Carnarvon, on resigning as chairman of Quarter Sessions, commented proudly on the manifold improvements in the force brought about during the previous two years. He claimed that earlier 'there was great discontent in the force, the standard of height had been lowered, the numbers had fallen off, the general level of intelligence and physical strength was stated to be lowered, the government inspector had reported in strong terms on the general position of the force, and the vacancies in the body could not be filled up on the existing terms.' Lord Carnavon with pardonable satisfaction then contrasted this dismal state of affairs with the happier situation which he himself, he claimed, had been instrumental in creating. 'During the last eighteen months (and it is perhaps right I should add in every instance on my recommendation as chairman) a succession of measures has been adopted which have entirely reversed the previous state of things, the numbers, the height, the intelligence of the men have been brought back to the original and proper standard, the whole force has been reorganised, a Department of Detective Officers has been trained and added to it, the pay has been increased, the men are contented and efficient, and the government inspector has pronounced his entire satisfaction.' Other gains were that the difficult questions of the rent paid by members of the constabulary living in stations and lodgings had been adjusted to the satisfaction of all parties. Furthermore, a very large amount of arrears in the repairs of police stations and buildings which had accumulated had been cleared off. By 1878 the disposition of the Hampshire police was as follows. Apart from the chief constable, the force consisted of 12 superintendents, three inspectors, 26 sergeants and 229 constables.

The two senior superintendents had an annual salary of £152 18s., the next five had £141 8s. 9d.; and the other five £130 15s. 10d. The superintendent appointed as deputy chief constable received £18 5s. a year extra. Each of the inspectors had £101 17s. 11d., and from superintendents and inspectors alike £10 a year was deducted for rent. Sergeants received £76 0s. 10d. subject to a deduction of £6 9s. 3d. for rent, if living in a police station. The first-class constables had £60 16s. 8d., second-class £56 5s. 5d. and third-class £51 14s. 2d. The deduction for rent of married men living in lodgings was 3s. 6d. a week for sergeants and 2s. 6d. for constables. The one detective inspector received £109 10s. a year and the two detective sergeants £86 13s. 9d. each. The various divisions with their respective officers in charge were: Alton, Superintendent William Cheyney; Andover, Superintendent John Bennett; Basingstoke, Inspector Robert Brinson; Fareham, Superintendent James Littlefield; Gosport, Superintendent James Homingold; Kingsclere, Inspector Joseph Waters; Lymington, Superintendent George Troke; Odiham, Superintendent Charles Stephenson; Petersfield, Inspector William Masterman; Ringwood, Superintendent William White; Romsey, Superintendent Edward Kellaway; Southampton, Superintendent Harrison Stannard; Winchester, Superintendent Thomas Fey; and Isle of Wight, Superintendent Edmund Horan. The last-named also acted as deputy chief constable.

It is interesting to compare this state of affairs with that of 1859, nearly twenty years before. The number of divisions had been slightly reduced but several familiar names appear, still in the same rank, if now in a different setting. Mr Horan, Mr Fey, and Mr Stannard had all been in command of divisions in 1859, and in 1878 they were the old guard of the hierarchy. Perhaps here is fit substantiation of the time-honoured legend of the longevity of superintendents!

Besides the broad framework of the organisation of the force, other items of change may be noted. In the late sixties and throughout the seventies of the 19th century an impressive volume of reforming legislation was carried through by the governments of the day. The work of social and political reform, made necessary by the remorseless advance and increasing complexity of industrialisation, went on throughout the entire period. But it is perhaps the case that the peaks of legislative enthusiasm were apt to come in the years following each of the three great Parliamentary Reform Acts, of 1832, 1867 and 1884. Each political advance seemed to stimulate a spate of further reforms in other fields. The result, only half-realised by men at the time, was the emergence of a whole new pattern of national government. As a consequence of piecemeal legislation, British government was gradually extending its concern to all sorts of social, economic and industrial activity. The indispensable foundations of government of a modern state were being created, albeit haphazardly. Inevitably, this created problems of application and enforcement, which involved the activity of the police. What were to be the limits of that activity? Where were the lines of demarcation to be drawn? In his report of Easter 1871 Captain Forrest drew attention to the fact that 'the constabulary are performing the following duties, for which there is no authority, either by act of parliament or by permission of the Secretary of State,' and he went on to suggest 'either that the sanction of the Home Office be obtained, or that the constabulary relinquish the duties, as the performance of them without authority may involve the loss of a portion of the government grant towards the maintenance of the constabulary – inspectors of cattle, impounders of cattle, inspectors of hawkers' licences, inspectors of county bridges, assistant excise officers, and assistant surveyors of highways'. A few months previously the Home Secretary had expressed the opinion that the only additional duties that could be undertaken by the police 'with advantage to the public service and without interfering with their ordinary duty' were the inspection of common lodging-houses; the relief of vagrants to the extent of police acting as assistant receiving officers and giving tickets to persons applying for admission into workhouses; the inspection of nuisances; and the inspection of weights and measures. In a later communication, however, the Home Office was at pains to point out that its earlier directive was not to be read as interfering with the directions of any Act of Parliament devolving upon the police the duty of carrying out its provisions, such as the Contagious Diseases and Workshops Regulation Acts. 'In all such cases the directions of the particular act must be followed independently of any control by the Secretary of State.'

All this added to the perplexities of the chief constable, who was repeatedly subjected to demands from different divisions within the county for more policemen to be sent there. The agitation for a greater police effort in the New Forest area has already been mentioned. Another example was the outcry from the Isle of Wight. Sir John Simon, a Member of Parliament, voiced the opinion current in the island that it was getting less than a fair share of the police resources of the county. While the Isle of Wight had one-sixth of the population, and paid one-sixth of the rates, they had only one-eighth of the police. There was a unanimous feeling that there was not sufficient protection to property by the police at their disposal. East Cowes, for example, had a population of 3,000, but only one police constable, who had to be on duty day and night with a beat of four miles. Little wonder that there were undetected crimes! Once some forts under construction were completed there would be no fewer than 400 artillerymen in one district and 'they all knew what to expect from such an accession of soldiers'! Some unsympathetic observers remarked that surely more police could be spared for the disturbed areas since it was well known that, apart from Aldershot, the Hampshire police had a very easy life.

Be this as it may, the recruitment and maintenance of police officers remained a nagging problem. Recruiting posters appealed for candidates to come forward who possessed the necessary qualifications; they had to be under thirty-five years of age, to stand clear 5 ft. 7 ins. without shoes, to be intelligent and able both to write and to read writing. Also each man had to be free from bodily complaint,

2 Constabulary recruitment poster, 1876.

of a strong constitution and able and active, 'according to the judgment of the chief surgeon of the constabulary, by whom he will be examined'. Nevertheless, a high rate of wastage continued to prevail, largely owing to ill-health of one sort or another. Perhaps after all life was not so easy and no doubt all sergeants and constables were grateful when in 1875 the number of days leave in the year was increased from four to seven.

At this time great annoyance to the public seems to have been caused by the large number of vagrants who roamed about and the police were hard put to cope with the problem. As was to be expected in a county containing major army and navy depots, many of these wanderers were deserters from the armed forces. And at the very end of 1874 complaints were made by the War Department of 'a want of activity on the part of the police forces in apprehending and bringing to justice deserters from the army and the militia'. The cause of this lack of zeal was, as might be expected, financial: that this was so was recognised in a further Home Office circular of May 1875. This stated that the Secretary of State for War had observed 'that the police labour under the difficulty that on the one hand, in many places, the local authorities do not repay them the expenses they may have incurred in apprehending deserters and conveying them to the place of committal; whilst on the other it has been the established practice of the War Department not to allow such expenses as chargeable to army rates'. The Home Office then went on to say that orders would be given by the War Department for the repayment of the necessary expenses incurred, provided that with the reward they did not exceed the sum of 40s., prescribed in the Mutiny Act as the maximum sum to be paid for the apprehension of a deserter.

Another matter of concern both to the government and the general public was the superabundance of pedlars at large, some of them of very dubious character. In 1871 the Home Secretary announced in the House that his attention had been called to the wholesale manner in which the requisite certificates had been granted by the police in defiance of what seemed to him to be the plain provisions of the law. The duty of granting these certificates was entrusted to the police in order that it might be discharged with care and vigilance; but all too frequently they had given certificates to tramps of whom they knew nothing, except that they had happened to lodge a night in a town. In many other cases they had given certificates to convicted felons. He went on to say that the government was concerned at the abuse of pedlars' certificates for purposes of begging and that it might be proper to empower the police to refuse licences in cases where they thought they were to be used for such purposes. Thereafter some tightening up was attempted, and Captain Forrest emphasised the need for strictness and regularity of administration in this matter.

But the number of vagrants continued to increase throughout that decade. In October 1879 the chief constable drew his men's attention to the fact that 634 more vagrants had been relieved than in the previous quarter; of 20 unions only four had shown a decrease in the number of individuals accommodated. The Guardians of Stockbridge Union, indeed, had complained of the increase and commented bitterly that out of the 101 vagrants who had applied for relief to the local police in their capacity as relief officers, only two had been refused. Here was gross laxity! In General Orders Captain Forrest observed wrathfully that 'If Sergeant Fox, who acts as assistant relieving officer does not show a greater amount of zeal and discretion it is not unlikely that he may end his days in a workhouse himself.' Nor was Sergeant Fox alone in disgrace. Of 174 who applied to Andover Union only five were refused; of 173 who applied to Ringwood Union again only five were refused. No fewer than 254 had applied to Romsey, of whom only 11 were refused, while at Christchurch all 109 applicants had been accepted. To quote General Orders again 'These figures speak for themselves and tell how little discretion has been used by the police as assistant relieving officers and how little zeal has been shown by officers in charge of divisions to suppress vagrancy, and relieve the charge under this head on the county rate.'

A peculiar type of begging about this time was that practised by the protégés of the 'Padroni'. These were the unscrupulous individuals who imported into this country children bought or stolen from their parents in Italy, or elsewhere, and employed them as beggars, either openly or under the guise of selling images and trinkets, or playing musical instruments. The Home Office pointed out that such children would probably come within the provisions of the Industrial Schools Act of 1866, either as a child begging alms or found wandering and without proper guardianship. Application, therefore, could be made to the justices for the child to be sent to a certified industrial school.

Exploitation of this sort was not the only fate threatening young people last century. Mortal illness was far more commonplace then than is the case in our happier circumstances today. From time to time poignant items appear in force orders concerning gratuities – pathetically small – awarded to police officers on the death of their children. And, of course, year by year there was a grim toll of infanticide. An instance of this is signified by a notice issued by the police in 1867, which offers £50 reward for any information leading to the 'Discovery and conviction of the murderer or murderers of a newly-born male child, who was found dead in the Basingstoke Canal'. There is, unhappily, nothing unusual about such a crime; but it serves to show that some types of misdeed are always with us. Today children are more comprehensively cared for than in the 19th century. It is also shamefully true that very often even today they are in even greater need of such care and protection.

Additional tasks for the police were presented by the passing of the Army Corps Training Act in 1876. This measure was one of the many ripples of anxious concern with military affairs which had grown in the British nation with the dramatic appearance, as the dominating power on the Continent, of a united and martial Germany. Certain areas in several counties were set aside for purposes of military training and it became a police responsibility to assist the military authorities with the maintenance of law and order in those areas. In Hampshire the area containing the camp was at Petersfield Heath Common and one sergeant and six constables were assigned for duty there. Provision was also made for other constables to be kept available in reserve for employment in case of necessity. The Home Secretary indicated that he would be prepared to entertain claims for any extra expense the county might be put to on this account; and that if the camp were inconveniently far from the police station and it were necessary to attach the police to the camp headquarters, both camp equipment and rations would be issued free to the police. However, the chief constable was not to take it upon himself to send extra police without notification and a formal request from the general officer commanding. Thus when Captain Forrest sent additional men to Petersfield 'in the interests of the ratepayers', the Home Office held out no hope of the government defraying the expense as these officers could not be deemed employed for military purposes. What *was* a proper duty in this connection was the listing of the names and addresses of the owners of sheep and cattle on unenclosed ground within the area and the forwarding of this list to the special commissioner concerned.

In April 1878, when European war seemed likely in consequence of the crisis in the Balkans, a royal proclamation called out the army reserve. Twenty-four constables of the Hampshire force were likely to be affected and assurances were sought that, when these officers were called into active service and the vacancies thus created were filled, facilities should be granted to the 24 to rejoin the force in the same rank; and that they should not lose any benefit in the way of superannuation allowance in consequence of this interruption of their service in the constabulary. On some previous occasions Captain Forrest had succeeded in securing the exemption of policemen who were members of the reserve from attendance at training.

The everyday work of the police was profoundly affected by the fact that they were carrying out law enforcement in a mainly rural county. Many of the orders issued to the force were of seasonal application and mirrored the routine of agricultural life. From mid-July to the end of September the constabulary were directed to do duty in plain clothes two days a week, the better to guard the cottages of farm workers left unprotected through the long summer days. A likely source of trouble, of course, was the host of vagrants on the move about the countryside, encouraged in their rovings by 'bad weather and the depression of trade'. Large numbers of bills warning vagrants and beggars were displayed in each division and one half-penny per bill was allowed for paste. In the same connection some officers found themselves being moved from place to place for temporary duty during the hop-picking. A more unpleasant problem was that presented by swine fever and members of the force were reminded from time to time of its depressing symptoms, including dullness, temperature, a feeling of chilliness, a disinclination to move, diarrhoea, congestion of the eyes and nostrils, tenderness of the belly, sickness, giddiness, and ultimately delirium. Diversity of interest was provided by the frequent need to assist neighbouring forces on special occasions. Also in 1879, as on many subsequent occasions, substantial detachments were sent to reinforce the police stationed at Bournemouth, to help them preserve peace and protect property on the night of 5 November. 'The constabulary will travel in plain clothes, except Sergeant Daniels, taking their uniform with them in a carpet bag or other convenient form so as to disguise their being police constables. On arriving at Bournemouth they will walk quietly to the police station, avoiding any act likely to betray them. They will report themselves to the officer in charge and put on their uniforms. Refreshments will be provided for constables on the following scale – ¾lb. cold meat, 1½lb. of bread, and 2 pints of beer for each police constable – 1 pint of beer only to be given previous to going on duty.'

Bournemouth did not always have such convivial associations. Three constables were promoted and commended in December that year for 'securing a man at night with a revolver, six chambers of which were loaded'. The constables had information that the person had loaded firearms in his possession 'with the avowed object of shooting two persons resident at Bournemouth'. By their courageous conduct the policemen very probably prevented the murder of one or two persons and very likely the suicide of a third. Brushes with malefactors were sometimes less successful. In April 1880 a constable was reprimanded and reduced in rank for disgraceful conduct, but the chief constable forebore dismissing him the service since 'his stupid actions may in some degree be attributed to the very severe blows which he received on his head when on duty at Overton in April 1870 (ten years previously) at which time he was set upon and nearly killed by six or seven ruffians, in consequence of his having detected two of them stealing a sack of greens'. Such assaults were commonplace, of course, not just in Hampshire but throughout the kingdom. As *The Times* commented in 1877, 'The friendly feeling of the public towards the police force is … very far from universal. If the policemen is the natural protector of some classes, he is not less truly the enemy of others.' The article pointed out that there was no other country in Europe in which a grave assault on a police constable would be passed over as lightly as in England. Elsewhere it was regarded as a sort of treason against the majesty of the state. 'We are more lax here, and the consequence is that among the lower classes of criminals the policeman is considered as fair game. To knock him down, to kick him, to jump upon him, to maim him if possible, is all counted as one of the best day's amusements.' *The Times* pointed out that the police were compelled to face dangers from which every other class of civilians is exempt. 'Their day's duty leads them into strange adventures, and such as the rest of their countrymen may be thankful not to share with them.'

In 1877 Sergeant Sillence, who had just been promoted and moved from the Isle of Wight to Totton, had a strange adventure of his own. One night he was on his way to Eling Cross for a conference with some of his men and while passing the *Anchor Inn* at Eling he heard a great disturbance. Sillence knew that the inn was kept by an old man of 90 who was assisted only by his two elderly daughters, so he hastened to investigate. On entering the passage leading to the bar he received a blow on the jaw which knocked his helmet off. He was confronted by five drunken Irishmen who were furious that the landlord would not serve them. Recovering his helmet and strapping it under his chin Sergeant Sillence drew his staff and forced the five trouble-makers into the passage. He was more active than the drunken rowdies and gradually forced them down the passage. In one of the adjacent rooms a private club meeting was being held, but the members were content to help the sergeant by voice alone; they timidly held the door open an inch or two and shouted 'Lock them up, Sergeant, lock them up,' but made quite sure that they were involved no further. Sillence forced the Irishmen out of the house on to the quay and immediately the door of the house was shut and locked behind him. Alone and in the dark the police officer confronted his five assailants. Luckily there was a little recess and standing in this he faced them and knocked them down as they came at him. Thereupon four of the Irishmen ran away as fast as each could get up. The fifth was hit so hard that his eyebrow was cut off, he was unconscious for twenty minutes and the sergeant's staff was split in two. The unfortunate rowdy was locked up and then Sergeant Sillence having obtained assistance went on board the coal brig whence the Irishmen had come and arrested two more. The two others he was unable to identify. A few days later one of the three prisoners was sentenced to four months' hard labour and the other two to three months apiece. The courage of Sergeant Sillence was even more marked in that the ruffians, in attacking him, had armed themselves with fire-irons.

Sergeant Sillence was promoted to superintendent on 20 November 1879, and shortly thereafter was involved in another dramatic case, in connection with the so-called 'Barrett Outrage'. An old couple, Mr and Mrs Bloomfield, resided in their own house at Barrett, near Southampton, Mr Bloomfield received a decoy telegram asking him to come to Southampton at six o'clock that evening to arrange about some work. At that hour two young men knocked at the door of Bloomfield's house and were admitted by a domestic servant. They pushed past her into the house, found Mrs Bloomfield and demanded money from her. She refused this demand, whereupon one of the men pulled out a revolver and shot her in the head, a portion of the bullet lodging in the skull. Mr Bloomfield then appeared upon the scene, was tackled by the men and had several shots fired at him, but fortunately he was not hit. A man from a neighbouring brick field came to Mr Bloomfield's assistance and was shot through the throat. The two assailants made good their escape from the house. Mr Sillence pursued his enquiries and eventually these led him to a house in Cambridge Terrace, Southampton. The landlady stated that there was a man in the house answering the description that was given and indicated his room. Mr Sillence had several men with him, but he had posted these around the house lest the man should try to escape from one of the windows. The superintendent had to go upstairs himself, accompanied only by the landlady carrying a lamp. Just as the door of the man's room was reached, the woman fainted and Mr Sillence barely caught the lamp as it fell to the floor. Then the outside handle of the door came off and Mr Sillence summoned one of the constables to help him get the door open. This was done and immediately the superintendent encountered a big bulldog. 'But I gave him a clout with a stick, and sent him out of the room.' The man was standing by the side of his bed undressed and Mr Sillence, mindful that the fellow might be armed, quickly pounced on him and held him down, 'handing him his clothes a little at a time to put on, and then we took him to Bitterne Police Station'. The revolver was later found on a plantation near Mr Bloomfield's house. The murderous outrage created a great sensation in Southampton and the prisoners were threatened with violence by a large crowd when they were driven through the streets to Barrett where it was necessary to attend to take Mrs Bloomfield's evidence, she being too ill to be moved. On the very morning that sentence was passed upon the men, Mrs Bloomfield died; but, fortunately for the criminals, two doctors had certified before the trial began that the shot in the head had not accelerated her death. In General Orders the chief constable recorded his high approbation of the conduct of the constabulary and especially of Superintendent Sillence. The latter was to be appointed deputy chief constable in 1895.

Courage and diligence in the performance of one's duty were not enough, however. Patience and steadiness under provocation were equally necessary qualities in a police officer confronted with rowdyism. In 1880 a detachment of Hampshire police had once more gone to Bournemouth to assist the local constabulary in the preservation of peace and protection of property. They had acquitted themselves admirably, until after midnight, when tempers became frayed. A blow was aimed at the officer in charge, who responded by making 'an aggressive movement with the section under his immediate charge, which although injudicious might not have led to ill consequences had it not been for the misconduct of a subsection under Sergeant Russell'. This small group had been stationed up a hill, from which stones had earlier been thrown at the police. Thereupon they 'did seriously abuse their authority as police constables and by using violence where no violence was necessary' they conducted themselves in a manner disgraceful in the members of an organised constabulary. They themselves committed the very acts it was their duty to prevent other persons from committing. 'They created a disturbance which it was their duty to prevent and brought discredit on the Hants Constabulary.' As a result Sergeant Russell was reduced to the rank of a first-class constable, and a Police Constable Stevens was dismissed the service.

1878 saw the birth of a new type of religious organisation, the Salvation Army, which was to make a dramatic impact on many of the social problems of the day. Well-bred and cultured persons stood aghast at the flamboyance and sensationalism of the 'Army', but its effect on broad masses of the poor, the uneducated, the degraded and the humble was outstanding. The Salvationists with superb courage adopted the techniques of demagogy and with drum and trumpet went to the people to win their loyalty against the powers of darkness. Captain Forrest, whose prejudice against dissenters will be recalled, was unlikely to regard such an unconventional body as the Salvation Army with much favour. Doubtless he was confirmed in his attitude by the apparent threat to law and order presented by the 'Army's' meetings and processions. A number of disturbances took place in Basingstoke and Whitchurch, when the activities of the 'Army' provoked violent antagonism on the part of other citizens. An order of March 1881 referred to the way in which the 'Army's' proceedings were causing annoyance and obstructing the highways and directed police officers to do all in their power legally to prevent the 'Army' from such activities. If at all possible a collision was to be avoided and the leaders of any demonstration served with a summons. If the 'Army' collected a crowd in or near a village the highway would be obstructed and 'it would be for the police to prove that an obstruction was caused. It is not absolutely necessary that any person should be actually obstructed – if the crowd is so great that it filled the width of the highway so that a vehicle could not pass, that would be an obstruction.' The Home Office was appealed to for advice and responded in a rather unhelpful way. The justices were informed 'that while it is their duty by every means in their power to preserve the public peace, they must at the same time exercise their discretion … as to whether the conduct of a body of persons in persisting in parading the town of Basingstoke in procession is likely to produce a riot and serious disturbance of the peace. The magistrates should give notice to all persons intending to take any part in any processions that it cannot be permitted. The forming of the procession should be stopped, each person being told the reason why it will not be allowed.' If all efforts at persuasion failed, however, sufficient force should be at hand to deal with any eventuality. The Home Office concluded its advice with the unexceptionable statement that 'it would be easier to prevent the procession from forming than to deal with an excited crowd after a collision has taken place'. For all that collisions did take place and throughout the decade the Salvation Army's activities were the occasion of tumults.

Another case of police enthusiasm outrunning discretion occurred at Fareham in May 1881. A disturbance broke out in the *Vulcan* public house, P.C. James entered, and was set upon by three sailors who beat him up and took his truncheon. The unfortunate constable returned to the police station and reported what had happened to Superintendent Kinshott. The superintendent went with the constable in search of the sailors, who were from colliers in Fareham Lake, but failed to find them. However, they encountered Sergeant Drew and P.C. Hodson, and the superintendent instructed the sergeant to look for the men who had committed the assault and if they were in the town to apprehend them. On no account, emphasised Kinshott, was Sergeant Drew to go on board a ship at that late hour of the night. Drew was not to be put off. He subsequently got information that the sailors were aboard the *Sarah King* and without reference to his superior officer, allowed the injured James, Hodson, and a third constable to board the vessel, which was anchored about fifty yards off the quay. The three sailors were reinforced by four others and 'a serious fight took place in which very hard blows were struck on both sides. The constables were overpowered and had to leave the vessel.' Doubtless they did not stand upon the manner of their going! Summonses were taken out against the constables for assaulting one of the sailors, and warrants were issued against the original three sailors for assaulting P.C. James. When the cases came up before the bench at Fareham, they were withdrawn on the application of the solicitors on both sides; but a black mark remained against the police. Captain Forrest pronounced that he was 'unwilling to deal seriously with the son of a late much-valued officer of the constabulary whose meritorious services are so well remembered by all who knew him and who is himself possessed of more than average education and intelligence and has the health and muscular power which should lead to his advancement in the service – but these advantages are as nothing in the police service unless accompanied by a proper sense of discipline, of the necessity of complying with the orders of his superiors and … discretion'. The chief constable went on to hope that the episode would be a warning to Drew and that he would by future good conduct prove that the clemency shown had not been wasted. He hoped too that Sergeant Drew would 'emulate the conduct of his father and will some day attain the same rank and deserve the same good opinion of his fellows'. The reference here was to Superintendent Drew who had died in 1872 amid widespread encomium.

A more successful display of zeal occurred the next year when a valuable mare was stolen from Odiham 'by a man of medium height, dressed in long dark overcoat, hard black square-crowned hat, and tight-fitting trousers or breeches and gaiters'. So quickly did the deputy chief constable act in circulating information that within forty-eight hours the missing animal, 'heavy in foal', was recovered at Marchwood. This incident serves once again to remind us of the pre-eminent place in everyday life then occupied by the horse. In the days before motor cars, the horse was as vital to the movement of society and the economy as are what the Buchanan Report referred to as 'our beloved monsters' in the second half of the 20th century. Theft of animals was a major problem for the police, as was their regulation and supervision. 'Foot-and-mouth' and other ailments repeatedly attacked the cattle of Hampshire and the counter-measures taken were in large part the responsibility of the police. One aspect of social reform in those decades was the growing concern with public health and the legislation necessary to enforce it. In matters of everyday sanitation the police themselves were far from impeccable. The wells on which some police stations were dependent for their water were occasionally found to be poisoned. Cess-pools were not always given the careful attention they warranted. In July 1881 the chief constable directed that the following instructions were to be displayed in the police stations at Bitterne, Christchurch, and Eastleigh: 'The cess-pools have been fitted with floats to indicate when they are full to the level of the drain inlet. The cess-pools are not to be allowed to fill higher than that level or the drains will get stopped. The liquid in the cess-pools is to be pumped out frequently and in small quantities distributed over the gardens. The cess-pools are not to be allowed to get full and then emptied at one pumping and on one place, but the liquid is to be distributed generally over the gardens.' The purity of water available in police stations, as well as efficiency of drainage, was a recurring preoccupation of senior police officers at this time.

The enormous problems created by the coming of the internal combustion engine might lie in the future, but other mechanical vehicles were already at large. Traction engines were snorting and grinding about the countryside and a shower of complaints of the noise, nuisance and danger of these machines was directed at the chief constable. He ordered that the bye-laws relating to them should be more strictly enforced in future. Another nuisance was dealt with in 1883, when the constabulary was ordered to 'deface, pull down, or otherwise destroy' bills headed 'Prevention better than cure. French letters', which were being posted throughout the county on walls and gates. Less enticing wares, perhaps, were offered by all sorts of doubtful characters who thronged to the frequent fairs which it was the duty of the police to supervise and regulate. Presumably many a labourer was cheated of his hard-won cash by cardsharpers and other tricksters – certainly warnings enough about the prevalence of the latter were given to the police, officers detailed to attend the fairs and race-meetings. There too a sharp look-out was kept for deserters. One such was Cornelius Rubrik, who had deserted from H.M.S. *Sappho* in New Zealand and despite or perhaps because of his having a wife and family there, was supposed to be on his way to England. That the force contained many alert and perspicacious officers was shown towards the end of 1883 when P.C. Hood was complimented by Captain Forrest on his sagacity. A young girl had broken out from the home of her uncle at Fair Oak, stolen some money and vanished. However, Hood ascertained that a female answering the description had been seen going towards Winchester. He went there, searched all beer and common lodging-houses without result and finally apprehended the girl on a train at Winchester Railway Station in the early hours of the next morning.

A different type of operation from supervising fairs was that mounted in connection with a royal visit. In May 1885, Queen Victoria visited Netley, and it is interesting to see that the order dealing with police dispositions for the occasion is a direct adaptation of a similar order of three years before, with only the names and ranks of those concerned somewhat altered. Five years later, however, when the Prince and Princess of Wales visited Bournemouth, much more lengthy and elaborate orders were necessary and without doubt succeeded in ensuring the smooth procedure of the occasion.

In 1886 one Albert Edward Brown was convicted of a murder at Worthy and the effective work of the police officers in bringing this case to a satisfactory conclusion was commended by the chief constable. The latter recorded in orders his 'sense of the intelligent and persevering manner in which the case was worked out by Superintendent Sillence and Inspector Lawler, without any assistance from the Public Prosecutor, who declined to take up the case until the prisoners had been committed for trial'. The two officers had collected and put together a mass of circumstantial evidence 'in a manner that would have been creditable to a solicitor in the habit of dealing with such intricate cases'. It is significant to note that Captain Forrest considered that one essential cause of the success was the 'intelligible telegrams' sent from Totton by Superintendent Sillence to the Detective Department of the Metropolitan Police. This was an example of the advantage of quick and decisive action, and of using the wires in an intelligible manner. From the tone of these remarks, it is clear that very often the wires had *not* been used in an intelligible manner in the past and that this triumph was a sign and a wonder.

In the following year a police constable displayed outstanding courage, and secured his promotion from the second to the first class, by grappling with, and overcoming, an armed man. About one o'clock on the morning of 2 November 1887, P.C. Chant heard cries of murder, and at once proceeded to the place from whence the cries came. He found a soldier threatening to shoot a prostitute and showing every sign of carrying out his threat. He promised to shoot any man or woman who came near him. Chant called upon the soldier to give up his rifle, but he refused and threatened to shoot the constable. The police officer closed with the soldier, wrested his rifle from him, warded off a thrust from the bayonet which the soldier then drew, secured the bayonet and arrested the soldier. Thus 'by his intrepid conduct and contempt of danger' P.C. Chant 'probably prevented murder, or serious bodily harm, to some innocent person'. Another example of courage came in 1889 when P.C. Gough saved the life of a boy, John Barton. Hearing cries for help, Gough found the child in the River Test, being carried away by the tide. Bravely he plunged in and brought the child safe to land. The Royal Humane Society presented Gough with an Honorary Testimonial in Vellum for his courage and humanity.

No one saved the life of little Percy Searle, nine years old, who was found at the Pallant, a lone place, in the night-time, at Havant, with his throat cut. A small boy said that he heard cries and had seen a tall man run away. An old rusty two-bladed clasp-knife was picked up about eight yards from the body. It appeared to the police, however, that the boy who gave this evidence, Robert Husband, was himself the killer, and he was apprehended. He was later committed for trial at the Assizes, where he was tried and acquitted.

Praise was lavished on the force as a whole in September 1890, when the Head Constable of Southampton wrote to Captain Forrest to express his appreciation of the help given by the Hants Constabulary in coping with a dock strike. This dispute lasted for more than a week, and the 50 Hampshire police officers were called upon 'to perform very arduous duties and for very long periods, yet they were always ready and never complained'. The head constable also remarked that 'Had I been unable to obtain your men, as was the case with the Metropolitan Police, I can hardly conceive what the result would have been, as it was with fifty of the Hants Constabulary and sixty of my own men I was able to keep a crowd of several thousand strikers within bounds and prevent them doing any serious damage until the arrival of the four companies of the Yorkshire Light Infantry when the combined police and troops cleared them away.' Perhaps the reference to the Metropolitan Police was not meant as an implied rebuke. For they had troubles and to spare of their own. The previous year had seen the great London dockers' strike, a landmark in trade union history, which had lasted for several weeks, and put a great strain upon the patience and resources of the capital's police.

Throughout the second quarter-century of the Hampshire force's existence, the formidable character of Captain Forrest was to be found at the centre of all activity. As has already been shown, he could be harsh and autocratic, and perhaps unjust. Yet it is impossible to withhold admiration for the devotion and drive he brought to the work of governing the force and of hammering it into an increasingly efficient organisation. He could bestow praise and commendation most generously. He could also scourge slackness unmercifully. Repeatedly he thundered against infringements of the regulations regarding uniform and even more against any inadequacy or lack of zeal in the performance of day-to-day duty. There was the unceasing problem of drunkenness. But also there were constables who lost or damaged equipment, ruined their uniform and failed to keep such things as lanthorns in good condition. In March 1889, out of 23 lanthorns inspected in Odiham Division, 'twelve were either out of repair, or had been tampered with by incompetent tradesmen, in place of having been forwarded to headquarters for repair'. Clearly, the monthly inspection could not have been properly carried out for a long time. Another activity which aroused the anger of the chief constable was that of constables' writing to the press, very often to complain of the general conditions of police service or to bemoan some exercise of authority by Captain Forrest himself. Where such letters were anonymous, his wrath was matched by his contempt. He himself was never averse to proclaiming his views on paper and at the beginning of 1875 found himself in an embarrassing position when the Earl of Normanton complained that the chief constable had sought 'in most forcible terms' to influence his attitude on a member of the Public Works Committee, with which Captain Forrest had been having acute differences.

Vivid and masterful language was certainly directed at a Sergeant Gilbert, who was scarified in General Orders for his want of activity and energy and in particular 'his neglect of night duty and not visiting conference points'. Week after week 'idle and frivolous excuses are made by him for this neglect of duty. If he has to attend Petty Sessions or other duty, he neither does duty the night before nor the night after, thus taking two nights in bed where a police constable would be allowed, probably, to miss one conference point.' The hapless Sergeant Gilbert had displayed his torpidity in more than one division and each superintendent who encountered him was soon eager to have him posted elsewhere. However, the chief constable did not consider it right 'to pass such an officer on from division to division at the expense of the county'. Gilbert's faults were such as lay within his own power to cure. 'It by no means follows that once a sergeant, always a sergeant,' warned Captain Forrest, adding grimly, 'There are other sergeants who will not be hurt by remembering this.'

All such admonitions apparently left Sergeant Gilbert unabashed, and his downfall soon followed. In March 1879 the chief constable visited Whitchurch Police Station where Gilbert was in charge, and was horrified at its condition. The building was altogether dirty, and 'one of the front bedrooms was more like the residence of a dealer in bones and rags than that of a respectable sergeant of police'. The county had not long since gone to the expense of filling up a dead well, constructing a water closet and connecting with the main sewer. But what was the use of such consideration when, in disregard of the properly constructed ash hole, refuse of all sorts was scattered in the yard, thus bringing about the very same offensive smell that the authorities had been at such pains to eliminate? All this negligence in itself would have been enough to cause the chief constable to reduce Sergeant Gilbert to the rank of police constable, bearing in mind his previous bad record. In addition, however, there was a report against him for having used 'insulting and provoking language' to Inspector Kinshott, in charge of the division, who told Gilbert that he was more drunk than sober. With his customary facility, Sergeant Gilbert had brought forward several witnesses to prove he was not drunk. 'But,' announced Captain Forrest, 'he was not accused of having been drunk but of being more drunk than sober – i.e. off the balance.' There was no doubt that his demeanour towards his superior officer had been so insulting that the latter was warranted in concluding that the sergeant was not in his right senses. Furthermore, he had been in such a state that he could not read the labels on the police constable's clothing. Thus Gilbert's doom was sealed, and he was forthwith reduced to the rank of first-class police constable.

Nor did the officer in charge of the division escape censure – he should have exercised stricter supervision. Well might Captain Forrest repeat the old saw 'If you want a thing well done, do it yourself. If you don't care how it's done, get someone to do it for you.' In January 1879 a Sergeant Gibson was reprimanded for not himself investigating a complaint of drunken brawling in a pub, but through idleness sent only a third-class police constable to clear the tavern and manage two or more drunken men on his own. To give one more instance, in October 1880 Sergeant Lowe was admonished to display more zeal and activity in the discharge of his duty. A gipsy encampment on New Down, Ventnor had to be removed, and the sergeant, in place of undertaking this difficult and troublesome duty himself, sent merely a second-class constable to deal with the situation. Thus he had avoided 'a very unpleasant duty on a very wet morning'.

We have already seen what a lofty conception of his duties Captain Forrest held and how wide he considered the scope of his authority to be. He had no hesitation in extending his forceful comments to the families of those serving under him. In 1887 the chief constable in General Orders regretted that the opinion had been forced on him that if Sergeant Gibson had his deserts he would be reduced to the rank and pay of a constable. In the preceding ten years, since his promotion, Gibson had been reported five times for neglect of duty; and now 'he and Mrs Gibson have encouraged some very young constables at Gosport to write a letter to the chief constable which Mrs Gibson posted, containing an insinuation, rather than a direct accusation, that the superintendent had not reported to the chief constable an irregularity which had occurred at the station, thinking, no doubt, to damage the superintendent. They were very much disconcerted on discovering that the matter had been fully reported, and that the chief constable unknown to them had visited Gosport Police Station and disposed of the case in a way which appeared to him the most expedient, seven days before their letter was written. Thus the little game of Sergeant and Mrs Gibson was exposed and spoilt.' The 'little game' of revenge against the superintendent had been provoked by the series of adverse reports and fines inflicted on Sergeant Gibson for neglect of duty. For on one previous occasion at least he had failed to make a proper entry in his occurrence book and been reprimanded for taking upon himself the discretion and responsibilities of his superintendent. Captain Forrest expressed himself as reluctant to inflict a punishment on an old officer of 26 years' service which would reduce not only his pay but also his pension but it was impossible to allow such constant reports against Sergeant Gibson to continue. 'No doubt in this last business Mrs Gibson is a great deal more to blame than her husband, but a police officer, if he has the misfortune to be wedded to a meddlesome intriguing woman, should control her and so far as police business is concerned must be held responsible for her actions. The chief constable hopes this will be a caution to both Sergeant Gibson and his wife, for most assuredly if they adopt such underhand means of endeavouring to injure any senior officer, they will find it a case of the *Biter Bit* ...'

A rather less unsavoury fall from grace was the lot of Sergeant Somerville in 1889. It might be said that it was his excessive generosity that had led him astray, for, driving one day in the county cart from Droxford to Fareham, he gave a lift to a female, in conscious defiance of the standing orders against the use of the conveyance by other than authorised persons. Fortune was against him, for when nearly at Fareham the horse broke its knees. He reported the accident but said nothing about 'having a female in the cart, which showed that he was perfectly aware he was doing wrong in driving her in the county cart'. The divisional superintendent, on the instructions of the chief constable, questioned Somerville, who claimed that he did not know the young woman and that he had never seen her before. He had merely overtaken the girl carrying a basket and offered her a lift, which had gone smoothly until the collapse of the wretched horse. 'Such is the story told by a sergeant of the Hants Constabulary' sneered Captain Forrest. 'It seems rather more like what might have occurred years ago when a man-of-war arrived in port from a foreign station, and the women used to flock to the beach and sing "Please, Waterman, ferry me over to a good ship called the *Fame,* For I've got a husband on board, but blow me if I know his name!" than an incident that could occur in a disciplined constabulary force at the present day.' Thus stern rebuke was seasoned with the chief constable's characteristic humour. In the upshot Sergeant Somerville was fined one week's pay and deprived of the use of the horse and cart. For the future he had to perform his duties on foot.

A more searing example of Captain Forrest's style of admonition is to be found in the reproof given to Superintendent Brinson in September 1880 as a consequence of his slackness, ineptitude and lack of imagination. A Mr Frank Swinbourne, when bathing at Bournemouth, either lost or had stolen from his pocket ten pounds in cash and two cheques, one of them for over twenty pounds. He reported his loss to Sergeant Alexander, who 48 hours later passed on his information to Superintendent Brinson. It apparently went no further. No entry was made in the occurrence book either in Ringwood or Bournemouth, nor was the information circulated to the police beyond Ringwood Division. The whole thing 'was treated by Superintendent Brinson not with the suspicion, said to be natural to police officers, that a crime had probably been committed, or if lost that the property might have fallen into dishonest hands, but with that innocence of youth which believes everybody to be good. The loss of a handful of gold and silver, a few cheques and a bank note or two was treated as of no consideration … The innocent mind of the superintendent was not disturbed with the idea that there might have been a robbery. No information was even circulated of the loss. Ringwood Division was treated as a little world of itself, a fool's paradise. The chief constable hopes Superintendent Brinson's mind is now opened and that he will take a wider view of the world in general. Ringwood Division is not Hampshire – Hampshire is not the United Kingdom – the United Kingdom does not even keep within its boundaries all lost or stolen property. Thieves will go beyond the seas. Stolen and lost property finds its way over the sea.' So with heavy sarcasm Superintendent Brinson was castigated. Doubtless the treatment rankled and very probably he was more watchful in the future. It was the latter result that was important for the well-being of the force.

However, the chief constable's strong words and firm action did not always go unchallenged. In 1881 there was tortuous discussion among the county authorities of the case of Sergeant Abraham and in that controversy voices were heard very critical of Captain Forrest's harsh and unbending attitude. In November 1880 when the police had been engaged in dealing with the customary 'Guy Fawkes' riots in Bournemouth, certain acts of violence were said to have been committed by a sergeant. An enquiry was held which resulted in the chief constable having a strong impression that Sergeant Abraham had been the guilty party; and the latter, when he left the chief constable's office, was convinced that he was about to be punished for an offence of which, as it was afterwards proved, he was innocent. The sergeant had been ordered to return to his station at Gosport, but before doing so, he went for a drink in the *St James's* tavern in Winchester. A few days later he was again called to headquarters and the chief constable, having in fact found out that a Sergeant Russell was the guilty party, acquitted Abraham of the charge brought against him. The chief constable then, however, accused Abraham of having entered into idle conversation with civilians in a public house and uttered remarks of a highly insubordinate character.

The evidence on which this charge was based rested solely on a statement made by Third-Class Constable Scanlan, who later deserted. It further came out that the tavern pointed out by Scanlan as the one in which Abraham had made his comments was quite another from the *St James* and one which Abraham had never entered. Sergeant Abraham admitted he had spoken improperly, under the stress of his indignation, but denied emphatically having made use of the expressions attributed to him viz., 'If the chief constable takes off my stripes, I will throw up my uniform and report to the magistrates at Gosport, and get my case before the Police Committee.'

Despite this explanation and apology, the chief constable on 29 November issued an order reducing Sergeant Abraham to the rank of first-class constable and at the same time instructed him to remove from Gosport to Shipton, 43 miles away. This Abraham refused to do. He remained firm in this attitude, even after the serious consequences of it were pointed out to him. He maintained that the removal allowance of 1s. per mile was quite inadequate to remove his family and effects so great a distance. Furthermore he regarded his posting as an additional punishment and quite unjustified. However, he admitted that he had refused to obey the chief constable's order and the upshot was that Abraham was called on to resign. A memorial to the County Court was presented on his behalf and the whole matter was referred to the Police Committee. From this in turn came the exhaustive debate on the powers and conduct of the chief constable.

On the one side it was urged that Abraham had certainly acted in a blameable fashion but under circumstances of great provocation. Considering his long service and the fact of his having been wrongfully charged, it was to be regretted that, having admitted his fault and apologised for it, he had been treated with such severity. Nevertheless, he *had* been guilty of insubordination and for that reason the committee found themselves unable to recommend the chief constable to reconsider his sentence of reduction. They did suggest, however, that 'whenever so large a force is required on special service, it is desirable that it should be commanded by the chief constable in person and that so important a responsibility should not be placed on subordinate officers'. Following on this it was proposed that in all future cases of reduction of non-commissioned officers, of enforced resignations and of dismissals, the chief constable should report in writing the circumstances to the Police Committee for their information and guidance. Surely here was a threat to the authority of the chief! Was not this proposal calculated to undermine his influence? Many thought so. But others were influenced by the argument of Captain Field, R.N., that 'the discipline of the police force could be maintained only upon principles of justice'. No one with experience of command in the armed services would have listened to the third-hand tittle-tattle brought to him; the more so as the reported tittle-tattle had been uttered in a public house, not in the presence of policemen and thus having had no injurious effect upon the police force. Officers in the habit of commanding men would not have listened to such reports, but would only have admonished the man and sent him away gratified and contented and sorry he had ever uttered such words at all. The chief constable had lost a golden opportunity, for it would have been god-like to forgive a wrong! The more so since it might very well be held that Abraham had been provoked into disobedience by an order which itself was unlawful. For it will be remembered that by the report of the Committee in 1867, presided over by Sir William Heathcote, it had been laid down as a cardinal principle that men were not to be removed as a punishment.

On the other hand it was argued that Captain Forrest had acted completely within his lawful authority, as defined in the Acts 2nd and 3rd Victoria, which provided that the chief constable at his pleasure might dismiss all or any of the constables and should have the general disposition and government of the constables to be appointed. Moreover, surely it was inadvisable and unjust that the court should interfere with the discipline of the force. The chief constable alone was strictly responsible for this discipline and for the force's management and general efficiency. The Court of Quarter Sessions had power to remove the chief constable if he were incompetent or unworthy of the office but so long as they considered him to be qualified to be at the head of the force they must trust him, and had no right to interfere with the exercise of his discretion. In the end a motion critical of Captain Forrest was dropped and the affair blew over. As for Abraham, he had compensated himself by gaining a post in the Portsmouth force.

Clearly the incident detracted not a whit from the chief constable's self-confidence and zeal in hammering his subordinates into acceptable modes of conduct. Orders streamed out dealing with all sorts of activity, desirable and otherwise. Policemen were forbidden to indulge in free rides on the foot boards of luggage trains. Even legal travelling by rail was frowned on. The chief constable had observed a disposition on the part of sergeants and constables to avail themselves unduly of this form of transport, to the detriment of the proper fulfilment of their duties. For only by patrolling the roads did policemen afford a feeling of security to the countryside through which they passed and success-fully keep an eye on highway and vagrancy offences, irregularities and nuisances of every sort. They were enjoined, when in court, not to sit lounging back in their chairs with legs stretched out as if perfectly indifferent to the court and without responsibility of any kind for its proceedings. They were reminded that, in accordance with the Instruction Book, they were not to sign any document without making themselves acquainted with the contents. This last injunction was inspired by the case of a travelling 'supervisee', William Fox, who sometimes went about the country selling nuts, and to aid him in his commercial activities was apt to display a paper bearing the signatures of several police officers, not one of whom it turned out had the faintest idea of what it was they had signed. Each in turn had affixed his name just because other police officers had already done so. As might be expected, Captain Forrest had a suitable tag to apply to such sheep-like behaviour. 'Four farthings make a penny, one fool makes many.' Some 'fools' were of senior rank. In 1884 Superintendent Paine, who had previously been repeatedly cautioned by the chief constable for his general want of knowledge, was sternly scolded for having 'thought proper to pursue his own ignorant course, till he has nearly brought disgrace and disaster on a constable of his division, and through him on the general body of the Hants Constabulary'. In a well-meant endeavour to trap an unlicensed dealer in game, Paine 'in self-satisfied ignorance' had induced one of his constables to sell a pheasant to the suspected person, thus rendering the unfortunate policeman himself liable to penalties for the unlawful selling of game. The crowning humiliation for the superintendent came in the chief constable's order that 'except in the most ordinary routine of police business', he was to refer to headquarters before taking any proceedings whatever!

More severe punishment came upon a Constable Meacham, who had brought discredit upon the force by joining in a party given by dishonest servants in their employer's house at Broughton. This sordid carouse had not broken up until 4 a.m. Far from protecting property, more especially in the absence of the owner, Meacham had assisted in misusing it. He was dismissed the service and in addition fined a week's pay.

Pecuniary obligation of another sort fell upon Inspector Duke in 1885. He had been directed to order a carriage and a good pair of horses to meet the Government Inspector at Andover Railway Station. But the officer had complied with the order by sending 'a pair of "old screws" one without legs and the other without feet'. These unhappy beasts were so lame that after four miles' travelling the Government Inspector and the chief constable had to get out and walk. The two dignitaries were eventually picked up by a mineral water van going its rounds and through the kindness of the man in charge were driven again to the nearest railway station. The consequence was that Kingsclere Division, which had been paraded for inspection at Whitchurch, waited in vain for the Government Inspector and finally was dismissed unreviewed. The expenses incurred in parading the division were to be borne by Inspector Duke.

The imperative need for discretion and impeccable conduct on the part of police officers was once more brought home strongly by another incident which gave rise to disciplinary action. In May 1888 Detective Sergeant Young and Sergeant Butler set out to escort one John French from Hartley Wintney to the railway station at Winchfield, en route to Aldershot. The prisoner was charged with setting fire to the furze on Hazeley Heath. Just after passing the *Phoenix Inn*, the two sergeants heard some shouting which they believed to emanate from the inn and to be directed against them. Instead of steadfastly marching on to Winchfield they rashly turned back to the *Phoenix* with their prisoner and became involved in a noisy altercation with the landlord's wife and sons, the landlord himself being ill in bed at the time. Tempers ran high, but fortunately no physical violence took place, though it was later asserted that Detective-Sergeant Young brandished a walking-stick in a threatening manner. Thereafter a letter was received by the chief constable from one of the landlord's sons complaining of the officers' conduct, of what were claimed to be false accusations and of their insolence. It was also alleged that they appeared to be under the influence of drink at the time.

Upon investigation by the deputy chief constable it was established that there was no substance in the last charge, at least. But both Young and Butler were admonished for their lack of discretion and good sense. It was entirely due to this lack 'that they laid themselves open to the charges brought against them; more than this, they might have been assaulted and also have lost their prisoner; perfect command of temper and indifference to taunts are amongst the first qualifications of a police officer. The credit of the service demands and the public expect it.'

Such a *contretemps* on licensed premises was likely to touch the chief constable on the raw. For earlier that same year he had received an application to allow a Sergeant Hale to receive a testimonial upon his removal from the district of Yarmouth. This removal had been ordered by Captain Forrest on receipt of complaints against the sergeant of want of police supervision and inattention on the part of the constabulary to the interest of the ratepayers. So the chief constable scrutinised the list of subscribers to the proposed testimonial with understandable suspicion. Nor was he surprised to find that nearly a third of them were licensed victuallers and refreshment house keepers! 'It does not require a person to see through a milestone to account for the neglect of police duties in that district.' The sergeant was not allowed to receive the testimonial.

An act 'of negligence and folly' that required marked punishment was that committed by First-Class Constables Hale and Kimber in 1888. Investigating the theft of some poultry, they visited an encampment of gypsies and grew suspicious of one Albert Smith because his boots corresponded with footmarks found near the place from which the poultry had been stolen. So far so good and in their eagerness the two constables actually told Smith of the similarity between his boots and the footmarks. But then they went off elsewhere in pursuit of their enquiries, neglecting to take possession of the boots. They returned later only to find that Smith had decamped. Later he was apprehended and charged but at the subsequent trial was acquitted; for in the meantime he had very naturally removed nails and altered the appearance of his boots so that evidence of similarity was wanting. Out of respect for their previous good character Kimber and Hale were not reduced to the second class, but merely fined a week's pay each.

Worse than such folly was the practice of 'shuffling' or malingering. At the beginning of 1890 First-Class Constable Hurford was ordered to report himself to Inspector Paine at Bournemouth. The very day on which he was supposed to arrive in Bournemouth Hurford wrote to the inspector to say he was unwell and unable to move. Inspector Paine, of course, only received the letter the following day. Forthwith he requested the medical officer in charge of the district to call upon the constable. This the doctor did and found that Hurford 'was downstairs dressed, very slight fur on tongue, no pulse rise, no raised temperature and could detect no lung mischief. I do not see what he is to go on the sick list for, in my opinion he is quite able to come to see you, and I can see no tangible reason why he did not go to his duty yesterday, he may be developing one of these colds but if so it is very slight.' In consequence Police Constable Hurford was called on to resign from the service.

The next month a characteristic thunderbolt fell upon Inspector Paine, now in charge at Basingstoke. The chief constable had visited the police station and had found it dirty and discreditable, the cupboards in the dormitory more like a marine store dealers' establishment than a county police station. Inspector Paine was instructed to mend his ways and to keep the place clean in such a way that it might 'in future be a credit to the constabulary, in place of being … a disgrace to a home for lost dogs'. The chief constable was nothing if not impartial and universal in his reproofs. Some months later he inveighed against the indiscipline and skylarking which seemed to be going on in the police station at Gosport, in which all ranks were involved. According to a report made out by Superintendent Catchlove against Second-Class Constable Butler, 'there seems to have been a sort of running fight of irritating nature and manner between Superintendent Catchlove and the police constable for about thirty hours, all of which is very detrimental to discipline, and it is derogatory to an officer of the rank of superintendent to wrangle with a police constable'. Resident in the police station were, besides the superintendent, one detective-sergeant and two sergeants, who must all have been aware of the disorder and to have suffered it to go on under their noses until it had grown so big that it came to the notice of the chief constable himself. One and all they were warned that if they could not maintain proper discipline at the station, they would, one and all, be dealt with severely.

No less evident than his endless concern to maintain and improve discipline was Captain Forrest's anxiety to use both advances in hygiene and new mechanical devices to the benefit of his men. In 1883 authority was secured for the inspector at Bournemouth to hire a tricycle 'which would be of great assistance to him and add considerably to the efficiency of the police in that district'. So useful did this machine prove that a few months later a special shelter and gate were provided for it. Towards the end of 1885 there was another sign of Bournemouth's eager awareness of technical advance; it was suggested that the police station there might be made the centre for communication by telephone with different parts of the district in case of fire. However, the authorities considered that such a development might lead to confusion and rejected the scheme. Nevertheless, as has been seen, both the telephone and telegraph were in increasing use, as was the developing science of photography. And at the end of 1888 advantage was taken of an offer by the Western Counties Telephone Company at Southampton, whereby the police stations at Bitterne, Woolston, and Shirley were connected by a private wire at the cost of £50 per annum. As for hygiene, the chief constable had amply demonstrated his horror of filth and constant preoccupation with such matters as the provision of pure water at the police stations and the effective disposal of waste. In 1874, for example, illness was caused, at Bournemouth again, by lead poisoning in the water supply of the station and Captain Forrest conferred with the county surveyor as to changing the lead cistern for one of galvanised iron.

By 1890 the force had once more increased in size and changed in organisation. In 1882 the Bournemouth Division had been formed and placed under the charge of Inspector Alexander, who was directed to supervise all police duties 'within the Bournemouth Commissioners' district and in the country in their vicinity, to the south of the River Stour'. In 1885 the force gained four more constables who were stationed at Aldershot, Boscombe, Bournemouth, and Hamble respectively. The authorised strength was now, apart from the chief constable, as follows: 12 superintendents, one detective inspector, four inspectors, two detective-sergeants, 31 sergeants, and 251 constables of all three classes. Consequent upon the Local Government Act of the previous year, in 1889 the borough police of both Basingstoke and Newport were amalgamated with the Hampshire Constabulary, which meant the addition to the enlarged force of one inspector, six sergeants and 15 constables. This gain, however, was more than cancelled out the following year when on 1 April 1890 the Isle of Wight became a separate administrative county. Forty-seven officers of the Hampshire Constabulary were thus transferred to the new independent island force, comprising one superintendent, one inspector, seven sergeants, 14 first-class constables, 16 second-class, and eight third-class. The next month the Home Secretary authorised the augmentation of the force by nine more constables and simultaneously the four constables on duty at the expense of the Bournemouth Commissioners were taken on the authorised strength of the force. The total strength of the force, of all ranks, was now two hundred and ninety.

By this time, too, the authority governing the police in the county had changed in form and character. The Local Government Act of 1888 had set up county councils, and given them some share in the administration of the police by substituting for the justices alone, joint committees of county councillors and justices. The Standing Joint Committee had appeared. In the same period other changes took place in the status of individual police officers. In 1887 they gained the right to vote in parliamentary elections, and in 1893 an equivalent right in municipal elections.

BOOK 3
1890-1915

Captain Forrest retired on superannuation in March 1891 and was succeeded as chief constable by Captain Peregrine Henry Thomas Fellowes. This officer had had an active and varied military career, and was appointed by the Standing Joint Committee from among 74 applicants. He was in his fortieth year, strikingly handsome, and seems to have been the very model, the 'beau ideal', of a Victorian gentleman. After service at the Royal Military College, Sandhurst, he joined the 31st (East Surrey) Regiment in 1873 and was appointed adjutant in 1880. Then followed several years of employment in Australia, chiefly at Melbourne with the Victorian military forces. There he was successively deputy assistant adjutant-general and assistant adjutant-general, with the local rank of first major and then lieutenant-colonel. He held these posts with distinction and was highly regarded. On his return to the United Kingdom, he resumed command of his company and was stationed with them at Tipperary. From there he took the fateful step of applying for the post of Chief Constable of the Hampshire Constabulary.

Captain Fellowes' term of office was to be brief, and to end tragically. In October 1893 he was fatally injured as a result of his brave action in attempting to stop a runaway horse. At about ten o'clock in the morning of 2 October a Mr and Mrs Best were travelling in their trap from Chilland to Mottisfont, when their horse took fright at a restive cow which was being led into Winchester Market. The horse shied, throwing the couple from their conveyance and then, slewing round, bolted back towards the city with the empty trap. Coming upon the steep road leading down to the constabulary headquarters the terrified animal lost control of itself and thundered down the slope at a terrifying pace. Three constables who were on the point of entering the quarters quickly formed themselves into a line across the road, intending to try to stop the runaway. At the same moment Captain Fellowes issued from the main gate, on his way for a day's relaxation off-duty. Instantly grasping the situation, he placed himself by the side of his men, completing the cordon across the road. As fate would have it, he was at the end of the line, nearest to the high stone wall surrounding the police headquarters. The horse swerved towards him and he made a belated attempt to get out of the way, but failed because of the wall. The shaft of the trap struck him in the side with appalling force, hurling him several feet; but the horse, continuing in the same direction, lost its balance and fell and for a

3   Captain P.H.T. Fellowes
Chief Constable, 1891-93.

moment Captain Fellowes, the horse, and the trap were all in a heap together. (Certainly the wheel of the vehicle passed over him.) The three constables ran to help their chief and carried him, half-conscious, indoors. Doctors came and it was ascertained that, in addition to a broken collar bone and thigh, and a dislocated knee-cap, Captain Fellowes had sustained a grave internal injury which was diagnosed as a severe laceration of the liver.

For two or three weeks thereafter the chief constable was desperately ill, but then slowly he began to improve and hopes grew of his complete recovery. At the end of November, however, he had a relapse, suffered great pain in his chest, complained of cramps in his leg, and died at five minutes past two in the morning of the 30th. Characteristically, he had employed some of his last waking hours in conversing cheerfully about his plans for action on his return to duty and in particular had taken an interest in matters concerning the constables' recreation room.

At the inquest the coroner expressed heartfelt sympathy for the widow and her six young children, and added that one could not help feeling that the unfortunate deceased had died while doing his duty and in trying to save the lives of others. Very probably others might have been injured by the runaway horse and vehicle, but for Captain Fellowes' heroism. He had done what he could and if a man had to be taken in such a way it was 'a mournful and melancholy satisfaction to say he died in the execution of his duty'. As the *Hampshire Chronicle* put it: 'It is impossible to foresee the inscrutable ways of Providence, but Captain Fellowes' appointment would seem almost to have been ill-fated, for soon after coming to Winchester he contracted a long and serious illness owing to the defective state of the drainage at the constabulary quarters, and now in a sense he may be said to have fallen at the post of duty, or to have met his death by an action which the promptings of a noble nature and a courageous heart inspired him to in the hope of saving others from the risk of danger.' The same journal also remarked that its earlier judgment of Captain Fellowes, as one combining a pleasant, genial disposition with admirable qualities as a disciplinarian, had been more than realised by the experience of the past two and a half years, 'and the excellent work he was enabled to do even within so short a period is likely to prove of enduring benefit to the force'.

There is no doubt of the chief constable's kindliness and benign interest in his men. He took pleasure in informing the force, through General Orders, that Third-Class Constable Matthews, 'who has been suffering from a severe attack of influenza, was taken in to the police seaside home at West Brighton for seven days, where he was most comfortable and well cared for'. And from the end of August 1891 instructions were given that in future all births in the force were to be notified to headquarters, while in the meantime a return of all children of police officers, giving their sex, date of birth, and place of residence, was to be made. The combination of this benignity with concern for the discipline and good name of the force is demonstrated by Captain Fellowes' comments on the outcome of what the press termed 'the Aldershot scandal'. This had arisen from the action of the police in arresting a Mrs Millard and her daughter and from the charges brought against the latter. One night in Aldershot Police Constable Bradbury was arresting Mrs Millard for disorderly conduct, when her 17-year-old daughter Alice came up and directed at him a stream of grossly abusive language. She too was arrested by Bradbury, and charged with both drunkenness and being a disorderly character. Sergeant Cottle, who was also involved, went farther and accused Alice Millard of being a prostitute. According to the prosecution later, these charges against the girl were wilful and corrupt perjury. The two police officers were duly placed on trial for perjury at Winchester Assizes and the case aroused national interest. This was a time, unhappily by no means unique, when the police service was subject to a great deal of adverse criticism, much of it ignorant and malicious. Strenuous efforts were made to prove that the girl Millard was chaste and of respectable reputation. A medical examination, made at her own request, established her technical virtue; on the other hand, the police carried their point that they 'had constantly seen her in the lowest company, and in houses which were frequented only by women of the class named'.

In the result, the jury pronounced Police Constable Bradbury, and also Sergeant Cottle, 'Not guilty' of perjury, judging that the officers honestly believed in the truth of their charges. 'The issue of the Millard case,' growled the *Birmingham Daily Post*, 'is a victory for the police, but it is one of which they have no reason to be proud. The police are acquitted of the charge of perjury in swearing that Alice Millard, whom they had "run in" was a girl of loose character, but the jury found them guilty of negligence in not making enquiries as to the character of the girl between the time of her arrest and the police court proceedings which resulted in her acquittal.' The *Post* went on to comment sourly, 'Mistakes, we know, will happen in the best regulated families, but then we expect them to be frankly acknowledged, apologised for, and rectified. The Aldershot police evidently prefer to aggravate their offence by striving to justify it.'

For his part, Captain Fellowes expressed his 'extreme satisfaction at the acquittal of these officers, of whose innocence he was never in doubt'. At the same time he thought it his duty to point out the danger of preferring a vague charge instead of one of a definite character and emphasised that this caution was intended especially for young constables. He then commented understandingly, 'Police Constable Bradbury had probably a dislike to charge his prisoner with assaulting him in the execution of his duty and consequently made another charge against her which, as events have shown, was very hard to prove. The honest opinion of the jury has averted a blow which would have been seriously felt by the police at Aldershot, by the force in general, and which would to a certain extent have affected every police officer in England.'

Captain Fellowes was to meet his untimely death because of a runaway horse, and it is ironical that just over a year previously he had occasion to commend the courageous conduct of Third-Class Police Constable Christopher 'in stopping at the imminent risk of his life, a runaway horse attached to a trap in Wellington Street, Aldershot ... at a time when the street was crowded with people and vehicular traffic. Had it not been for the plucky conduct of the police constable, most serious results would in all probability have happened. There cannot be a doubt that Police Constable Christopher has by this action, not only deserved the thanks of the community, but has in addition reflected credit on the whole force.' The constable's name was noted for promotion. Perhaps this gallantry helped to cancel out the unsavoury light which the 'perjury case' had seemed to cast upon the police. The incident is also a reminder that traffic problems, accidents and fatalities are by no means peculiar to the era of the motor car. The horse presented not just a problem, but also a temptation. For it had come to the ears of the chief constable that members of the force, when on duty at race-meetings, had indulged in betting. 'Such a practice is most reprehensible and must be discontinued.'

Though universally considered a kindly and generous man, Captain Fellowes could no more brook slackness than could his formidable predecessor. In 1892 he had occasion to reduce his chief clerk, Superintendent Bowles, to the rank of sergeant, and Inspector Paine was reduced to first-class constable. Nor were these isolated cases. In November 1891 Superintendent Russell had been reduced to the rank of first-class constable for 'committing irregularities in his accounts'. Less dramatic was the punishment of Second-Class Constable Boyde, who had foolishly allowed a prisoner to escape by letting him enter his cottage unescorted to fetch his coat, without taking any precaution to prevent his leaving at the back. The chief constable allowed Boyde a week's unpaid leave to try to recapture the prisoner, but all to no avail. Consequently Boyde was reduced to third-class constable. Captain Fellowes regretted having to do this as he had had excellent reports of Boyde hitherto, but felt 'he must mark his sense of displeasure at such gross carelessness'.

From the beginning of 1891 there had been an increase of pay for all ranks. First-class superintendents were to have an addition to their pay of 3d. per day after five years' service and further increments of 3d. per day after ten and 15 years. Superintendents of the second and third class, and inspectors were to receive similar additions, except that there was no mention of any further increment beyond the 3d. per day they were to receive after ten years' service. Sergeants and first-class constables were to have an addition to their pay of 1d. a day and an increase of 1d. per day at intervals of two years up to ten years' service. Second-class constables were to have an extra 1d. per day, an increase of 1d. per day after two years' service, and a further increase of 1d. per day after four years' service. Lastly, third-class constables were to have an addition to their pay of 2d.

per day after one year's service. Although at most these increases amounted to only a shilling or so per week, it has to be remembered that three-quarters of a century ago even a penny had considerable purchasing power.

The next year the pension scale, which had been adopted by the police authority in 1890, was amended as regards the age limit as follows: 'The limit of age, below which a constable is not entitled to retire on a pension without a medical certificate, shall be fifty years, or in case of a constable above the rank of sergeant, fifty-five years.' There was also a further slight increase in strength, as the Home Secretary authorised the addition of six second-class sergeants and four constables to the force and that the drill instructor should rank as sergeant-major. The total number of the county constabulary was now 311 men.

Captain Fellowes was succeeded as chief constable by Major St Andrew Bruce Warde, whose term of office was to equal in length that of Captain Forrest for Major Warde was to remain chief constable until 1928 and to preside over the force throughout the tumultuous opening decades of the 20th century, including the portentous years of the First World War. The arrival of motorised transport on a large scale, the impact on everyday life of modern warfare, the changes inherent in an increasingly complex and mobile society – all these created problems with which inevitably the police had to contend. It is a truism that all periods are periods of change. Yet seldom in British society have there been such broad and deep changes as occurred during this time. Between the 1890s and the 1920s stretches a tremendous quagmire of technical advance, social dislocation, and armed violence. Across the whole distance, Major Warde directed the activities of the Hampshire Constabulary. It was a memorable chief constableship. Indeed, it is worth remarking that in the whole of its existence the force has had only eight chiefs. Major Warde's tenancy of the post was one of the longest. He assumed command on 26 February 1894.

Regardless of this change of leadership, necessitated by the tragic death of Captain Fellowes, the work of the force went on ceaselessly. In 1893, 30 Hampshire officers were sent to help the Nottinghamshire police to suppress the riots taking place in that area in connection with the coal strike. This help to their comrades in another county laid certain burdens upon the Hampshire force. Until the end of October that year, no more passes were to be granted and then only under special circumstances. The contingent returned on 6 November, just two months after their departure, and evidently they had performed this special duty most efficiently. The chief constable from his sickbed made known to the force his great pleasure in the fact that the discipline and conduct of those officers and the cheerful and willing manner in which they performed their duties had been most favourably commented on by the chief constable of Nottinghamshire. Superintendent Payne, who had commanded the party, and Sergeant Daniels were specially mentioned as having been of great assistance to their host.

Other duties which came round year by year were those brought by the need for extra surveillance during the hop-picking season and by the special arrangements made necessary by military manoeuvres. The nightly watch on Laverstoke Mills was maintained as it had been since 1865, and in 1897 one constable was 'cautioned for having neglected his duty by failing to pull five check clocks' there. Traffic accidents abounded, and frequently gave occasion for displays of alertness and bravery on the part of the police. In the summer of 1898 First-Class Constable Ballard was commended for the presence of mind and prompt action shown in stopping three horses attached to a bus; the animals had run off during the absence of their driver. The Standing Joint Committee granted the sum of £2 to the constable as a reward for his meritorious act. A similar act was performed by First-Class Constable Jennings, who stopped a bus with a pair of horses attached which had bolted from the *Grand Hotel* in Bournemouth, while Second-Class Constable Haigh was commended for his attempt to stop another runaway horse in the same town. Another second-class constable, J.H. West, was praised for rescuing a child from being run over by a carriage in Aldershot.

The perennial problem of tracking down and arresting deserters and other miscreants from the armed forces occupied a good deal of attention. In 1898 the Under Secretary of State at the Home Office informed the chief constable that the War Office, following the example of the Admiralty with regard to sailors, had requested that soldiers in uniform, when in the custody of the civil power, should not be marched through the streets. 'I am to request that in such cases cabs or other covered carriages may be employed. The cost of providing such conveyances will be recoverable from army funds, and the Secretary of State is informed that the general officers commanding districts will be directed to arrange to pay locally expenses of this kind on being properly vouched by the police.' The resultant arrangements were affirmed in General Orders in August 1899, whereby all prisoners were to be conveyed from Winchester Railway Station to H.M. prison in cabs, at a fixed tariff. Mr Parrott of Station Hill, Winchester, had contracted to take four persons or under, per journey, at 1s. 6d.; and five persons or more, at 6d. each. It was also provided that a sixpenny telegram be sent direct to Mr Parrott, notifying him of the number of prisoners and escort, the time of arrival, and where from. 'A bill will be made out on Form 13 and handed to Mr Parrott for signature.'

Another return called for from each division was one showing how stray dogs were destroyed at each police station and, if poisoned, the kind of poison used. It was ordered that for the future prussic acid would be used for the purpose, thus ensuring the beasts a painless death. Divisional officers were to purchase a syringe for use at each police station; the syringe was to be charged with the quantity required, the dogs' mouth opened, and the acid shot down its throat. The order added helpfully, 'The quantity required to a terrier is about half a dram, and three-quarters of a dram for a larger dog.' It was also stipulated that the necessary prussic acid would be purchased each time it was required and not kept in hand.

In 1898 a so-called 'Gypsy Diary' was issued to each sergeant in charge of a sub-division, and also to the appropriate sergeant at the divisional station, in order that a careful record might be kept of the gypsies in each district. On the basis of statistics supplied by the constables on the beat, numbers and other relevant particulars were to be noted. 'The column "Remarks" is intended to include any observations which are likely to be useful, such as whether the gipsies refused to move on when requested to do so by the police, whether they had permission to remain, etc.' Superintendents were instructed to inspect the gypsy diaries quarterly and to initial them and to ensure that they were kept up to date against the time of their production at inspections.

By this time the force had once more increased in strength. The Home Secretary had approved an addition of one inspector, two sergeants, and 27 constables to take effect on and from 1 April 1898. This brought to 381 the total number of the Hampshire Constabulary. The new officers were to be distributed in the following manner: Alton, Petersfield and Winchester divisions received one additional police constable each, Fareham four, and Southampton five; Bournemouth gained one inspector, one sergeant, and 11 police constables, while the mounted police acquired one sergeant and four police constables. Two years previously the chief constable had secured a new and improved scale of pay, announcing contentedly, 'The pay of the Hants Constabulary having hitherto compared unfavourably with that of other forces, the chief constable determined to endeavour to have the former placed upon a better footing. He is happy to be in a position to state that his efforts in that direction have met with success. In notifying the new scale of pay the chief constable feels assured that he can rely upon all ranks showing their appreciation of his efforts in their behalf and of the success they have met with at the hands of the Standing Joint Committee, by evincing, if possible, increased zeal in the performance of their duties.' This last comment perhaps echoed an earlier warning that Major Warde had given with regard to promotion. 'Promotion is slow in the force, and there are numbers of good men waiting their turn for promotion. So that when a constable is selected for advancement he must prove himself worthy of such selection, otherwise another man will be given the chance he has thrown away.'

1897 was the year of Queen Victoria's Diamond Jubilee and the Hampshire police both shared in the national rejoicing and benefited from it. Major Warde secured approval of his recommendation to the Standing Joint Committee that an extra three days' pay be given to all ranks to commemorate the occasion. Earlier he had on his own authority granted three extra days' leave to all ranks and now here was some cash to match it! Certainly the chief constable expressed the hope that every member of the force would thoroughly enjoy the holiday.

In the following year Her Majesty visited Aldershot on 6, 7 and 8 July and naturally much work fell upon the police by way of preparation and supervision. The chief constable was unable to oversee arrangements there personally, but he announced that he had been notified that all had been satisfactory and that the duties had been carried out in a very creditable manner by the police concerned. He desired to express to the officer in charge, Superintendent Hawkins, 'his appreciation of the satisfactory manner in which he discharged his onerous duties on this occasion'. Major Warde stressed the fact that he was 'very pleased to find that the mounted police fully justified his reliance upon them and performed their duties in a sturdy and reliable manner, controlling their horses well and turning out smartly'. All those engaged on duty at the review were granted one day's extra leave.

Indeed, Major Warde during his term of office made a point of taking a steady interest in the welfare of his men, not least in respect of leave. Annual leave was increased from one day off each month to one day off each fortnight. He took steps to secure better housing for the constables. As early as August 1894 it was notified in General Orders that 'Officers in charge of divisions will be held responsible that all their constables are decently and comfortably housed and will send in a report of any house which they consider unsuitable.'

A keen cricketer himself, he did a great deal to encourage sport and recreation of all sorts and to emphasise the importance of proper recreation. He pronounced himself thoroughly in favour of divisional annual matches and outings for wives and children of police officers, and countenanced subscriptions being received from magistrates and others, though discretion, of course, was to be shown by officers in charge of divisions in this matter. 'No subscriptions are to be received from any person directly interested in any licensed business, the reason for which is obvious. A list of subscribers, stating their occupation and an annual account of expenditure will be kept for the information of the chief constable of those concerned.'

For if Major Warde was kind, he was also firm. Anxious for the well-being and happiness of his men, he was even more concerned to maintain the highest standards of integrity. Again and again he insisted on the imperative necessity of this. In 1894 one constable was called upon to resign from the force for using unlawful violence to a prisoner and 'for telling a falsehood when giving his evidence'. After mature deliberation, the chief constable decided that, in the interests of both the public and the police, the constable should leave the service. 'It is with regret that the chief constable has arrived at this decision, as hitherto the police constable has borne a very good character and has all the appearance of making a smart and efficient officer. But it is due to the public that they should be able to feel implicit confidence in the integrity and uprightness of our officers when giving their evidence.' The chief constable added that he hoped that the whole unpleasant incident would serve as a warning to the members of the force never to allow themselves to deviate in the smallest particular from strict accuracy and absolute truth when giving their evidence.

Other orders concerned with discipline and correct procedure throw interesting light upon the circumstances of the day. Police officers were directed to report any irregularity or neglect of duty on the part of their superior officers. In cases where a constable was found drunk, he was not to be questioned until he was sober. For over-indulgence in drink still remained a great problem and a prime agent in disrupting discipline. Major Warde pointed out that as a rule a single charge of giving way to drink unfitted a man to remain in a police force. It being the duty of the police to deal with drunkenness on the part of the public, constables had no excuse for similar lapses. If a police constable therefore 'chooses to risk his position and the credit of the force, he must expect to take the natural consequence, viz. dismissal'. Members of the constabulary should bear in mind that, in dealing with reports against constables, the first consideration was to afford an example to others and so safeguard as far as possible the interests of the public and ratepayers and the credit of the force. One first-class constable was reduced to the third class and cautioned for not reporting a supposed robbery to his superintendent until 25 hours after receiving the information; and when he did get around to reporting the occurrence he was dead drunk, and in plain clothes. The wearing of uniform correctly and the whole matter of dress generally continued to be a main concern of the police authorities. From the end of 1893, all ranks were permitted to wear a white linen collar, 'provided that such collar shall not in any case show more than one-eighth of an inch above the tunic'. The collar was to be fastened to the inside lining of the tunic collar. 'The collars, if kept clean, should give an improved appearance to the wearer,' and, added the order optimistically, 'It is hoped that all ranks will avail themselves of this concession, so that uniformity may prevail.' In dirty weather sergeants and constables were invariably to wear their gaiters when on duty. 'In putting on gaiters the trowser legs should be slightly drawn up, so as to enable the trowsers to be folded neatly down over the top of the gaiters.'

As might be expected, casualness in dress was only too likely to creep in, especially in the smaller country stations. Sergeants and constables were reminded that it was always necessary to wear a coat when attending to callers. In 1899 the chief constable was apprised of 'a habit of constables sometimes enforcing ejectment warrants in plain clothes and smoking whilst performing this duty'. Such irregular conduct was forbidden for the future, but as a concession it was agreed that old uniform could be worn on these occasions. Another practice forbidden was that of taking constables away from their beats for the purpose of whitewashing police stations, which ought always to be done by station men. And in the summer of 1900 strong disapproval was expressed at the habit of using regulation belts as razor-strops. It was expected that better care would be taken of the gloves issued with the opening of the new century. Superintendents were allotted two pairs of brown leather annually, one of which was for driving, and also one pair of white leather, to be replaced when necessary. Inspectors had the same allowance. Plain-clothes officers had to be content with only the two pairs of brown leather annually, while sergeants and constables received merely one pair of white cotton gloves annually and another pair of black wool every second year.

Over against this mass of petty administrative detail must be set the solid achievement of the force to which a remarkable tribute was paid in the summer of 1899. In the course of an address to the Grand Jury by Mr Justice Wright, he drew attention to the Annual Report of the Inspector of Constabulary for the Southern Counties of England and Wales. In that report Hampshire is the only county with reference to which the observation was made: 'I cannot fail to remark that the apprehension of offenders, in proportion to the crime committed, is exceedingly favourable in the county of Hants.' Mr Justice Wright went on to hope that the chief constable and the officers and men under his command would receive the recognition due to them for this extremely satisfactory state of things. He commented that the number of charges and offences committed had increased in the county, but it had to be borne in mind that this was the natural result of greater skill and zeal in following up crime. The chief constable published the substance of these remarks in General Orders, and in doing so 'desires to express his gratification and to convey his personal thanks to the members of the force which he has the honour to command by having brought such credit on the force by the manner in which they have carried out their duties. He feels that the force is working with him with their hearts as well as their heads and this fact makes it doubly a pleasure to him to study their interests in every way in his power.'

That Major Warde did so study the interests of his subordinates, there is no doubt. As mentioned above, he had secured an increase in annual leave. He made it clear that he had no objection to constables spending their leave at home if they wished, but in such case they had to be prepared to attend promptly to any call which might be made upon their services. However, should any considerable time of their leave be taken up by such calls, the chief constable would be ready to consider an extension of leave. In the meantime, he trusted that those members of the force who took advantage of this order would do so 'in the same spirit which governs its issue, and will not become unduly familiar with the residents in their respective beats nor commit any irregularities that the chief constable would be likely to disapprove of'.

In the last decade of the 19th century some details of police work were changing. The task of inspecting weights and measures, which had been a continual preoccupation of the force, apparently ceased in 1891 with the appointment of inspectors of weights and measures. The county was divided into three districts for this purpose, with a new non-police inspector in each, and the police officers who had hitherto been responsible were instructed to hand over all the impedimenta of the function. Copies of the imperial standards of weights and measures, beams, scales and all articles, except books and forms used by the police superintendents, were to be transferred against appropriate receipts.

In 1894 pocket books – with pencil attached – were issued to every sergeant and constable, and it was impressed upon them that entries in these books 'will relate to matters connected with police work only (such as reports of robberies, descriptions of thieves and suspected persons, statements by witnesses, prisoners, etc.) and are to be made in a legible and careful manner for future reference if necessary'. Another innovation in 1895 was the appearance in October of that year of General Orders in typescript, in place of the manuscript used up till then. This bold experiment did not last, however, for at the beginning of August 1896 there was a reversion to the older style, and the typewriter did not regain the day until the First World War.

Towards the end of 1898 the practice grew up of making more effective use of the resources of the Metropolitan Police. An order was issued that, in cases of burglary where there was a chance of the offender being identified, application was to be made to headquarters for permission to take the witness to New Scotland Yard for the purpose of seeing the photographs of criminals. Yet, still, a great part of the Hampshire force's activity remained bound up with the predominantly rural character of the county. General Orders were largely taken up with measures designed to identify, isolate, and prevent such diseases of animals as swine fever. Though at the same time care had to be exercised to ensure that notices of sheep scab and other afflictions were not posted on such inappropriate places as church doors. Under Section 23 of the Customs and Inland Revenue Act of 1878, the police possessed full powers to take proceedings against persons who failed to comply with the Act by keeping dogs without licence; and from March 1899 the police undertook these proceedings as a regular duty. One half of the penalties exacted were payable to the Police Pension Fund, and the collectors of Inland Revenue were authorised to pay a moiety of the costs incurred in prosecutions by the police, where the costs were not recovered from the defendants. The duties placed upon the police in connection with the whole business of local taxation licences were inclined to be of an invidious nature, and some years later the chief constable stressed that it was of great importance that they should be carried out with discretion and invariable civility. He then instanced a case in which a police officer observed an individual wearing a signet ring and thereupon enquired of the man whether he had taken out a Licence for Armorial Bearings! 'The chief constable strongly disapproves of such action as being offensive, unjustifiable, and inquisitorial.'

In the meantime, events were taking place in the wider world which were to have profound and momentous effects on Great Britain, the British Empire, and the whole international scene. In October 1899 Kruger's troops invaded

Cape Colony in South Africa, and Britain was plunged into the Boer War, the biggest of all her colonial conflicts and one the consequences of which are being unfolded even today. Some British troops were already in South Africa – indeed their gathering there had been the pretext for Kruger to issue his ultimatum – but many more were to be needed in the next two-and-a-half years before the bitter struggle was concluded. Reservists rallied to the colours and the departure of these men had an impact on the Hampshire Constabulary as well as on many other spheres of civilian life. At a meeting of the Standing Joint Committee it was resolved, with the subsequent approval of the Secretary of State, that members of the force who were reservists and who had been called upon for active service be enrolled upon 'a list of supernumeraries without pay' and be permitted to rejoin the force on the termination of their military engagement. This was well enough as far as it went, inasmuch as it secured the future employment of the reservists. But what of money for their dependents? Now appeared a most striking instance of comradeship and generosity. Members of the force of all ranks came forward and agreed to a subscription to help support the wives and families of their colleagues ordered to the front. The chief constable was keenly appreciative of this and affirmed that 'This evidence of the feeling of *esprit de corps* which exists in the Hampshire Constabulary affords their chief much pleasure and pride.' Happily the need for such generosity soon ceased. The Standing Joint Committee resolved that while constables who belonged to the army reserve were on active service, payments out of the Police Fund were to be made on the following scale: in the case of each married reservist an allowance of 10s. a week to his wife, who was also to be permitted to remain in the police cottage, rent free; in the case of single reservists an allowance not exceeding 6s. a week in the discretion of the chief constable to any person whom the reservist is legally liable to maintain and to whose support he has contributed. This may seem little enough to later eyes but perhaps this marginal security for their loved ones did something to strengthen still further the excellent morale of the reservists. In a message wishing the members of the force a happy Christmas and new year, the chief constable could not 'refrain from alluding to the terrible ordeal the country is undergoing through the sufferings and loss of life in South Africa and expressing his appreciation and admiration of the cheerful spirit and keen zest with which our reservists have answered the call to take their places at the front'.

The first batch of reservists to go numbered 20 in all, comprising 14 married men and six single. A second group of 12 went off in March 1900 and again there were more married men than single, seven to five. Nor were the first casualties long in coming. In April 1900 the chief constable regretfully notified the death of Police Constable Frank Rymell who had been one of the first reservists to go and who had fallen victim to dysentery. 'This constable bore a high character in the force, the members of which will without any doubt join with their chief in sympathy for Mrs Rymell.' The police were naturally concerned with the welfare of their own colleagues and their families but in addition the war imposed other responsibilities. Officers in charge of divisions were ordered to direct constables to ascertain if there was any case within their respective beats of wives of soldiers or militiamen who had not received any assistance from the Soldiers' and Sailors' Families' Association. Whenever such a case occurred, the officer in charge of the division was to transmit the relevant facts to the secretary of the association, Colonel Little, at the same time sending a copy of their communication to headquarters. The instruction also cannily suggested that it should be stated whether any assistance was being received from any source.

The same spirit of economy was perhaps evident in a decision of the Standing Joint Committee in January 1900, which reduced the allowance paid to the wives of reservists to only 8s. a week 'in view of the increase of 5d. per day to the wives of reservists from army funds'. Other matters of financial administration about this time included a reminder that all children born to police officers should be reported to headquarters for entry in the register. Should an officer be killed on duty and a pension recommended to his wife and children, only those children that were registered would qualify.

In June 1899 First-Class Constable Jennings was commended for his prompt action in a case of larceny at Meonstoke. He had traced the two men suspected on his bicycle, and had arrested them at Guildford with the stolen property in their possession. Indeed, the bicycle was coming ever more frequently into use as an almost indispensable aid to police work. From early in 1898 constables using their own machines were entitled to a special duty allowance in the same manner 'as when going by train or route march'. The Standing Joint Committee sanctioned an allowance of 15s. per year to each officer in the force who owned a bicycle and used it for police purposes. This allowance started on 1 January 1898, and was payable quarterly. Major Warde later secured authority from the Standing Joint Committee to increase the allowance for the upkeep of the bicycles to the sum of 30s. per year. Officers in charge of divisions were to be responsible that the machines were in fact used by the individuals to whom the allowance was granted and were to inspect the machines each month to see that they were kept in serviceable order. Precisely what interpretation was to be put on the term 'serviceable' is open to doubt, for in 1902 an order insisted that all cycles ridden by police officers were to have brakes! Perhaps this stipulation came none too soon, for the previous year Second-Class Constable Deacon was commended for his smartness in hiring a bicycle and following a motor car which was being driven furiously at Worthy ... 'resulting in his overtaking it in Winchester' – though certainly motor transport then was far less speedy than it has since become. However, in 1906 the chief constable referred in a letter to Lord Winchester to a case of a motor car driver being summoned for travelling at a rate of 21 miles per hour.

The force continued to grow in strength. In 1900 the Home Secretary approved of an addition of two sergeants and 17 constables, to take effect on and from 1 April. Fareham Division gained two constables, while Alverstoke, New Forest, and Bournemouth gained one each. Odiham Division acquired two more constables and one sergeant, while the Southampton Division gained no fewer than five constables and one sergeant, while the remaining five constables were assigned to patrol the railway extensions then under construction in different parts of the county. The Hampshire Constabulary now numbered 406 officers of all ranks. Apart from the chief constable, there were 15 superintendents (five first, six second, and four third class), two inspectors, one sergeant-major, 48 sergeants and 339 constables (134 of the first, 130 of the second, and 75 of the third class). By the end of the year there had been a further addition of two inspectors, one sergeant, and 18 constables. Some improvement, too, had taken place in the matter of pay, at least for the higher ranks. From March 1900 first-class superintendents received an annual salary of £170 6s. 8d. as against £152 1s. 8d. before; while second-class superintendents went from £141 8s. 9d. to £150 11s. 3d. In addition each superintendent was to be entitled to 6d. a day extra after five years in the rank, of whatever class. In somewhat melancholy vein the chief constable trusted 'that all those officers affected by this revision may have good health given them to enable them to enjoy its benefits to the full'.

Nothing is more striking in Major Warde's career than his extreme sensitivity to the welfare and good morale of his men, and his eagerness to be appreciated by them as a friend, as well as a commander. Consequently his hurt was all the greater when he felt on occasion that his benevolence was not reciprocated and his trust betrayed. In May 1900 he had 'observed some letters in the *Police Review* purporting to be written by men of the Hants Constabulary relative to alleged grievances'. He pointed out that it was against regulations for constables to write to the newspapers, and further that 'however willing and anxious he may be, not only to be made acquainted with any legitimate wishes of the men in a proper manner, but also to carry them out if possible, the fact of men disobeying existing regulations must necessarily put it out of his power to consider any wish however reasonable'. He hoped that proof had not been wanting during the time that he had been at the head of the force that he had the welfare of its members always at heart. 'The only reason he has for drawing attention to this matter is solely in the interests of the force and in order that his hands may not be tied to the detriment of those interests by the acts of a few thoughtless members.'

Far worse than thoughtless were the acts of a sergeant and a constable who were both dismissed the service for conniving together to produce a list of false convictions against a prisoner, and thereafter making a false report to their superior officer respecting these alleged convictions. This wicked conduct

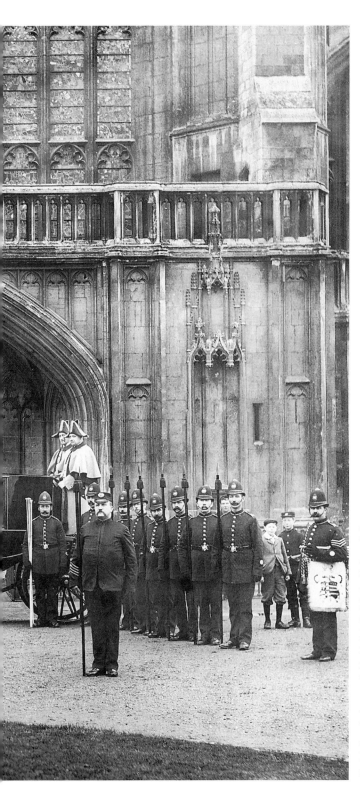

4 Judges' Escort at
Winchester Cathedral,
Hampshire Assize,
Sunday, about 1900.
Officers in foreground:
left – Deputy
Chief Constable of
Hampshire, Julius
Sillence.
Seen to the left and
behind DCC Sillence
(with officer's hat) is
the Head Constable of
Winchester City Police.
right – Sergeant Major
Perkins, Hampshire
Constabulary.

5 Superintendents of the Hants Constabulary, August 1900. Back row: Supt Courtney, Supt Jacobs, Supt Silver, Supt Griffin, Supt Hawkins, Supt King, Supt Wakeford, Supt Bowles; Front row: Supt Daniels, Supt James, Supt Hack, Supt Sillence D.C.C., Supt Foster, Supt Hale, Supt Payne.

hit the chief constable hard. On entering into the enquiry relative to the charges preferred, he could not for a moment believe that facts would be forthcoming to bear out such charges. 'To his consternation and deep regret they have been fully proved.' Major Warde, in General Orders, went on to observe that it was a very remarkable fact that throughout the whole country the fullest confidence was evinced in the police, and that they were always treated with respect 'which is infinitely to their credit considering the nature of their duties'. He quoted the opinion of an experienced chairman of a county bench to the effect that 'The whole machinery of Society may be said to turn daily, even hourly, on the integrity of the police.' Major Warde commented further: 'That it should be possible in the year 1900 for a police officer to commit such an atrocious act as to produce a false conviction against a prisoner well knowing it to be false is a terribly serious blow to the confidence implicitly placed upon police evidence.'

The chief constable trusted that should there be any policeman in the force who might at any time be tempted to colour his evidence in the slightest degree 'or to deviate one hair's breadth from the exact truth, he … will realise that such an offence will be dealt with in one way and one way only, namely by the severest possible punishment'.

A happier note is that struck by Captain F.J. Parry, one of Her Majesty's Inspectors of Constabulary, who on his retirement asked the chief constable to say goodbye for him to all the members of the Hants Constabulary and to tell them how very sorry he was to sever his connection with them. In carrying out Captain Parry's wishes, the chief constable expressed his deep personal regret at the severance. Once more Major Warde's deep sensitivity, and desire to be well thought of by his fellows, shines forth. After paying tribute to Captain Parry's interest in, and material help for, the welfare of the force, Major Warde remarked, 'He has also shown the chief constable so much invariable kindness that the remembrance of the connection resulting from their respective positions will always be a bright spot in the chief constable's police life.' Major Warde was always highly appreciative of any kindness or courtesy bestowed on him and, by extension, on the men under his command. The reverse side of this was an extreme consciousness of his own honour and dignity. He wished to like people and to be liked by them; but often he was disappointed and his feelings outraged. He could well understand, too, the meaning of bitter grief. In December 1901 Superintendent Morgan died, in consequence of a severe attack of typhoid fever which had prostrated him for five weeks. In his order notifying the force of this loss, the chief constable remarked that during his illness Morgan had shown exemplary patience and his end had been peaceful. The death of this officer in the prime of life was a serious loss to the force, all members of which were surely united with their chief in profound sympathy for the widow. Major Warde then added the characteristic comments, 'Superintendent Morgan was an upright honourable man and his courteous manner was appreciated by all with whom he was brought in contact. The chief constable personally feels his loss very keenly.'

Typhoid was one menace. Another was smallpox, a horror which has in our own day become a rarity in this country, thanks to the advance of medical science and the unremitting vigilance of health authorities. Early in the century it was otherwise and in the first weeks of 1902 there was an outbreak of the disease in Hampshire. Some constables who had been vaccinated within the previous three years hastened to be re-vaccinated as an additional safeguard and it was notified that any who wished to be so treated might have it done free of expense. In the same connection the Standing Joint Committee authorised the chief constable in July 1902 to abolish sick stoppages completely. Major Warde announced that he felt he had incurred a very serious responsibility in taking this step, but nevertheless was confident that it was a right and proper

one. Once more in General Orders one catches the authentic tone. 'He feels deeply this additional mark of confidence which the Standing Joint Committee have shown in him as head of the force and he earnestly calls upon those over whom he has the honour to be placed as their chief, to do their best – no man can do more – to serve their county honourably and diligently in all respects. So far as is in his power the chief constable will never cease to

6 The Hampshire Constabulary mounted branch in 1901, on a fortnight's course under riding master Parr, RHA, Royal Artillery barracks, Aldershot. (*Left to right*) Sergeant Smith, P.C.'s Hewett, Green, Aylesbury, Stone, Plowman, Miles and West. The mounted branch remained an important ingredient of the force until its eventual demise in the 1920s when the motorcar began to take over as the preferred method of transport.

watch closely over the interests of the force and all he asks for in return is that its members will carry out their duties in such a manner as to justify his efforts on their behalf.'

At the beginning of the 20th century the population of Hampshire was over 400,000 occupying a total acreage not far short of one million. The figures for each of the then 14 divisions are set out below:

Division	Acreage	Population
Alton	61,759	16,345
Andover	103,851	20,063
Basingstoke	74,719	21,482
Fareham*	101,176	44,751
Alverstoke	3,878	28,884
Kingsclere	68,504	13,034
New Forest	108,691	28,151
Odiham	61,750	61,487
Petersfield	58,391	15,020
Ringwood	97,897	21,935
Romsey	58,690	14,432
Southampton	23,003	37,106
Winchester	119,222	20,826
Bournemouth	5,769	59,762
	947,300	403,278

*This includes the part of the Parish of Cosham, with an acreage of 955 and a population of 657, which was to be transferred to Portsmouth Borough on 9 November 1904.

These show that the main clusters of population were in the vicinity of Aldershot, Portsmouth, and Bournemouth. These totals are derived from the census taken in 1901, the year of Queen Victoria's death. To many living at the time it seemed almost as though a world had ended, as well as the longest reign in British history. Comparatively few persons could remember any other monarch than that small superb lady who had presided so dutifully and courageously over the period of our greatest magnificence. Throughout the whole of its existence, the Hampshire Constabulary had been striving to maintain the Queen's peace: now, with a new century and a new reign, the police in common with all other British subjects looked once more to a king. The coronation of King Edward VII, and the ceremonies and celebrations consequent upon it, brought extra duties to the police and also extra rewards. In commemoration of the coronation three days' pay was granted to all ranks and all officers who were on duty at the subsequent Royal Review at Gosport were awarded an extra day's leave.

In July the next year King Edward held a grand Review of Troops at Aldershot and the police performed their relevant duties in a most praiseworthy fashion. The chief constable published his appreciation and emphasised that his thanks were due to Superintendent Hawkins 'for the satisfactory arrangements made and for having imbued those under his command with that feeling of *esprit de corps* which is of so much value in helping to maintain the high reputation which the chief constable feels justified in believing the Hants Constabulary to possess'. An extra day's leave was granted to all ranks involved. The chief constable's pleasure was vastly increased by a letter from General Sir John French, Commanding 1st Army Corps, Aldershot, in which the distinguished soldier proffered his thanks 'for the excellent work done by the police under your command … They had a very difficult task which they carried out to the great satisfaction of all concerned.

I can assure you it is a great pleasure to us all to know what good comrades and friends we soldiers have in the whole body of Hants Constabulary headed by yourself.' To crown all came a letter from a royal equerry, which conveyed to Major Warde 'His Majesty's satisfaction with all the police arrangements on the occasion of his visit to Aldershot on the 8th instant'. It had seemed to the king that all the arrangements had been very well carried out and reflected credit on all concerned.

A less spectacular preoccupation at this time was that concerned with the handling, re-arrest, and cautioning of prisoners. It was provided that cabs conveying prisoners to Winchester Prison would henceforth drive into the prison yard, instead of escort and prisoners alighting in the road as before. In January 1903 it was settled that the Winchester City Police would re-arrest all prisoners on discharge from the prison, who were wanted by the Hampshire force either on another charge or for re-commitment: they were to be handed over by the city police to Superintendent Sillence, the deputy chief constable, who in turn would detain them to await an escort or send them back to prison, as the case might be. In the summer of 1903 a new order was issued with regard to the cautioning of prisoners. The need for this had arisen because of a difference of opinion among judges as to whether or not prisoners in custody should be cautioned. Some judges would not allow statements made by prisoners to be given in evidence unless a caution had been given, with the result in some cases that valuable evidence was shut out. The chief constable had consulted the Home Secretary on the subject and sought his advice. That dignitary held that because of judicial dissension it was not possible for him to 'lay down any rigid rules as to whether prisoners in custody should be cautioned or not, but he thinks that in certain classes of cases it is advisable that a caution should be given'.

Consequently the order stipulated that a constable was not to try to draw a statement from a prisoner; he was to caution him that anything he said might be used in evidence against him. It was a breach of duty in a police officer to put questions to prisoners in his custody, and 'learned judges have, in many cases, reprehended such conduct'. However, it had to be borne in mind that every officer was justified in apprehending on reasonable suspicion and that, in cases of suspicion, it may frequently be perfectly right for a peace officer to ask questions of a suspected person not in custody, provided such questions be fair and adapted to the particular circumstances. A constable's duty was to listen attentively to everything a prisoner said and, as soon as possible, to write down what he had heard for the purpose of refreshing his memory. A constable should not allow a prisoner to sign a statement. In all this the foreshadowing of the later 'Judges' Rules' is clearly to be seen.

At any rate the Hampshire Force seemed to acquit itself well in view of these uncertain judicial complications. In December 1904, at the conclusion of the assizes, Mr Justice Wills sent a letter to Major Warde in which the judge expressed his appreciation of the county constabulary. 'The standard of conduct and intelligence has been generally high, and I can say the same, and I say it with pleasure, of the veracity and fairness of the constables and their superiors as witnesses.' The judge went on to say that of course he attached the greatest importance to these qualities. 'A great part of the difficulty of administering justice and arriving at right results is gone when I feel that I can rely upon police evidence, and I am glad to think that the fine force under your command deserved very high commendation in these important respects.' Naturally the chief constable was delighted and lost no time in transmitting his pleasure to all his subordinates. He thanked them for having earned this tribute from Mr Justice Wills and hoped that by continuing to carry out their duties to the best of their abilities, with absolute honesty and fairness, they might earn similar commendation in the future. To mark the happy event an extra day's leave was granted.

Major Warde was ever rightly jealous of the reputation of his force and saw clearly that this depended in large measure on good relations with the public. The principle he always endeavoured to inculcate in the minds of the members of the force was that of 'putting themselves into other peoples' places'. In his own words, 'when they are carrying out their duty let them consider what would be their feelings were the position reversed, and let them act accordingly with feeling and consideration'. This injunction arose out of an incident in 1903, when a complaint was made to the Home Secretary that a decided want of consideration had been shown in the issue of a commitment warrant following on a summons, for riding a bicycle without a light, before all possible steps had been taken to recover the fine by other means. The Home Secretary had expressed himself very strongly on the matter and the chief constable took the opportunity of once more impressing upon those under his command the need to display the utmost care and consideration in carrying out their duties towards the public.

A landmark in the changing character of British society, and of police activity made necessary in consequence, was the Motor Car Act of 1903. Again, in issuing orders in connection with the enforcement of this Act the chief constable emphasised that, while every effort ought to be made to prevent reckless and dangerous driving, 'this act will be put into force in a fair and reasonable manner and care will be taken to avoid unnecessary or vexatious interference'. The orders drew attention to the requirement that a car only travel at such a pace as was considered consistent with the safety and comfort of other users of the road. In crowded or narrow streets, or at sharp corners, cars were obliged to travel slowly. If complaints were made that the speed limit of 20 miles per hour was being exceeded in any particular locality, or if it came to the knowledge of a superintendent that such was the case, he was directed to take action in the following manner. A precise distance of either 220 or 440 yards was to be measured on the road, and a constable stationed out of sight of the approaching motor car five yards in front of the first point. As the offending vehicle passed him he was to take the time with a stop-watch, and simultaneously signal with a white handkerchief to another constable stationed opposite the end point of the measured distance. He too was to be out of sight if at all possible and was also to take the time with his stopwatch as the car passed him; at the same time, he was to signal to his colleague. Thus the two witnesses as to speed required by the Act would be provided. To complete this basic 'speed trap' a third constable wearing uniform was to be placed a little further on to stop the car if necessary or, if unable to do so, to take its number as it passed him. It is interesting to note that 'a margin of five miles an hour over the speed limit of twenty miles an hour will be allowed'. Thus the police in a sense were interpreting the law in such a way as to reconcile it with practical circumstance and common sense. Again, during the month of January 1904, when the Act was first to come into force, superintendents were to use discretion with reference to any omission to comply with the regulations. Perhaps this benevolent attitude lingered overlong with certain members of the force. For in August 1907 Third-Class Police Constable Alexander was dismissed the service for 'having on the 6th instant stopped a motor car on the Salisbury Road, Romsey Extra, and informed the occupants that there was a police trap at the bottom of the hill'.

Very quickly the number of cars registered increased and far exceeded the number expected by the county authorities. So, naturally, did the number of drivers licensed. Thus instead of each division having a copy of the register, as originally intended, it was arranged that only one central copy be kept at headquarters, to be the source of any relevant information required. The number of prosecutions likewise increased and apparently the stop-watches mentioned above were in constant use; for it was ordered that each month they should be tested by a watch-maker in each division. Even in those first years of the motoring age restrictions were closing in on the eager driver. Areas in which speed was strictly limited multiplied. In 1912 cars passing through certain parts of Basingstoke were limited to a speed of ten miles per hour.

Meantime the humble bicycle remained an increasingly important tool of everyday police work. Indeed, on the eve of his retirement in 1906, Mr Sillence, the deputy chief constable, who had witnessed the introduction of the bicycle into the force, expressed the opinion that 'in my humble judgment it is the very best thing that could ever have been introduced. Bicycles have been of the greatest service.' In February 1904 Sergeant Eades and Constable Pope were highly commended for 'their praiseworthy perseverance' in tracing a horse, cart and harness stolen at Aldershot. These officers continued their enquiries on bicycles for several days, finally arresting the thieves and recovering the stolen property at Birmingham. By the end of that year the Standing Joint Committee

7   Sgt Padwick at Droxford, *c*.1905.

on the recommendation of the chief constable increased the bicycle allowance
to £2 per annum and also removed the previous limit as to number. Naturally,
superintendents were ordered to report on the condition of new bicycles when
the allowance was applied for and to inspect the machines monthly to see that
they were kept in serviceable condition and were in fact used by the officers
to whom the allowance was granted. Some years later all police bicycles were
equipped with rear reflex red lights, which, it was laid down, were to be attached
to the back stay of the machine. Care was to be taken that the light was so fixed
as to be mostly horizontal. These lights had been supplied to police bicycles
and carts throughout the county by the Automobile Club in order to advertise
the value of such aids when being overtaken by other vehicles; and to try and
bring about a more uniform and better standard of lighting of all night traffic.
With customary caution it was laid down that 'when an officer leaves the service
the light will be forwarded to headquarters with his cycling outfit'. In 1912
the bicycle allowance was again increased to £3 per annum. Nor was the care
of the machine itself the sole concern of instructions. The conduct of police
cyclists had also to be regulated. In February 1913 police officers on bicycles
were directed to 'salute by dropping to the side the arm furthest away from the
person saluted'. However, the order added sagaciously, 'Circumstances may arise,
such as when cycling down hill, when this may not be possible, having regard

to the side upon which the brake is fitted, and in this case the arm nearest to the person saluted will be dropped.'

The telephone came ever more into use in these opening years of the 20th century. There are continual references in General Orders to stations acquiring the necessary apparatus. In 1906 the police stations at Fleet, Romsey and Emsworth were connected with the National Telephone Company, and had the numbers of 8, 9 and 10 respectively. In 1908 the stations at Petersfield and Hartley Row were brought into the system. Hythe Police Station was added in 1910 and the police cottage at South Hayling the following year. As the use of the telephone spread, it became necessary to alter some station numbers, as the system became more complex. In July 1914 the number of Tidworth Police Station was changed from 33 to 83. It had been earlier established that all police stations were limited to a certain number of calls each year. A record of these was of course kept. If the limit was exceeded during the year an extra charge was made and if the allotted number was not reached a rebate was allowed for the unused calls.

Alterations in the strength and organisation of the force continued to take place. The parish of Steventon was transferred from Kingsclere to Basingstoke Division at the end of 1904. The next year a subtle modification in the force resulted in an increase of one inspector and a corresponding decrease of one sergeant. In 1907 the force gained three sergeants and 14 constables; of the latter ten were added to the first class, and four to the second. Six of these additional constables were to be stationed at Bournemouth, four at Alton and the remainder distributed singly in Basingstoke, Fareham, Petersfield and Ringwood. One of the new sergeants was placed at Bournemouth, one at Fareham and the third replaced a constable at Andover. Further changes were necessitated by the Police (Weekly Rest Day) Act of 1910. This measure was to be brought into operation on 1 April 1914, and in the few years preceeding, preparations were gradually set in train for its realisation. From 1 November 1912, superintendents were to arrange for the police officers in their divisions to have one day off in every fourteen, the time to reckon from 8 a.m. to 8 a.m. Each officer was to have his leave on the day fixed and no exchange was to be allowed. In every case, of course, these arrangements were to be subject to the exigencies of the service; but in cases where a day was fixed and afterwards cancelled another day was to be substituted. Already certain increases in the strength of the force had been realised, to meet this new situation. From April 1912 five more sergeants and ten more constables had been distributed over the Basingstoke, Fareham, New Forest, Odiham, Southampton and Winchester divisions. With a view to bringing the Act fully into operation by 1 April 1914, further increases to the force were sanctioned according to the following schedule: 20 constables by 1 April 1912, another 20 by the same date in 1913 and yet ten more by 1914. The first two of these three infusions were to comprise six first-class, six second-class and eight third-class constables, while the third, smaller one, was to be made up of four,

four, and two in each class. One or two other petty alterations came in 1913, when Bournemouth gained an additional sergeant and a first-class superintendent replaced one of the second class. In August of that year the chief constable was pleased to announce that the Secretary of State had approved of the fixed number in each class of constable being dispensed with. Thus the way was clear for promotions to be made more readily from one class to another without waiting for vacancies to occur and, in general, promotion for the future was facilitated.

One consequence of this increase in strength and of the attainment of more leisure dependent on it, was the discontinuance of the police outings that Major Warde had earlier been glad to encourage. The requirements of the service would not admit of police officers having one day off per week, annual leave and outings in addition. So the outings had to go. No further contributions for the purpose were to be solicited or received from the public. Such money as was already in hand could be devoted to the recreation rooms, to the purchase of books, or to those local afternoon cricket matches which the chief constable indicated that he would still be pleased to sanction.

At the end of February 1914 a General Order announced that the police weekly rest day would finally be brought into operation on 1 April next, and set out details of the arrangements for this and also for the annual leave of inspectors, sergeants, and constables. The annual leave of ten days was to be taken in one period between 1 April, and 31 October in each year. The weekly leave accruing would be added. A fixed number of constables would be on leave each month, over the whole period, in every division according to its size and subject to the exigencies of the service. The constables would be notified how many would have annual leave each month and they could arrange among themselves accordingly. 'Failing such arrangements the superintendents will fix the leave.' Superintendents were also to arrange the weekly leave. The annual leave of inspectors and sergeants was to be arranged as most convenient for the working of the division. Lastly, no annual leave was to be granted until a constable had one year's service.

This amelioration of conditions was in harmony with the general trend of social reform in Great Britain in the years before the First World War. Reform was in the air and there was then a spate of legislation relating to the conditions of industrial labour. In 1908 coal-miners secured an eight-hour day and in 1910 the conditions under which shop assistants had to carry on their work were defined and regulated. Workmen's compensation, the creation of labour exchanges and the establishment of control by the Board of Trade over the wages and conditions of many industries; all were part of that great structure of welfare which was created nearly a century ago and on which all the later achievements of 'the welfare state' were to be based. Life, though still very hard for very many, was becoming a little easier. The promise of better things was eagerly looked to. In the meantime, ever more people had a slender store of leisure and increasingly diversified ways of spending it. As has been seen, organised sport, especially football and cricket, was firmly established. The modern Olympics were initiated in 1908. The Boy Scouts and the Boys' Brigade were opening up broader horizons for youth. It was the last golden age of the English Music Hall. For some, those years before 1914 were indeed 'La Belle Epoque'; for all, it compared favourably with earlier times. But if there was greater comfort, there were also higher and more desperate tensions, abroad as well as at home.

All the great powers of Europe were arming, all were racked by fear and ambition, all were locked in the grip of formidable alliances and mighty rivalries. This was true even of Great Britain, which for so long had held herself aloof from any permanent connection with any other great power. The Anglo-Japanese Alliance of 1902 astonished the world and decisively breached Britain's traditional isolationism. The ententes with first France and then Russia drew this country inexorably into what was in effect an anti-German alliance. From 1907 the General Staffs of the French and British forces planned jointly for the contingency of a European war. The deadly naval race with Germany mounted in intensity as the years went by. The British Army had learned the humiliating lessons of the Boer War and under the brilliant guidance of Lord Haldane at the War Office had transformed itself into the small but superb force which was to acquit itself so gloriously in 1914. Behind it stood the new Territorial Army, drawing increasingly for its leadership on the many officers' training corps which sprang up in universities and schools at that time. In those years Great Britain and the other powers were at peace, but it was an armed peace. The military and their activities were becoming more and more a centre of attention in this country and their manoeuvres in Hampshire made demands upon the police. In the summer of 1910 one sergeant and three constables were directed to report themselves to the Provost Marshal of the Second Division in Aldershot for duty with the headquarters of 'Red Force' during the manoeuvres about to take place. Similarly, one mounted sergeant and six constables on bicycles were allotted to the First Division and an equivalent group to the Second.

The rations, tent, waterproof sheets, forage and line gear for the horses were supplied by the military authorities. Pay and subsistence for the sergeants and constables was to be at the rate of 4s. and 3s. per day respectively. Bicycle allowance was 1d. per mile and to provide additional groceries 4d. per day was allowed, which was to be recovered from the men in cases where they were attached to, and fed with, an army unit. The duties of and instructions to the constables and directions for motors, carriages, etc., attending the manoeuvres, were issued to each police officer accompanying the different army forces. An interesting point was that 'arrangements have been made with the chief constables of Wiltshire, Dorset, and West Sussex, that should the Hants police find themselves in either of those counties they will be attached to that police force and will be under the orders of that county constabulary and will therefore obey all orders given there by officers of a superior rank as they would in their own county. All cases of crime that may come under their notice will be handed over to be dealt with by the local police.' The same conditions were to apply to constables from the three counties named coming into Hampshire. Finally, 'the police of this county in the manoeuvres area will also render what assistance they can to the military authorities whilst the troops are in their district.'

As well as being overshadowed by tensions abroad, Britain in the first years of this century was torn by partisan vehemence and bitter dissension. It was a time of growing social dislocation. In industry there were many strikes and in many of them the threat of direct action was to be discerned. There was the furious controversy over the various suggested measures of social and political reform, especially those concerning the powers of the House of Lords. There was the extraordinary outbreak of violence on the part of those valiant champions of women's rights, the Suffragettes. Above all, the fearsome Irish problem overshadowed British politics and infected the whole of public life with a sinister ferocity. Feelings ran high; there was something hectic and fevered in the air and violence lurked, ready to spring. If British society as a whole was more comfortable than ever before, it was also more uneasy and disturbed. In this, perhaps, is to be found the true deep-lying cause of the spectacular disturbances at Winchester in May 1908, the so-called 'Russian Gun' Riots.

Half-way over the wide crossing at the end of Eastgate Street and within a stone's throw of the statue of King Alfred there had stood for many years one of the numerous Russian guns captured in the Crimea. It had come to be regarded as a convenient meeting place for gatherings of the Salvation Army, or for open-air temperance meetings. Certainly multitudes of people passed it day by day, taking it for granted as a humdrum feature of the scene. However, there had grown up in the city a tradition that on no account must the gun be interfered with. The weapon itself was mounted on a carriage and surrounded by sturdy iron railings. Only the neighbouring trees lent some element of beauty to the scene. A pageant illustrative of Winchester's history was then being prepared, and possibly with this in mind the mayor, Alderman Forder, thought it would be both appropriate and pleasing to have the gun and carriage cleaned and re-painted, the site on which they stood re-gravelled, and the ugly iron railings removed. He placed his suggestion before a meeting of the General Purposes Committee of the Town Council and the members agreed that the gun itself would thus be shown off to best advantage. The council as a whole sanctioned the scheme. But opposition quickly appeared. On 13 May a protest meeting was held against the proposal to remove the railings and thus interfere with the traditional sanctity of this civic totem. The principal speaker at this meeting was a Mr Joseph Dumper, a house-painter known to many in the city. He had once been a prominent worker on behalf of the Good Templars. He was now to gain notoriety as a leading figure in what were afterwards sometimes called 'The Dumper Riots'.

As a result of an indignant gathering round the gun, a written petition was forwarded to the mayor, who passed it over to the town clerk to lay before the next meeting of the General Purposes Committee. Such a meeting was not scheduled to take place before the last Wednesday in the month and the Chairman of the Committee, Alderman Cancellor, afterwards denied strenuously that he had received any formal protest, although naturally he and his colleagues had been aware of the general sentiments of the protest meeting. Not having official intimation of any protest, Alderman Cancellor gave instructions for the work to go forward, but did not specify as to what hour the railings should be removed, that point being left to the discretion of the surveyor. That gentleman, thinking that there might be opposition if the work were done at an ordinary hour, used his discretion with the best of intentions. To avoid disturbance and protect his own workmen he gave orders that the railings be removed at four o'clock in the morning. Thus, by the time most people were about, the railings were already cleared away and stored.

It was not to be expected that those who had organised the previous protest meeting would meekly accept this *fait accompli*. By word of mouth the information spread that another meeting was to be held that evening. Later the same day a hand-cart bearing placards announcing the meeting was wheeled about the city and finally Mr Dumper himself was to be seen driving around in a pony and trap, to the sides of which were affixed printed posters inviting Citizens to attend an indignation meeting at the gun at half-past seven. Rumour and excitement flourished. By the appointed time several hundred persons of all ages were gathered round the gun and some youngsters were cheerfully perched astraddle on the weapon itself. The police were present, of course, but kept discreetly in the background. In the light of later developments it is significant that some soldiers, who had come to see what happened, were ordered back to barracks by the military police.

Promptly at half-past seven Mr Dumper appeared, accompanied by a younger man equipped with a cornet, which he used with enthusiasm and increasing frequency. Dumper clambered on to the centre of the gun, while his trumpeter found a perch at the muzzle end. He was greeted with cheers, which the cornet echoed. Then he embarked upon a rabble-rousing rambling speech which was certainly effective in screwing the tension of the crowd even higher. He began with a denunciation of the press, always a popular ploy with politicians, because of some comments made concerning the earlier meeting. Proceedings took a lighter turn when he next led the crowd in singing 'Auld Lang Syne'. After this choral interlude Dumper got down to business. 'For the benefit of those not at the last meeting I am going to repeat the names of the gentlemen who are guilty of this mean and contemptible action.' He mentioned in turn the names of nine members of the council, each name evoking groans of varying volume and accompanying blasts on the cornet. Dumper went on to assert that as the mayor and council had received a protest from the previous meeting, they should have taken no further proceedings. 'They should have stopped neutral until the thing was settled either by them or by the citizens.' He continued, 'If the council were feeling justified in what they were doing, why did they employ men at an early hour this morning? It puts me in mind of a midnight poacher or a midnight burglar; in fact, I sum it up in a few words – their deeds are so evil that they daren't come to the light. I take it by the action they have been guilty of this morning they are totally ignoring the wishes of the citizens of this city … I'd like to mention this fact – this being our glorious Empire Day – only this afternoon that honourable gentleman has been educating the children how to build up an empire; that is on the one hand, but on the other hand this morning he has been teaching us citizens how to pull down an empire by taking away this protective barrier.' All this was punctuated by cheers and toots on the comet. 'I think it is time that someone – because I quite agree we have no Ratepayers' Association in Winchester, and it is now time the working man, if no one else won't, took up the strain against the wasteful way in which our mayor and corporation do their work.' Cries of 'Hear, Hear,' and other acclamations of 'Joe'. Mr Dumper continued, 'I gave three reasons at the protest meeting why they should not remove the railings, and one and all agreed unanimously that they were three real reasons why they should not move them – you can see as well as I can see that this gun will become an intolerable nuisance with children without the rails. The gentleman who was so kind as to have the rails put round put them there for a specific purpose – to prevent people getting into trouble and also to protect this relic of the Crimean veterans. They say "Building an Empire" – where's the respect for the British soldier?' Here was a shout of 'They ain't got none.' 'Where's the respect for the British working man? – I tell you these corporative bodies it behoves you and me as men of common sense to keep a watchful eye over them. If they contend what they were doing was right, I'd like to know why they came at such an unearthly hour to pull down these railings.' At this point, there were shouts of 'Night poachers' and 'Robbers'.

There was a great deal more in the same style, with Dumper using all his considerable demagogic skill and his undoubted popularity to link this trivial affair of the railings with the destiny of the British Empire, the honour of the British people, and the integrity of British local government. He poured scorn on the explanation allegedly given him by some of the councillors – that the railings had been taken down only that they might be repainted ('Where's the railings gone, Joe?'!). He charged his audience to take note of the names of the civic dignitaries he had read out, and to bear their motives in mind at the next local election. 'Now you electors of the City of Winchester, I hope that you will take the names I have read out; I hope you will ponder over them, and I am going to say the more you ponder over them the worse you'll think of them, and remember as they tumble out of office never to return them again.' Finally Dumper moved from denunciation of the past action of others to the instigation of fresh action by his turbulent and high-strung audience. 'I propose that we make a demonstration through the city, and to leave no stone unturned to tell them. Are you agreed?' The answer came in a wave of cheering, loud shouts of 'Yes' and jubilant blasts on the cornet. 'Now we will go round to the mayor's.' Amid fresh cheering Dumper was hoisted shoulder high and, surrounded by the crowd, was carried along to the front of the mayor's residence.

By this time the crowd had increased in number to nearly three thousand. Many were there out of mere idle curiosity and many women and children were to be seen. However, there were also many present who were in earnest and who had by now been stirred up by Dumper's demagogy. Excitement was intense as the mob surged towards the mayor's house. They were met by a dozen policemen led by Head Constable Felton, who were lined up on the edge of the pavement in front of the doorway. One or two stones were thrown and windows broken. Dumper proclaimed that the reason they had 'gathered outside his worship's residence was to condemn the action of the corporation in removing the railings, and there'll be no rest until they are put back'. The crowd was soon persuaded that the mayor was not at home and began to move off. Head Constable Felton divided the multitude into two, turning one half off down Lower Brook Street, and the other along Silver Hill. The disturbance, however, was far from over. Violence mounted. In the crowd were many youths who evidently had come with pockets full of stones, fully determined to make use of them. As they moved away from the mayor's house, every public street lamp was smashed, and many were extinguished. In the High Street the *George Hotel* had two large windows broken, and stones were hurled through the face of the town clock. As well as many shop windows, the pageant offices were favourite targets. 'At every noise of smashing glass the crowd cheered as though they had achieved a glorious victory,' the *Hampshire Chronicle* reported. The demonstrators also burst open the gates of the pageant ground, scattering a rehearsal then in progress. Tents were slit, a piano smashed, a chariot burned and the remains thrown into the River Itchen to the accompaniment of triumphant cheers. The earlier excitement, still strongly tinged with good humour, had now grown into fury and the demonstration had developed into a full-blooded riot. The slender resources of the city police were powerless in the face of such overwhelming numbers. The mob then surged back to the gun itself for, by that mysterious general will which so often directs the action of a crowd, it was determined that the next move was to unlimber the gun – the very weapon which the protesters earlier had maintained should not be interfered with. With the aid of ropes the gun was hauled off its carriage and thundered to the ground. Cheers and laughter rang out again. Dumper was placed on the carriage, ropes were affixed, and away lumbered the house-painter, the central figure in a wild barbaric triumph, acclaimed by the yells of the crowd, his progress marked by fresh waves of glass-breaking. An especially favoured target was the house of the city surveyor, Mr W.V. Anderson. Several of his windows were smashed, and the gateway of his residence damaged. The windows of property belonging to several other councillors were also broken. It was clear that the situation was becoming out of hand, and the temper of the rioters increasingly ugly.

What happened next in the train of events is not altogether clear and soon became a matter of controversy between the Mayor of Winchester and the Chief Constable of the Hampshire Constabulary. The former was later to suggest that the latter had interfered with the legitimate authority of the mayor, while Major Warde implied that it was only by his own common sense, tact and discretion that the situation was appeased and even worse trouble averted, and the good name of Winchester preserved. In consultation with some members of the Watch Committee, in his own home, Alderman Forder resolved that it would be advisable for the military to be called out in aid of the civil power. Major Warde came into the affair in the following way. At about 9.30 p.m., he maintained, he received a telephone message from the Officer Commanding the Rifle Depot, stating that the Mayor of Winchester had requested the aid of troops to quell disturbance in the town and asking for Major Warde's advice about sending them. The chief constable emphasised that he had no jurisdiction in the city, and was unaware of all the circumstances. The military commander acknowledged this, but repeated his request for advice, and stated that he himself thought that troops should not be sent. Major Warde replied, 'I think you are right. I cannot think this is necessary. I will at once go and see what is occurring.' He forthwith went into the town, found the turbulent crowd in the Broadway and spoke to the few town councillors who were present. Major Warde said that the mayor should be sent for and expressed surprise that he was not already present. A councillor went off to persuade the mayor to come, but did not return. So a short time later, as the crowd continued to clamour for their leading citizen, the chief constable himself went to the mayor's house, which he found to be guarded by some policemen and observed by a small crowd. Major Warde was admitted to the house and, according to his own account, said 'Mr Mayor, I have no right or authority to come to you save in the interests of your city. Shall I go, or will you hear what I have to say?' According to Warde, the mayor said he would be very glad to have his advice; and so the major pointed out to the mayor that he had countenanced a proceeding which he had known to be very unpopular and that it had been done under cover of dark; that he had taken no steps to uphold his authority nor to support the city police; and that he considered it his duty as chief constable of the county and having seen the state of affairs in the city, to point out to the mayor that his duty was to be at the Guildhall. In his own statement of his part in connection with the affair, Major Warde asserted that he then asked the mayor, 'Will you come with me?', to which the reply was, 'Yes, I will, but by the back way and you had better come that way too.' With characteristic pride and sensitivity the chief constable replied, 'I am not accustomed to go by back doors.' He left by the front, and later met the mayor again at the Guildhall.

Here the mayor once more tried to pacify the crowd, but to no avail. The mob closed in on the front of the Guildhall, there was more stone throwing and this in turn stimulated an upsurge of jeers, yells and cheers. In vain did Alderman Forder try to make himself heard and to tell the crowd that he would undertake that the railings round the gun would be replaced if that was their wish. The anger of the mob would not be assuaged, the voice of reason could not reach them. The redoubtable Dumper himself was sent for: he stood up on a balustrade and repeated the mayor's pronouncement. There were some cheers but they were soon swallowed up in the howl of disorder. Perhaps it was then that the mayor determined irrevocably to send for the military. He was descending the steps to the police office to telephone when a large piece of wood was thrown at him. Then came an ugly rush for the police station and Head Constable Felton gave the order to his men to 'draw staves'. This gave the mob pause, though the stone throwing continued. It was at this point, according to Major Warde, that following upon his advice, thirty or forty respectable citizens were sworn in as special constables. It was also now that Major Warde, mindful of his promise to the officer commanding troops to let him know whether he considered the military necessary, requested and secured permission from Head Constable Felton to telephone the barracks. The chief constable assured the commander that he saw no need for soldiers. Because of this message, it seems, the troops who had been on the way down were halted at the *City Arms Hotel* and returned to their barracks. Major Warde was still of the opinion that even a show of armed force was unnecessary and would redound adversely to the reputation of the city of Winchester. He himself was most active in trying to quieten the crowd, and, as the *Hampshire Chronicle* noted, 'At one point he scored when a noisy customer in flowery language was expressing his concern for the gun. Major Warde, turning to him, said, "I have been a gunner five and twenty years, and we love our guns", an observation which evoked a hearty cheer from those about him.' A second time the soldiers came from the barracks in answer to the mayor's call and again Major Warde was instrumental in having them sent back. He met the officer in charge of the troops as they were approaching, who asked the chief constable if they were wanted. Major Warde replied, 'In my opinion certainly not, it would be most unwise to bring them.' So the troops went back again, while the officer commanding them accompanied Major Warde to the Broadway. Later, yet another requisition for troops was made. The officer commanding, taking advantage of his presence on the spot, exercised his own judgment, and at once ordered the troops back.

About 1 a.m., as Major Warde afterwards stated, 'I went among the crowd and got a hearing as a citizen and advised them to disperse and go home. They said they would do so if I took away the two officers who had followed me into the crowd, it having become known that the soldiers might come down.' Here was evidence of the traditional English nervousness at even the appearance of military force. In any case, Major Warde replied, 'Certainly, the officers are here as my friends to help me to persuade you to disperse.' They then led a large section of the crowd away; later Major Warde returned to the Broadway, and remained until it was clear, about 1.30 a.m.

To the observer considering these events from the safety and calm of after-time, the orders and counter-orders from the mayor and the major might seem nothing but matter for amusement. Even to commentators of the day the whole episode appeared a mere low comedy of errors. In the words of the *Star* of 28 May 1908, 'It is necessary to go back to the experiences of Mr Nupkins to find a parallel to this humorous incident.' But it cannot have seemed funny to those caught up in the turmoil of the moment, desperately trying to do what was right and needful. Both Alderman Forder and Major Warde were seeking to do their best for Winchester in a trying situation. It may seem ironic that the civilian mayor was set upon calling out the soldiers while the chief constable, with his military background, was equally resolved that the army should not be brought into it. Perhaps Major Warde had greater experience of such disorder and more appreciation of the pronounced reluctance of British soldiers to become involved in such affairs. The then Secretary of State for War, Mr Haldane, dilated on the fearful dilemmas of army officers employed in dealing with civil troubles when he subsequently addressed a Select Committee of Parliament. According to the *Hampshire Chronicle*, 'He pointed out that the soldier was bound, like the civilian, by two general principles of the law: to go to the assistance of the civil power when required to enforce law and order and then not to use force more than was necessary to assert law and order. The soldier, however, differed from the civilian in that his menacing appearance might bring about the very disturbance which it was the purpose to prevent. For that reason in the War Office they were very averse from allowing the military to be employed in this way. They were compelled to obey the law, but while he was at the War Office he should always insist very strongly on this – that they should be called out legally and not illegally. They were called out illegally if called out under conditions which might be dealt with by a force less menacing.' Here surely was the very consideration that must have impelled Major Warde to send back the troops, thus countermanding the instructions of the mayor. The *Hampshire Chronicle* report continued, 'Mr Haldane differed from the proposition that when recommended by the civil power the officer had no discretion as to whether he went or not. An illegal requisition could not absolve the officer from his liability to the general law of the land.' Mr Haldane opined that if an officer were summoned to a disturbance, not knowing the facts, he was bound to go. 'But if, when he got to the scene, be found only a small disturbance, he would be committing an offence if he intervened. A commanding officer must, to a certain extent, exercise his own discretion, notwithstanding the requisition of the magistrate.' Mr Haldane concluded his remarks by stating that divided authority and responsibility was not a good thing, and with grim cogency, that it was better to have one man who could be hung if necessary.

The mayor, on the other hand, had his own fears and preoccupations. He was only too well aware of the slender police resources available and of the mounting destruction of property and danger to life. The total strength of the Winchester City Force was only 39, of whom ten were guarding the mayor's house. In the anxiety of that turbulent evening the actions and suggestions of Major Warde might well have seemed officious and arrogant and his attitude tinged with contempt. Certainly Alderman Forder disagreed vehemently with the chief constable's version of events and considered that it did not fairly represent the character and motive of his own actions. He maintained that Major Warde had refused to accompany him to the Guildhall and had subsequently interfered with his authority repeatedly by sending back the troops each time the mayor had requisitioned them. On the third occasion that he telephoned the barracks to know if he could have the assistance of the military the mayor was told that if he desired to speak to Lord Henniker, the officer in charge, he could do so in a moment as Lord Henniker was just coming in. When the mayor asked if he could bring down the soldiers again to quell the riot, Lord Henniker, according to the mayor replied, 'No, I will not: Major Warde says you do not want them.' On the mayor's insisting that he did want them and that, as chief magistrate of the city, he was determined to have order established in the streets, Lord Henniker replied, 'I shall not bring them down again.' The mayor indignantly said that he would report the matter to the proper quarter, whereupon his lordship's reply was 'You do'. Little wonder that subsequently the mayor congratulated himself on keeping his head and his temper and that, in common with his colleagues, he regarded it as most serious when the power vested in him by Act of Parliament was denied him. More than one of the civic fathers considered the action of the Chief Constable of Hampshire grossly impertinent. What had he to do with the city? What right had he had to come and interfere with the military? In particular, Major Warde's reference to leaving by the back door was bitterly resented by the city fathers who naturally took it as a slur upon their courage. In a letter to the *Hampshire Chronicle* which was published at the same time as Major Warde's statement, the mayor claimed that both the statement and the covering letter were 'in many respects grossly inaccurate, and do not fairly represent what took place with regard to myself'. On 2 June 1908, a letter from the Lord Lieutenant of the County, the Marquis of Winchester, was published, which evidently sought to reconcile the differences in the accounts of the mayor and the chief constable. Lord Winchester wrote to the editor of the *Chronicle*, 'In regard to certain correspondence appearing in your journal under the signatures of the Mayor of Winchester and the chief constable of this county, I am requested by the latter to say that at 9.30 p.m. on May 25th he received a telephone communication from the Officer Commanding Rifle Depot that the Mayor of Winchester had requisitioned for troops to quell the disturbance in the town but that he now understands that the actual message from the mayor was not received at the barracks until 11.15 p.m. (The mayor holds official acknowledgement to this effect from the officer commanding.) The chief constable regrets that he made use in his letter of words which may have been construed as reflecting on the personal character of the mayor and unreservedly withdraws same. His only object in making reference to the incident in the manner in which he did was to explain the statement made by the mayor to the council, which had been reported to him, that he, the chief constable, had refused to accompany the chief magistrate of the city to the Guildhall when requested. The mayor is now assured that the chief constable's action was prompted by a desire for the best interests of the city, unofficially and as a citizen, in advising the non-employment of the troops, the presence of whom in the chief constable's opinion might have led to a serious collision between a certain section of the citizens and the military.' This might well seem a dignified and successful reconciliation of the two sides in the controversy. It will be seen, however, that pride and anger were not so easily to be assuaged and, indeed, that Major Warde was deeply hurt by Lord Winchester's intervention.

On the following morning, Tuesday, 26 Winchester was in a state of unrest and excitement. The main thoroughfares were crowded with citizens, many out to inspect the previous night's damage and some, doubtless, to revisit the scenes of their excesses and all eager to indulge in gossip and speculation. The famous gun itself was a centre of attention. It lay on the road by the side of the carriage. The city surveyor went to the spot to make arrangements for the replacing of the gun on the carriage, and then of the railings round the gun. A score or so of the men standing idly by volunteered to hoist the gun back themselves. As some of them said, 'We pulled it down, we'll put it back.' So they fell to with chains and poles, but displayed more zeal than ability, with the result that nothing very much was achieved. The work was finished by the surveyor's own staff on the Wednesday morning and the railings were temporarily erected, being permanently restored on the Thursday. In the meantime, however, Winchester was to experience further alarm and tumult. At first it seemed as though this might not turn out to be the case. For although crowds were once more assembling in the Broadway, they appeared at first rather concerned to discuss the previous night's disorder, than to initiate a new outbreak of their own. Nevertheless, rumours and threats of fresh violence had been circulating all day and the authorities, belatedly acting on Major Warde's advice, had sworn in two hundred special constables to help the mayor maintain order in case of need. The body of specials comprised several officials and workmen employed by the corporation and also many of the men engaged on the work of cathedral restoration then in progress. It was considered diplomatic to keep these special constables out of sight unless needed and so they stayed in the Guildhall yard. Other preparations had also been made. From seven o'clock that evening all soldiers had been confined to barracks and the military were on the alert.

Time wore on and by nine o'clock the crowd had swollen to thousands and a change of mood had become apparent. There was a great deal of booing and catcalling and several free fights broke out. The sorely-tried Head Constable Felton and his men were continually jostled and the atmosphere once more grew ugly. The mayor was in the Guildhall accompanied by many of his civic colleagues and officials and he decided to try to address the crowd, to persuade it to disperse. As he appeared on the Guildhall steps he was greeted with an uproar of both cheers and groans. He persisted, however, and after a time was able to make himself heard. 'Citizens,' he cried, 'I do appeal to you to go home quietly for the good of the city you love. There is now no grievance, everything is in order, and do protect your wives and children and go home peacefully. I do appeal to you very much indeed; let us have peace and quietude in our city. Why make this demonstration?' Here he was interrupted by a voice implying that he had started the whole affair. 'I did not start it at all. You have your railings and your gun – I had nothing to do with moving the railings; I defy anyone to prove that I knew until eight o'clock on Monday that the railings were gone.' All this was shouted against a background of increasing noise, made up of groans, booing and cheering. Another free fight broke out at the front of the crowd and again the police were hustled. Then came various facetious demands from individuals in the crowd to see the special constables whom they knew to be at hand and whom they now cheerfully described as 'England's last hope'. Suddenly Joseph Dumper appeared on the balustrade to be greeted by cheers. When the clamour to see the special constables was renewed, the mayor dramatically pointed to Dumper and said, 'Here is one.' The effect of this revelation can be imagined. To their credit the city authorities had displayed shrewdness and initiative and enrolled the demagogic Dumper himself as a special. That worthy was now ready and willing to rally to the side of the law, as he considered that the object of his original agitation had been realised, in that the railings round the gun had been replaced. Once more he addressed the crowd, but this time he aimed his oratory not to arouse it, but to pacify its passions. He said, 'Citizens, I only hope and trust that you'll carry out the promise that you gave last night, that you will, as citizens do everything in your power to maintain order because you have got all you asked for. I think there is nothing more to be said. It is quite sufficient to justify all you have done and you are well repaid for all you have done. Now, take my advice, and go away home as peaceful citizens. Let well alone.'

Cheers greeted this conciliatory advice and two of Dumper's erstwhile supporters were so enthusiastic that they clambered up beside him on the balustrade, one of them calling for a rendering of 'the song of the Old Brigade'. To avert this fresh excess, the mayor quickly interposed to confirm the truth of what Dumper had just said and to repeat his injunction that everyone disperse and go home quietly. 'Go home and be loyal to your city and do keep order and quietude. I appeal to you. You are all sensible men and women, protect your city and do your duty.' Dumper again rallied to the mayor's support and called for three cheers for him. This elicited a mixed response of cheers and groans and then a call for 'three cheers for Joe Dumper', which were given with rare good will. To this tribute Dumper replied in a curiously moving and artless way, 'Now go home like good boys, or I'll never be your captain any more.' Perhaps it is too fanciful to see in this a humble echo of the young King Richard II admonishing the rebellious following of Wat Tyler. In any case Dumper's appeal had only an indifferent effect. The clamour to see the special constables was renewed and when one or two persons were admitted to the yard to see them, there was a rush to break in which the regular police repelled only with difficulty. Having failed to persuade the crowd to disperse, the mayor and his companions went indoors. For a time the noise and aimless milling of the mob continued. Then there was fresh cheering as an old man pushed through and mounted the steps. This was Sir Bampfylde Fuller, a former Lieutenant-Governor of East Bengal and a distinguished local figure. He in his turn had decided to try to pacify the multitude. Certainly, he secured a hearing from the crowd, which was beginning to thin out. He reminded the citizens of what his father and grandfather had done and that was what the gun stood for. No one in Winchester wanted the gun moved and as long as he, Sir Bampfylde, was there, the gun never would be moved. These remarks were applauded and there was a shout of 'Good old Bampfylde.' The old gentleman rejoined, 'Yes, boys, good old Bampfylde', which remark was accorded cheers and laughter. 'Listen, about these railings. The railings are not part of the gun. I don't care twopence whether the railings are there or not but if I had taken them down I would have done so at twelve o'clock in the day. Look here, listen, please. Hang it, we are all citizens of Winchester and we don't want to give the town a bad name. We shall be in all the London papers tomorrow and in *Punch* next week.' Waves of laughter interspersed these remarks and it became clear that Sir Bampfylde was succeeding in mellowing the mood of the crowd. He went on, 'Take my advice, and drop it. We will see it is all right, if I have to haul the gun up myself tomorrow. It is all right now. Take my advice and go home quietly. Good night.' To this dignified address many replied, 'Good night, sir,' and there were calls for three cheers for the old gentleman. Adroitly, Sir Bampfylde cried, 'Wait a minute, wait. Now look here, "Three cheers for the good old gun".' These were given and again Sir Bampfylde said good night and was rewarded with three cheers for himself. There was no doubt that the bulk of the crowd was now in a better humour; many drifted away and those that remained did so out of curiosity rather than a yearning for further mischief. Later that evening there were one or two stone-throwing incidents but no worse disorder arose in consequence. By ten o'clock the soldiers concentrated in the barracks were stood down. The cavortings and subsequent arrest of a few drunks were the only other focus of attention that night. By shortly after midnight, all was quiet and the 'Gun Riots' were at an end. But controversy concerning them continued.

At the centre of it all stood Major Warde, whom some saw as the saviour of Winchester's good name and the hero who had averted worse disaster and even bloodshed: and whom others considered to have been nothing but an interfering busybody. It has already been indicated how sensitive and proud he was in character. Certainly he felt hurt and indignant at the imputations put upon his motives. In particular, he clashed with Lord Winchester, the Lord Lieutenant, who had been unfavourably impressed by the chief constable and the mayor both issuing conflicting statements to the press so soon after the rioting. In a letter to Major Warde, Lord Winchester wrote, 'There now appears to have arisen insuperable difficulties to any arrangement being arrived at, chiefly owing to the unfortunate tendency of everyone in this regrettable affair to rush into print.' The chief constable took exception to this stricture and in replying to the Lord Lieutenant, wrote, 'As I said in my letters to the papers I make it a rule not to write anything for publication but circumstances may arise when it is not only advisable but necessary to depart from this or any other laid down rules. In my humble judgment such an occasion arose in this case. I do not think you would have come to the conclusion you apparently have that it would have been wiser for me not to publish the facts as I did had you seen me and heard what I have to say in the matter.' Major Warde then vented his bitterness at what he considered Lord Winchester's failure to support him. 'I certainly hoped and thought I might rely upon the full support of the Lord Lieutenant in this matter, as I am placed in a very difficult position, more especially as you have seen Colonel Herbert who thoroughly agrees with my action throughout and who, I think I am right in saying, saw my statement of facts and agreed with me there was no alternative but to publish it. It is not possible to put you in possession of the real aspect of affairs in a letter.' A main cause of rancour in the controversy that had developed was evidently the chief constable's reference to leaving by the back door, for he concluded 'I am sorry now I made any mention of the back door, but even this I can explain and I made the allusion in no bad spirit.'

The bitterness increased and others were involved in the controversy. Major Warde appealed to Sir William Portal, a member of the Standing Joint Committee, for support, and reproached him for his previous failure to give a full hearing to both sides in the dispute. 'You have told me I am one of your best friends in the county but you have forsaken me at a most critical moment.' The chief constable complained that he had been insulted by the Lord Lieutenant, and went on, 'He has since written to me and made no apology but threatened me that the Standing Joint Committee may be requested by him to investigate this matter – I have nothing to fear from such an investigation and have applied to the clerk to summon a meeting of the committee.' In another letter to Sir William, dated two days later, Major Warde again upbraided his friend for his failure to rally to his side and in feverish terms sought to justify himself as a man of honour and proud lineage. 'I do not want to preach, God forbid – I am humble in mind and have a poor opinion of myself – but I am proud of my name. I was obliged in the hearing of a hall-porter to take an insult lying down, from a sense of discipline, from one whom I do not acknowledge as my superior socially, although he is the Marquis of W—, and I am Major Warde. My family dates from before the conquest, and is without stain – my ancestors have refused to relinquish their name for titles – I am considered worthy of being a personal friend of, and addressed by my christian name by the king's brother – so as man to man I will not lie down under a threat from the Marquis of W— or any other man. My past life will I venture to think compare favourably with his.' After again invoking his past friendship with Sir William, Major Warde ended his emotion-charged letter with expressions of gratitude for all the help he had previously received from him. 'In fact as I have often told you, I feel I owe my appointment practically to you. I am a very poor man in means and that makes me all the more grateful. I cannot afford to go into "Society", neither do I wish to. My tastes are simple, I love my family and the county.'

Such was the passion with which the chief constable sought to defend himself and his conduct in the affair. He was consumed with the indignation of a man who, certain of his own integrity and good intentions, had been unjustly misunderstood and condemned by others. However, calmer counsel prevailed. Major Warde turned for advice to his eldest brother who recommended that he try to end the matter without a meeting of the Standing Joint Committee. Major Warde announced himself willing to redouble his expressions of regret and sorrow at having placed himself as chief constable in conflict with the Lord Lieutenant and for having embarrassed the committee. Perhaps this sudden change of front is yet one more illustration of the chief constable's volatile and generous character, at once proud and humble, confident and sensitive, swift to act and swifter to relent, if once convinced it was fitting to do so. 'On the advice of my eldest brother, whose shoes I am not worthy to black … I at once saw I ought to look at the matter from a higher and broader standard and under no circumstances ought I to put myself in conflict with the high office of the Lord Lieutenant, who is appointed by the king.' Even then he still hankered for an opportunity at some time or other to justify himself in the eyes of the Standing Joint Committee as to his 'back door' reference. But the point of crisis was past; and on 12 June 1908, Major Warde wrote to the Commissioner of the

Metropolitan Police, in the interests of the Mayor and Corporation of Winchester. The City Watch Committee had applied for the loan of six detectives from the Metropolitan Police for the famous pageant and probably owing to recent events this request had been refused. Major Warde wrote that he wanted to help the civic authorities all he could and in the name 'of our warm friendship' asked the commissioner to reconsider the matter and if possible send the six detectives. The whole turbulent episode of the Winchester Gun Riots seemed at length to have blown over.

Less than a year later, however, Major Warde made some unflattering references to the mayor and councillors of Winchester, in a letter to one of His Majesty's inspectors of constabulary, Captain Terry. The matter under consideration was the proposed consolidation of the Winchester City Police into the county constabulary. In discussing the set of conditions the city had submitted relative to this proposal, Major Warde wrote that if the city police were to be taken over, 'the sooner the "old order" of things and all appertaining thereto is swept away the better.' He pointed out that it was proposed to put the mayor and another member of the Town Council on the Standing Joint Committee. 'Now you know the class of men who are elected mayor – a recent Mayor of Winchester has lately been convicted under the Excise Act and fined some £60, this occurred a few months ago. Another Mayor of Winchester a few years ago was a publican in the town, his house had a bad name, he drank and subsequently committed suicide. Now from a point of discipline and of efficiency, I consider it would be in a high degree objectionable and inadvisable to have men of this calibre on the Standing Joint Committee and living in the city.' A crucial point was that 'The mayor has been accustomed to be chief constable practically of the police and referred to by the head constable who could do nothing of his own initiative.' Major Warde feared that if, according to the proposed arrangements, the Mayor of Winchester were to be a member of the Standing Joint Committee, there would be a dangerous undercurrent working against him. Furthermore he asked why Winchester should be specially represented on the Standing Joint Committee more than Aldershot or Basingstoke or any other town in the county. The only argument advanced, scoffed the major, was because it had a long and ancient history. But this was not enough. 'The Town Council of Winchester in the past have proved themselves utterly unfitted to manage their own affairs and especially as regards police management.' In another confidential letter to Mr Barrow Simonds he repeated the substance of these views and made an appeal to Sir William Portal 'to once again weigh in the balance the question of sentiment against what I consider necessary for the proper discharge of my office which becomes each year more responsible and onerous'.

This was certainly the case. As the pace and complexity of everyday life increased, so did the responsibilities of the police and of the chief constable. As well as important matters of policy and organisation, however, there was the steady grind of daily administration and the necessary careful watch on the discipline of the force. A General Order in February 1904 announced that 'cases have occurred where constables have stated they have been assaulted years ago when arresting prisoners, of which there is no record, and attributing their present illness to such assault'. In future no notice was to be taken of any such statement unless the constable concerned was examined by the doctor at the time of the assault, and a certificate forwarded to headquarters showing the nature of his injuries. A few months later a constable was fined a week's pay for having, when off duty, seen another constable in uniform lying on the public highway 'and not ascertaining the cause or attempting to remove him from the road'. In 1906 a third-class constable was similarly fined for having received a reward of 10s. from a gentleman to whom he handed some lost property and neglecting to report in accordance with 'paragraph 63, page 27, Instruction Book'. As the luckless constable had been so rash as to plead ignorance of the order relative to the receipt of rewards, he had in addition to copy out a page of the Instruction Book daily until he had copied the whole book. At the same time another constable was dismissed from the force for having 'illegally served two rate summons by placing them in a letter box at the residence of the defendant' and for having falsely endorsed the summonses as served personally on the defendant. A graver matter altogether was mentioned in a General Order of October 1906, which superintendents were charged to see that every constable took a copy of in his own writing. This dealt with the offences of missing conference points and making false entries in journals. The failure to attend strictly to conference points was a most serious offence, in that the whole system existed for the purpose of preventing burglaries and other such crimes. As for falsifying entries, 'The safety of the liberty of the individual and the just administration of the law depends upon the truthfulness and honest behaviour of the police.' Thus any untruthfulness or dishonest behaviour on the part of a police officer was likely to make him unfit for retention in the force. The chief constable reiterated his constant care for the interests of all the men under his command urging them to bear this concern in mind and let it influence them in avoiding the commission of serious offences and so spare him the painful duty of inflicting punishment.

In March 1908 'the practice of walking on the railway line from Cosham to Farlington' was forbidden and police officers getting off the train at Cosham to proceed to the race course were directed in future to travel by road. The following year a superintendent, on probation in that rank, was considered to have failed to justify his selection 'in that he has become addicted to drink and brought discredit to the force by not carrying out the responsibilities of his position in a straightforward and honourable manner'. He was reduced to the rank of sergeant. A more serious offence was that of a second-class constable in 1910 who had been foolish enough to ride a bicycle without a light on the main road at Itchen. He had run down and fatally injured a pedestrian. Adjudged guilty of conduct calculated to bring discredit to the force, he was permitted to resign, while in February 1914 another second-class constable was reduced to third class for grave neglect of duty. He had failed to examine a luncheon tray which he had brought to a prisoner and omitted to remove a knife before allowing the prisoner to have the food. The prisoner used the knife to cut his throat.

Less gruesome orders dealt with a variety of administrative matters, great and small. Superintendents were to ensure that whistles, no less than every other article of apparel, were in proper order and that the owner of each whistle should blow it when his equipment was being inspected. The death of any person whose fingerprints were recorded in the Habitual Criminal Registry was to be notified to the Registrar, Habitual Criminals at New Scotland Yard. Superintendents were to make enquiries respecting employment for juvenile offenders once they had been discharged from prison. The police were to keep in touch with them and help them where possible. When recommendations for promotion were made, it was to be stated whether the constable recommended was a cyclist. In July 1907 it was noted that in future licence duty need not be paid in respect of the county carts used for police purposes. In the same year the Standing Joint Committee resolved 'that the consent of this committee be not in future given to the acceptance of a testimonial or gift of a pecuniary value by any officer on retirement from the force'. A matter more nearly touching the contentment of the force was referred to in a General Order of November 1909, which announced that there were then no fewer than fifteen constables awaiting married stations, and that there would be no opportunity for future applicants to marry until these had been provided for, 'which will probably take twelve months or more'. The alacrity with which officers entered matrimony, without waiting for permission of the chief constable, was a matter of continual concern. In January 1909 a second-class constable was fined one week's pay and placed at the bottom of the list of constables awaiting married quarters, for thus marrying without superior authority. The next year another second-class constable was reduced to third class and to the bottom place on the list for a similar act of defiance. It is clear that the prudence and wariness exhibited by the chief constable in this connection was the product of anxiety to ensure that his married subordinates were properly accommodated and not of any hostility to the personal aspirations of individuals. Nevertheless, official obstruction had what was perhaps its inevitable result and a General Order of April 1911 stated that 'the number of constables making special applications to marry, in consequence of their intended wives being *enceinte*, is very much on the increase and in some cases under very discreditable circumstances'.

While Major Warde was vigilant to maintain a high standard of discipline, he was equally alert to any attempted encroachment upon his own authority as chief constable. In 1911 he rejected with contempt a letter from a Mr Hayward who was apparently interfering in a matter of force discipline by taking up the case of a constable dismissed the service. In a letter to Lord Northbrook, the chief constable commented that 'The Standing Joint Committee has invariably and without exception acted upon the principle that the chief constable is wholly and solely responsible for the discipline of the force and has on occasions when complaints have been made to the committee merely replied to that effect. I ask you in the interests of discipline to follow the same course with Mr Hayward and not to go further into the matter with him. If I am to be called upon to justify my action in carrying out the discipline of the force, this is not only contrary to the provisions of the Police Act but it would make efficient discipline an impossibility.' Major Warde went on to remark that he had been under discipline himself for the past forty years and 'I can assure you my education in the Gunners and my own instincts have taught me that no discipline can be satisfactorily maintained with harshness and injustice.' In a postscript Major Warde reminded his correspondent that Mr Hayward had himself been a constable in the Hampshire force and now had a son serving in the same rank. If Mr Hayward were not given 'clearly to understand that the chief constable cannot be interfered with in carrying out discipline, you can imagine what mischief might ensue!' Mr Hayward, however, was not to be disposed of so easily. Eighteen months later, in April 1915, Major Warde was aghast at a proposal to put him on the Standing Joint Committee: if carried out this might be indirectly prejudicial to discipline. 'At present the police look to their chief constable to watch over their interests. But with Mr Hayward on the committee, he would pose as their champion with, I believe, mischievous results.' Evidently Mr Hayward had supported his application to be on the committee by reference to his previous police experience. Major Warde was more than willing that this should be considered. 'He was only four years in the Hampshire Constabulary some fifty years ago. His record involves insubordination and he had to leave for committing an assault upon a woman – I think it stands to reason that a man in his position who is on terms of equality and familiarity with the police is not a suitable person to be placed as it were above their chief constable.'

Careless and unsubstantiated charges against the police were no more unknown then than now. In December 1915 the chief constable had to contend with criticism on the part of Lord Malmesbury that the police in Bournemouth were slovenly and that they managed the traffic badly. Major Warde later conceded that the earl had written in the friendliest spirit: at the same time he pointed out that he was bound to enquire into the serious allegations made against the Bournemouth Police in the most thorough way. This he did, the more so as Lord Malmesbury's letter had caused him so much surprise: '... from my own observation when at Bournemouth and from what I hear from time to time from reliable sources there, I know of nothing to justify the grave strictures ... with reference to the Bournemouth Police … Among other people, some heads of large borough police forces who have been staying in the borough from time to time have complimented the Bournemouth Police on their smartness and the manner in which they regulated the traffic.' Major Warde directly enquired of half-a-dozen members of the Standing Joint Committee who resided in Bournemouth and forwarded their comments to his lordship. None bore out the criticisms levelled at the police. Major Warde commented to Lord Malmesbury, 'I think you will agree with me that from whatever source your information emanates it is clearly unreliable and void of foundation. No doubt the disgraceful occurrences of some years back which caused me so much disquiet when a number of the Bournemouth Police were detected stealing articles from shops left unoccupied at night left an unfortunate impression behind. But all the evil doers were punished and cleared out.' The chief constable observed that Bournemouth lent itself in an unusual degree to burglaries owing to its large area and the great number of houses standing in their own grounds. A familiar modern note was struck by his comment that burglaries were also facilitated by 'the train service enabling burglars to come from London and return before perhaps burglaries they have committed have been reported to the police'. Nevertheless, the record of Hampshire, including Bournemouth, in detecting crime was good and compared favourably with other counties; and this even though 'The present day burglar is more often than not a respectably dressed man, which makes detection more difficult than it used to be.' Major Warde repeated that fair criticism was to be welcomed and might be decidedly helpful; but that criticism could not be considered fair unless it rested upon solid foundation. The chief constable feared that Lord Malmesbury had been influenced by idle and malicious stories and insisted that he had every reason to place full confidence in the superintendent in charge of the Bournemouth Division, who through long service had proved himself to be not only a thoroughly efficient police officer but also an honourable man who had the credit of the force keenly at heart. 'It has been impossible to clear the matter up without his becoming acquainted with the grave strictures passed upon the police under his charge and he naturally feels sore and hurt at such unmerited censure.' All police officers will applaud this comment, as appropriate now as in those distant days.

In June 1915 the chief constable announced that it afforded him 'great pleasure and gratification' that a revised scale of pay had received the approval of the Home Office and would take effect from the end of the month. In his customary fashion, he trusted that the force would always realise the warm affection he had for all its members and that they in their turn would extend to him their friendship, which he valued highly. To brighten further the good news, he held out the hope that 'it is quite possible in a few years' time he may again feel justified in applying for a further rise of pay'. Meantime, the three first-class superintendents were to have an increase of 1s. 2d. per day, while the seven other superintendents and the inspector were each to gain 6d. a day. Eleven sergeants promoted in 1901 and 1902 secured an increase of 3d. a day, 24 sergeants promoted between 1903 and 1908 gained 2d. a day, and five promoted in 1908 and 1909 were to gain 1d. per day. With regard to the constables, 70 of the first class who had been promoted between 1892 and 1905 were to gain 4d. a day, 24 of the same grade promoted between 1905 and 1907 were to gain 3d., and a further 25 of the same class, promoted between 1907 and 1909 were to have an increase of 2d. The 22 remaining first-class constables who had been promoted as recently as between June 1909 and 1911 were to gain 1d. per day. Lastly, 38 second class promoted between 1907 and 1909 were to have an increase of 3d. per day. In August of the same year special allowances were sanctioned by the Standing Joint Committee to constables while stationed in Bournemouth, to meet the high cost of living there. Second-class constables were to have on appointment 2d. per day extra, and after four years in that rank to be equated with the first-class constables and have an extra allowance of 1d. per day.

There is no doubt they earned their pay. Increasingly, public opinion regarded the cost of the police as a necessary expense and a sound investment; although, as so often, this view was arrived at only in consequence of hard experience. Certainly, this was the case with the ratepayers of Andover, who, in June 1914, found their town involved in riots of the kind which had struck Winchester a few years before. As with the earlier disturbances, so now the apparent cause of the Andover rioting was disproportionately trivial though perhaps more rational. A young girl, Phyllis Mary Beckenham, had twice appealed to the Andover borough magistrates for an affiliation order against one Isidore Harvey, the bachelor son of a prominent local business man, and twice had had her appeal rejected, on the grounds of a lack of corroborative evidence. On leaving the court on the second occasion the girl and her mother assaulted Harvey and in consequence were sentenced to be fined, or in default to short terms of imprisonment. They were allowed a week to pay but since at the end of that time they had failed to do so, they were taken to Winchester Gaol. Before the girl and her mother had completed their sentences of seven and 14 days respectively, however, their fines were paid by some anonymous sympathiser. For from the start many persons had rallied to the support of the two women, who were seen as the outraged victims of a callous villain. Thus when word spread that they had been released from prison, a large crowd began to gather at the railway station to await the arrival of the two heroines from Winchester. The fact that they came on a later train than the one expected served only to increase the size and excitement of the crowd. When at last Miss Beckenham, her mother and her baby alighted on the platform they were greeted by tremendous cheering. A procession was formed, with the girl at the head, and to the accompaniment of singing and what was later euphemistically described as 'rough music' – the banging of tin cans – the mob straggled along towards the High Street, growing in number all the time. Outside the shop owned by Mr Harvey senior, the crowd halted and, according to one newspaper, several individuals started singing, 'It's the poor that helps the poor when poverty knocks at the door.' Not poverty, but excited men then knocked repeatedly on the door of Mr Harvey's premises, but received no reply.

Violence followed in the form of stones and tin-cans hurtling through windows. Soon the windows of the confectionery shop, the cycle shop and the stationery shop opposite were all smashed, as were the windows of the upper storey on either side. The street was covered with broken glass and missiles of various sorts. The police, meantime, found themselves almost powerless to control the disorder. They were too few in number. Superintendent Jones himself was on leave, attending the funeral of a relative, and several other officers were away at the assizes then in progress. Sergeant Every was left in charge with only a few constables at his disposal. All that the few police could do in the face of the big crowd was to form a half-circle in front of the windows under attack, and try to prevent people coming too close and persuade them to stop throwing stones and disperse. This was all in vain. Sergeant Every realised he must have reinforcements and telephoned to the chief constable. Immediately Major Warde set out for Andover, gathering such police as he could on the way. However, it was not until nearly midnight that the police arrived by motor car and bicycle and even then it was quickly apparent they were too few completely to disperse the crowd. Major Warde quickly appreciated the situation and used his slender force to clear the main street where the damage had been done and keep the crowd back at either end of it. He aimed to keep the street clear, and to tire out the mob. This was achieved by about three o'clock the next morning, a Saturday.

A somewhat confusing element in the situation had been the appearance earlier of the fire brigade, in response to a suggestion that they use their hoses to clear the streets. Before the police reinforcements had arrived 'the members of the fire brigade, with their manual and hose cart, had turned out under Mr A.F. Beale,' and stationed themselves at the top of the High Street near a water hydrant, close to the *Angel Hotel*. No order was given to turn on the water, however, and it was generally agreed afterwards that this was wise, as a drenching would only have infuriated the rioters, while the brigade lacked the power of water effectively to break up the crowd. So the firemen stood there uneasily, the target of jeers and banter. Then their hose-cart was overturned by the mob and on the instructions of the mayor the firemen retreated to the fire station, pursued by ironical cheers.

On the Saturday morning the High Street presented 'a sight such as that of a Dublin street after a riot', according to the *Andover Advertiser*: 'Mixed with the hundred-weights of broken glass was confectionery, bicycles, and gramophones, with their accessories, and all somewhat damaged.' In the course of the day rumours of fresh impending trouble abounded and extra police, both on foot and mounted, were moved into Andover as a precaution. This strengthened force came under the direction of Superintendent Waters, as Superintendent Jones was still on leave. As evening approached, tension increased and was reflected in the numerous constables patrolling the main streets and mounting guard on the residences of borough justices in different parts of the town. All was quiet, however, until about eleven o'clock, when crowds emerged from the public houses. Rowdies started throwing stones at Mr Harvey's few remaining windows, and those belonging to other tradesmen were smashed. The police closed in on the High Street and about midnight formed a cordon and cleared the thoroughfare, though not without half-an-hour's brisk work, when the mob hurled stones and brickbats at the police and the latter used their truncheons. At length mounted police were brought up and idle onlookers were warned that the men on horseback were coming. This had the desired effect and hundreds of spectators scrambled away to safety, almost falling over each other in their anxiety to get clear. There was only one casualty in this flurry: an elderly woman, Mrs Waters, who was afflicted with deafness, apparently failed to hear the clattering approach of the horsemen and was knocked unconscious, suffering severe head injuries. One other individual, a man named Barnes, was also knocked down and received cuts and bruises. But the mounted police had arrived none too soon. Their colleagues on foot had been having a rough time. As the *Hampshire Chronicle* reported, 'Several were badly kicked about the legs, which left cuts and bruises. Mounted Constable Wilson received an ugly cut in the head, had to be surgically attended, and next day appeared with his head swathed in bandages. Superintendent Waters himself had a nasty cut on the shin and there is no doubt many in the unruly crowd retired home that night with cuts and bruises that it was policy to keep to themselves.' Order was restored about one o'clock on the Sunday morning.

Later that day many shopkeepers, fearing that the evening might bring a third outbreak of rioting, boarded up their windows and in one or two places there appeared a foreshadowing of the phrase to become famous throughout the country later in that fateful year. For on some of the boarded-up windows the proprietors affixed notices proclaiming 'Business carried on within as usual'. About two o'clock in the afternoon a crowd once again assembled, distinctly smaller than on the two previous days but quite as avid for mischief. As the mob moved down Marlborough Street many street-lamps were damaged and in Charlton Road most of the windows of a newly-built house belonging to Mr F. Beale were smashed in the same way. For a time the crowd lingered near the *Junction Hotel*, but then scattered in all directions as a strong force of police hove in sight. That evening the High Street was once more thronged, as people bustled to and fro, observing the signs of damage and doubtless looking forward with morbid eagerness to fresh excitement. But the police patrols were there in strength and kept everyone moving. As with the Winchester riots earlier, an important factor in restoring order was the absence of soldiers, many of whom, from the Tidworth Garrison, were habitual visitors to the town in the evening. On this evening, however, the military police had forbidden the town to soldiers in uniform. Another precaution taken by the police was a request to public houses to close an hour earlier than usual on a Sunday, at nine o'clock, and this was uniformly complied with. So the Sunday night passed off quietly. The large force of police remained in Andover throughout Monday and again patrolled the streets in the evening, but there was no more disorder.

Naturally the local press commented at length on the affair and due tribute was paid to the police, emphasis being put on their initial difficulties, arising from their scarcity. As the *Andover Advertiser* said, 'For its size and population Andover is about the cheapest policed place in the country and whereas in Winchester one falls over a priest or a policeman at every fifth step, in Andover their rarity makes them distinctly valuable.' Owing to the assizes and the holidays the only available police to begin with had been Sergeant Every and two constables. If twenty men had joined in assisting the police the first outbreak would have been speedily quelled and the town have been saved a 4d. rate. There were many present who should have assisted the mayor and the police to restore order but did not do so. The cost of the extra police alone may be a little lesson to those who pay the rates not to encourage disorder.' Compliments were paid to the efficiency of the police, as well as to the admirable way in which they had kept their tempers under severe provocation and their restraint in the use of force. 'On Saturday they had worked hard from eleven o'clock until 2.15 a.m., but in several instances the reply to a raised arm was the rejoinder to get off home and many times the result was that the advice was taken.' To be sure, there had been some minor *contretemps*. One constable on the Sunday night had been using some force to make one rowdy individual go down New Street rather than along East Street, when he had been thrown violently against an onlooker, who then thought he was being unjustly attacked. But for the most part the police had done the business expeditiously. In particular, the *Advertiser* maintained that the mounted men had been right to charge the crowd and not merely walk their horses into it. The latter course 'would have meant that the riders would have been dismounted in a couple of seconds, for there were plenty of country lads there who know the knack of lifting the heel of a rider so that he drops gracefully over the other side of his mount'. The *Advertiser* gloomily concluded its remarks on the affair by estimating that the cost to the ratepayers was likely to exceed the first estimates and would probably result in an increase in the rents of cottages. Finally, 'the disorder has drawn the attention of the papers of large provincial centres to Andover and the town has not received a very flattering character, while the exaggerated reports of the proceedings that have been spread in the district have had a distinctly adverse effect upon the

trade of the town'. Even more than a sense of shame, the dominant reaction
among the citizens was naturally one of concern for their pockets. Perhaps it
was this and a laudable concern to retrieve the reputation of his town, that led
one Mr Kendall to refuse to prosecute a man arrested for damaging some of his
property. Kendall remained unswayed by pressure from the mayor and the police.
'I am not here to be dictated to by anybody. I have not prosecuted the man and
I don't think I will. It is on the information of the police. I understood I had
to be here from the chief constable of the county and was here as a witness. I
have not expressed an opinion through the whole crisis and by prosecuting the
man I should be showing feeling in the matter.' To this Superintendent Jones
rejoined, 'If everybody behaved like you, where should we be?' Mr Kendall
retorted, 'I am a private citizen,' to which the superintendent answered, 'And we
are trying to protect you.' Here in a few words is the whole problem of the clash
between individual right and the necessary police function of maintaining order,
without which all rights are worthless. Despite all urging, Mr Kendall refused
to prosecute; but at least the police had the consolation of public praise from
the mayor, who referred to the state of affairs which had prevailed in the town
for the past three days and said that he thought the police had acted in a most
difficult situation with the greatest possible moderation and in a way which had
to be admired.

All lesser concerns dwindled to comparative insignificance with the British
declaration of war on 4 August 1914. Unrealised at the time, the coming of the
First World War marked the end of both an historical era and of a whole way
of life. British society was to be profoundly affected by the colossal struggle.
Fresh functions and responsibilities were thrust upon the police by the war
situation. Inevitably some members of the Hampshire Constabulary itself were
immediately affected. On 10 August the chief constable reported to the Standing
Joint Committee that 16 single constables and seven married constables who were
army reservists had been called for active service. Fifty constables of the First
Police Reserve were recalled, and the committee approved the extra expenditure
of £2,000 to cover the cost of the additional men. This First Police Reserve
consisted of retired police officers who had voluntarily placed themselves at
the disposal of the regular force in time of emergency. Furthermore, the chief
constable was authorised to enlist special constables into a Second Police Reserve
and to enrol paid members of the Second Police Reserve at 5s. per day. He was
also allowed to purchase 50 additional revolvers and ammunition. In October
the training of police officers in the use of rifles was approved, as well as an
allowance of 50 rounds of ammunition per man. An order had been issued giving
general information for the guidance of police armed with rifles or revolvers.
When they detected the approach of any person or persons whose actions were
suspicious, they were to challenge such person or persons by calling out 'Halt,
who goes there?' If a satisfactory answer to this challenge was not forthcoming

'the constable should, if circumstances permit, repeat the challenge and warn them that unless they stop he will fire, and if possible blow his whistle'. If the challenged persons still advanced or ran away 'and he has reason to infer from their actions or the surrounding circumstances that they are evilly disposed, it will be necessary for him to fire with the object of disabling them'. On hearing the sound of a police whistle or of shots any police in the vicinity were to hasten to the disturbance and give help. It was stressed that a report stating the cause of the incident and its exact locality was to be sent as early as possible thereafter to the divisional superintendent. The same order also indicated that arrangements should be made for an armed constable posted on a vulnerable point to be accompanied by a boy scout to act as messenger. And a few days later members of the force were warned that great care would now have to be observed in acting upon telephone messages in case they might be bogus ones.

One task which fell to the police was the supervision of the Aliens' Restriction Act of 1914. A notice in this connection warned that 'Registration will close at 12 noon on Wednesday, August 19th, 1914, after which date aliens will be proceeded against under the order.' In November 1914 a similar restriction order gave notice that 'persons of Ottoman (i.e. Turkish) nationality (other than inhabitants of Cyprus) are required to register themselves forthwith. Persons born in Egypt are Turkish subjects and must register.' However, persons born in Cyprus and producing passports issued in Cyprus 'or other satisfactory evidence of birth in the island' – were regarded as British subjects. The penalty for not registering was a fine of £100 or imprisonment for six months. Despite these moves to control the alien within, the chief constable reported at the end of October that a number of German seamen, many of military age, were residing at Beech Abbey, Alton, had not been interned and were apparently under no restrictions. Some of these sailors had caused public apprehension by roaming the streets in a drunken state armed with sticks. The Home Office was requested to arrange for their internment and shortly afterwards the whole group of 171 was transferred to internment camps in Stratford, London. Another group of foreigners required to register with the police was that composed of Belgian refugees, who had fled to this country in considerable numbers as the German onslaught struck their own small land.

Measures taken for the defence of the realm included regulations and advice concerning the possible approach of enemy aircraft. The chief constable advised that when bombs were being dropped, cellars were the refuges which offered the best chance of safety. At night time the most important precaution was to show no lights which would be visible from aircraft 'and enable them to identify the towns or other places on which they propose to drop bombs'. Outside lighting ought to be reduced to a minimum as long as there was a danger of air raids and if notice was received of the actual approach of aircraft all outside lights of every description were at once to be extinguished. In all places where the lighting of the streets had been reduced by order of the Home Secretary or of a competent naval or military authority, the use of powerful lights on motor vehicles was forbidden. 'Any person becoming aware of the approach of hostile aircraft should immediately inform the police in order that the alarm may at once be given.' This was to be done by the sounding of hooters or sirens in boroughs or urban and rural districts, or else by the ringing of church bells, or of bells in discord. Air raids on Hampshire and indeed on the whole United Kingdom were to be only on a puny scale in the course of the First World War. But orders such as these signalled the advent of war in a new dimension and the coming of new terror to the civil populations of the 20th century.

In those early days of the great struggle the police rendered help to the military authorities in all sorts of ways. Captain Norton, Deputy Assistant Director of Remounts, No. 1 Remount Circle, Southern Command, wrote to Major Warde in September 1914 'to acknowledge the very great assistance which has been rendered to purchasing officers and to me by the Hampshire County Constabulary since mobilisation was ordered. In very many cases purchasing officers have told me that without the assistance of the police they would have found it almost impossible to get through their tasks. I can speak from personal knowledge of the help given by the Petersfield Police, which has been invaluable, and should like to mention particularly the superintendent, whose energy, common sense and tact are admirable.' Other tributes to the energy and helpfulness of the police in connection with the complex business of billeting came from the Royal Marines; and Lieutenant-Colonel Mackenzie of the Argyll and Sutherland Highlanders expressed his thanks to the constabulary for their efficient and timely assistance, 'especially in staving off the evil of drink by their valuable help which was always most energetically given me by Superintendent Marshall: Christmas and New Year's day were most orderly as a result of the above.' The Hampshire Police were also active in securing the integrity of the various prohibited areas within their jurisdiction, such as Bournemouth, Christchurch, Lymington and Romsey; the urban districts of Eastleigh and Bishopstoke, Fareham, Gosport and Alverstoke, Havant, Itchen and Warblington; and the rural districts of Christchurch, Fareham, Havant, Lymington, New Forest, Romsey and South Stoneham.

In these and many similar ways the war affected the work of the Hampshire police. The great conflict overshadowed the force in other forms too and these more grim. On 18 January 1915, Major Warde reported to the Standing Joint Committee that of the 23 constables who had been called up as army recruits, seven had been wounded and one killed in action. These were only the first of many casualties.

BOOK 4
1915-1940

The war imposed many extra duties upon the police, in Hampshire as elsewhere. Some of these tasks, such as the registration of aliens and the enforcement of the Defence of the Realm Regulations, have already been indicated. Others included the conducting of enquiries on behalf of the military authorities and intelligence agencies; the furnishing of returns for allied powers of their nationals of military age; the management of billeting arrangements; the taking of censuses of horses, cattle, forage and potatoes; the application of food control orders; and the serving and enforcement of liquor control board orders. All this was in addition to normal police work and put the force under strain; this in turn was exacerbated by the rapid rise in the cost of living brought by the war. Prices steadily rose, as did wages in many spheres of industry. The police felt the pinch and more than ever the securing of better pay and allowances became a main pre-occupation. In January 1915 the Standing Joint Committee approved the grant of a war bonus of 3s. per week, to offset the higher cost of living. In October 1916 there was a further increase of 3s. per week and at the same time the weekly boot allowance was raised from 6d. to 1s. A General Order of May 1917 announced that all members of the force 'who had completed twenty-six years' service on May 19th, 1915, or who may since that date have completed that service', were to receive a deferred bonus at the rate of £26 a year for all service after that date and after the completion of 26 years' service. In the case of men who died in the service, the bonus might be paid to the widow, children or their relatives, as the Standing Joint Committee might determine, and the scheme applied retrospectively to men who had died or to men who had been permitted to retire since the date named. Again, the bonus would only be payable when the chief constable certified that the service had been in all respects satisfactory. It could be earned only during the continuance of the war and would not be paid until after the war, unless the officers concerned had meanwhile been permitted to leave.

Two months later the war bonus was increased from 6s. to 15s. weekly and in an order announcing this Major Warde in his usual style emphasised that, 'It gives the chief constable keen satisfaction that having taken all the members of the force into his confidence and sought their views he has felt justified in doing his best to obtain their realisation and that his anxiety on their behalf is at an end owing to his being successful. As their chief, nothing affords him greater happiness than to add in any way to their welfare.' The sudden steep rise in the war bonus testified to the sharp increase in food prices; for 1917 saw the German submarine campaign at its height and Great Britain in those terrible months came near to being starved out. A commendable aspect of this increase was the preponderant feeling in the force that the bonus should be alike for all members, whether married or single. In fact one division composed only of married constables voted unanimously for this system. The stress put upon consultation is significant of the growing feeling in those years throughout the British Police Service that some regular and effective representative machinery should be set up. For if the war years put the police system under pressure, they also awoke many people to the need for sweeping reforms. During the conflict, large sections of the British population became more mobile than ever before and long-standing barriers of region and class were weakened. For the first time it was brought home strongly to many policemen that conditions of service varied very widely from one force to another and that each of the 190 British police forces operated in almost complete autonomy. This new awareness was to have important consequences later.

An innovation brought by the war was the introduction into Hampshire for the first time of special constables and towards the end of August 1914 Major Warde issued instructions for their guidance. They were to be under the direction of Captain Lionel Wells, R.N., assisted by commanders in the various divisions. In case of need the 'Specials' were to be notified of where they were to attend for duty and were reminded of the importance of carrying their warrant cards at all such times. As badge of office, they were to wear the appropriate armlet on the left upper arm only when actually on duty, and in addition they were provided with a pocket book, handcuffs, truncheon and whistle. They were strongly reminded that the truncheon was the only authorised weapon, and no kind of firearm or other weapon was to be carried, except under special authorisation. The sage advice was offered that 'The regular police find it most convenient to carry the truncheon in the trousers pocket, as it is out of view and readily available when required. The display of a truncheon might be deemed provocative and therefore it is advisable not to display it.' Other useful suggestions were that the special constable should 'remember that a conciliatory demeanour often smooths away difficulties and that many cases may, by means of an exchange of names and addresses between the persons concerned with a view to process, be more satisfactory than by resort to the extreme action of arrest'. Most helpful of all, perhaps, was the recommendation to specials called out for duty to carry some food in their pockets. One of the duties taken over by the specials in 1917 was that concerned with air-raid precautions.

The atmosphere of war tension had some curious results. In June 1915 one Thomas Harry Richardson was charged under the Defence of the Realm Act. He had been found in possession of a paper bearing the portentous message:

'No. 2. The North Sea Fleet is located around the quarter on my chart marked T and Y. Five transports leave Southampton tomorrow and picked drafts of Kitchener's are being sent over within a fortnight.' This turned out, however, to be his answer to a competition in Cassell's *Saturday Journal*, and the case was dismissed. More serious was an occurrence in July 1916, when Superintendent Littlewood and Constable Bird were commended for their courage in dealing with an armed and violent man at Woolston. From the house occupied by the miscreant had come the sound of firing, and the housekeeper was found shot. At the time of the arrest the man was in front of the house threatening passers-by with a revolver, to the great danger of the public in general and of the arresting officers in particular. As a reward for this meritorious conduct £5 was paid to the superintendent and £2 to the constable.

A much uglier crime occurred in July 1917 when a girl of 15, Vera Mary Glasspool, was found dead in a copse off the Owlesbury to Longwood road just outside Winchester. She had been in service at Longwood House and had been walking to her home at the nearby village of Baybridge when she was attacked, strangled and stabbed in the throat. The inquest jury naturally returned a verdict of murder, but the killer, apparently, was never brought to justice.

In February 1915 Superintendent Wakeford received the King's Police Medal from the monarch himself, who shook hands with him, and said he was proud to meet him: and Major Warde noted that 'The special mark of favour on behalf of His Majesty towards one of his superintendents in whose interests the chief constable is always so much concerned, gives him much pleasure.' Even more gratifying was the award in June 1918 of the O.B.E. to the deputy chief constable, Mr Griffin. The chief constable's pleasure was enhanced by the fact of his long association with Mr Griffin, first as his chief clerk and then as his deputy chief constable. These official decorations could well be taken as marks of appreciation not only to the individual officers concerned, but to the whole Hampshire force. Later, other tributes were to be paid to the county police for all that they had done in willing co-operation with the various military and naval authorities in the area, during and immediately after the war. In December 1920 Major A.W. Gale, Road Transport Officer for the Basingstoke and Salisbury areas, wrote to the chief constable: 'In view of the closing up of the road transport offices at Salisbury and Basingstoke in the near future, I wish to bring to your notice the valuable assistance rendered me at all times by the various superintendents of divisions and the officers serving under them of the Hampshire Constabulary, particularly in the years of 1918 and 1919, the former when the department was created and a great deal of work fell on the police in rounding up all transport owners for registration and the latter during the railway strike. I have had many years connection with the police forces in various parts and I have never worked with a better lot of men than the Hampshire Constabulary. I wish them the best of luck.'

The police certainly deserved luck, but in addition aspired to more concrete benefits. In July 1918 the chief constable announced that he had 'laid the petition submitted to him in connection with pay and war bonus before the Standing Joint Committee with the result that an increase of 5s. per week to the existing war bonus has been sanctioned to take effect from the 15th instant'. He added with pride that this war bonus was now the highest flat rate bonus granted to any county force in the country. The Secretary of State, however, would not at that point sanction any increase of pay during the war. In September 1918 the Home Secretary did notify the Standing Joint Committee of his decision to fix a standard rate of pay for all counties and boroughs and announced that this scale would replace the one recommended by the conference of the group of counties and boroughs in which Hampshire was included. The conference had met in London in March, and Major Warde was the only chief constable on the sub-committee appointed to consider the matter and report back to the parent body. His suggestions regarding a scale of pay were in general adopted, as was his recommendation that it should come into force forthwith instead of waiting until the end of the war. The conference had decided that this should be contingent upon the government agreeing to pay half the net cost of the police. However, all was to be changed by the grave events at the end of August 1918: for the first time in the history of the British Police there was a strike.

The roots of this action were deep. As early as 1872 attempts had been made to create some sort of organisation to represent the views of the rank and file of the Metropolitan Police. A so-called 'Representative Committee' had been set up to formulate and express current grievances. But when the organiser of this committee had tried to establish it on a permanent basis, he had been dismissed the service for insubordination. A similar incident had occurred in 1890 and from then on there was a constant agitation for 'the right to confer'. At the beginning of the 20th century the Metropolitan Police Union was set up, which later expanded into the National Union of Police and Prison Officers. By 1917, the membership of this union had become considerable, despite every kind of official discouragement and it had been affiliated to the T.U.C. During the war years the various discontents of policemen had been focused and exacerbated by the growing hardships of everyday life; the long hours of duty, the extra tasks and the cost of living which always outstripped the level of pay. The soaring income of munitions workers provided a glaring contrast to the modest wages of the police and the discipline and self-restraint of the latter were put under strain. It must be remembered that at this time there existed no machinery through which policemen in different forces could raise with the Home Secretary any questions with regard to pay or conditions of service. Even within most forces no such machinery existed. If any constable made a complaint he might well be marked down as insubordinate. Collective complaints smacked of mutiny. There was no centrally-authorised code of discipline. All these factors contributed to the Police

Strike of 29 to 31 August 1918. It was in consequence of this that the Home Secretary for the first time decided to fix a standard rate of pay throughout the country. Out of this too came the setting up of officially-approved representative boards and of the Police Federation. Early in October 1918, the Chief Constable of Hampshire issued a memorandum to sound out opinion in his force and at the end of the month announced in General Orders that 'a considerable number of divisions see no necessity for a representative board but as other divisions wish this instituted he has drawn up rules applicable to the Hampshire Constabulary which are herewith forwarded for general information'. At the same time he once again voiced his appreciation of 'the fact that his unceasing efforts for the welfare of the force under his command are recognised and appreciated in the force and that he will always have the satisfaction of knowing that the result of those efforts has been to place the Hampshire Constabulary in the forefront with other forces as regards favourable conditions of service'. The rules provided that the initial election of representatives was to be held in each division forthwith and a list of elected representatives forwarded to headquarters by 27 November 1918. The election was to be by ballot and the senior officer of the division, next below the superintendent, was to act as returning officer. Every member of the division below the rank of superintendent was to be free to nominate one other member as representative and such nominations had to reach the returning officer six days before the election took place. Immediately nominations were completed the nominees were required to signify in writing to the returning officer their willingness to serve. Cards were then to be prepared bearing the name of each nominee willing to serve, set out in order of seniority, with a space opposite each name for the recording of the vote. Any other mark or writing on the card other than the regulation cross would render the vote invalid. The nominee receiving the highest number of votes in each division would of course be elected to serve on the representative board. If any officer were not willing to serve, that division would not be represented. Superintendents were instructed to afford the returning officer any necessary clerical assistance or other facility for carrying out the election in a proper manner.

In March 1919 the famous Desborough Committee was set up to review conditions of pay, service and pensions for all British police forces. Its recommendations met with a generally favourable reception but despite this there occurred in July 1919 the general police strike. This proved a failure and ruined the careers of those who had taken part in it. They were dismissed the service and only after several years were granted a very slight monetary compensation. Out of it all the Police Act of 1919 emerged, which, among other provisions, laid it down that any police officer who continued, after 15 September of that year, to be a member of any trade union or of any association which had for its object, or one of its objects, to control or influence the pay, pensions, or conditions of service of any police force, automatically ceased to be a police officer and lost all the powers of a constable. In drawing the attention of his own force to this provision, Major Warde proclaimed his confidence that members of the force which existed for the purpose of enforcing the law would themselves obey the law and that he did not propose to enquire, in individual cases, whether an officer who formerly belonged to a union had now absolved his membership. 'But it is important that all should know the full consequences of remaining a member of a union contrary to this enactment. These are as follows: Any constable who fails to comply ceases automatically to be a constable and neither the chief constable nor the Secretary of State has power to reinstate him. He loses irretrievably all pension rights; he can no longer lawfully be paid for his services; and, if he arrests any person after his disqualification and after he has lost his authority as constable, he becomes liable to pay damages to that person. One exception is made. If a constable was a member of a trade union before he joined the police he may, with the consent of the chief constable, continue to be a member of that union in order to receive the union benefits to which he is entitled.'

Already other General Orders had been issued relating to pay and allowances. The chief constable had secured the agreement of the Standing Joint Committee to a new scale of pay for sergeants and constables, dating from 1 April 1919. Constables on appointment were to receive 70s. weekly. Thereafter for each year of satisfactory service their weekly pay was to rise by 2s., so that a constable after ten years would receive 90s. a week. After a further seven years' good service and conduct his wage would rise to 92s. 6d. After a total of 22 years' service he would get 95s. a week. A sergeant on first being promoted would receive 100s. a week, and for each of the next five years he would gain an increase of 2s. 6d. The boot money was increased to 1s. 6d. per week and the stoppages for lodgings and payment of war bonus were discontinued for all ranks from 11 August 1919. At the same time it was announced that all constables appointed were now to be on probation for twelve months or more. 'Superintendents will report at the expiration of ten months if it is considered that each constable will qualify at the end of twelve months for advancement to the one-year service class. Should a superintendent at any time form the opinion that a constable is never likely to make an efficient police officer he will report to headquarters with a view to his being discharged without waiting for the twelve months to expire.'

As well as pay and allowances, new provisions were made concerning hours of duty. With effect from 1 January 1920, the principle of an eight-hour tour of duty came into force. The hours were to be three by day and five by night. Superintendents were instructed to arrange the duties of inspectors and sergeants in a manner to suit the requirements of their divisions. It was, of course, recognised that detective work and county police work generally could not be worked to fixed and limited hours and that it was impossible for a county constable to work fixed hours of duty in the same degree as a borough constable. 'On the other hand, the county constable has some advantages inasmuch as he is on duty as soon as he leaves his house or station, whereas the borough constable has to spend some time in travelling to and from the police station and parading for instructions.' Where a constable was called upon to extend his tour of duty by more than a complete hour, or to do duty outside his normal hours, time off in lieu was to be given within a reasonable time, and at the start of 1923, it was intimated that annual leave could now be taken at any time throughout the whole year.

An interesting minor offence which became current after the First World War was the wearing of distinguished decorations, genuine or false, by persons not entitled to do so. A General Order of July 1920 informed the force that on the reverse of the Victoria Cross were engraved the rank, regimental number (in the case of a soldier), surname, initials and unit of the recipient together with the date of the deed in respect of which the award was made. 'If, therefore, any person is found wearing an unengraved cross it is almost certain to be spurious and a full report will be forwarded to headquarters as a complete list of those entitled to wear same has been supplied by the Home Office.'

A notorious crime perpetrated in 1920 was the so-called Thruxton murder which took place on the road at Thruxton Down, near Andover. One Sunday morning a labourer, Mr Burridge, discovered a dead body lying under a hedge by the road-side as he was cycling past. It was established that the victim was one Sidney Spicer, a Salisbury taxi-driver, and that his murderer was a 35-year-old army deserter, Percy Topliss. Topliss had hired Spicer to drive him to the railway station at Andover Junction and on the way had shot him dead and robbed him. He left the body beside the road after making some attempts to conceal it and then drove off in the direction of South Wales. At some point on the journey he picked up another soldier. As soon as Burridge had discovered the body he informed the police, who rapidly circulated the number of the car and a description of the two wanted men. Thanks to this swift action and the resultant nation-wide press publicity, the car was discovered abandoned at Swansea the following day. Topliss's companion was soon arrested and charged with being an accessory to the murder and with harbouring Topliss, but eventually was cleared of both charges. Meanwhile the hunt for Topliss went on and, as might be expected, from all over the country came reports that he had been seen. Later Topliss was tracked down and cornered in Cumberland and at Penrith, more than five weeks after attempting to murder a farmer and a policeman, he was shot dead by another police officer after a gun battle. Thus ended this bizarre episode in the history of British crime. Even today, however, the place where the murder took place is often referred to as Topliss Hill.

In January 1923 a war memorial to those members of the Hampshire Constabulary who had fallen for their king and country was unveiled by the Lord Lieutenant in an impressive and moving ceremony. The memorial itself was in the form of a monumental approach to the flight of steps leading to the headquarters building in Winchester and, thus placed, had to be passed by everyone visiting the county police station. Placed on either side of the steps were two stone piers or pillars inscribed with the names of the 21 officers of the force who had given their lives. The whole had been designed by Captain A.L. Roberts, the county architect. The proceedings were favoured with beautiful weather and attended by a large and distinguished company representative of the county, the constabulary, the armed services and families and friends of the fallen. Each division was represented by the superintendent, one sergeant and a detachment of constables. In addition there were several contingents of special constables and a large number of ex-sergeants and ex-constables of the force, as well as many of the general public. The Duke of Wellington, in his capacity as Chairman of Quarter Sessions, invited the Lord Lieutenant, Major-General The Right Honourable J.E.B. Seely, C.B., C.M.G., D.S.O., to unveil the memorial. This the latter did, but not before he had paid a remarkable tribute to the Hampshire Constabulary. In the course of his address, he said '... I think it ought to be said what good services the Hampshire Constabulary rendered during the war. We are here today to commemorate those who gave up their lives. No fewer than twenty-one members of the Hampshire Constabulary were killed in the Great War out of 540 of all ranks who were ready and anxious to join, so much so that a special order had to be issued to say that it was not possible for them to join and retain all their pension rights. In spite of that order many of the Hampshire Constabulary surrendered those rights in order to serve at the front but I am glad to hear from Major Warde that after all they were allowed to count their time spent in the army for pensions. Of course, it was not possible to allow too many of the constabulary to go as they had vitally important duties to perform. That was the case in all counties, but especially in Hampshire, where there were so many great military camps. I have seen from the testimony of the officers commanding those various camps of Canadians and Americans and of our own troops that you were vitally important in fulfilling many duties of maintaining order and other duties specially devolving on the police ... I have always thought and said that Hampshire is the best ordered county in England. If that is so, and I make bold to say it is, it is largely due to the Hampshire Constabulary and it must be a pleasure and delight to you, Major Warde, after nearly twenty-nine years' service as chief constable, to reflect that the force which you have so ably commanded should have rendered such valued services in the Great War.'

The Lord Lieutenant continued with a special compliment to the special constables present. 'When the members of the constabulary went to the war you came forward to fill their places and augment their number. The king, whom I represent in this county, has more than once testified his royal approval of the great services you have rendered and I can only endorse his words on his behalf, and say that the whole community, from the king downwards, thanks you for what you did.' Later in the proceedings the Lord Lieutenant informed the assistant chief constable, Major Nicholson, that he was greatly impressed with the fine appearance of the men and had never seen a finer guard of honour. In a General Order after the ceremony the chief constable expressed his deep satisfaction that the tribute to their fallen comrades had been of such an impressive nature 'and that the Lord Lieutenant of the county should have felt justified in giving voice to such remarkably high testimony to the character of the force which it is the great privilege of its chief to command'.

Less happy publicity had come to the force concerning the appointment, at the end of 1922, of this same Major G. Nicholson as assistant chief constable. For this gentleman was son-in-law to Major Warde and had been sworn in as a constable only three weeks before his appointment. These circumstances gave rise to unfavourable comment, as did the seeming abruptness of Major Warde's act in choosing him and the absence of any other candidates for the position. In the quarterly meeting of the Hampshire County Council the whole business was discussed at length. Several speakers emphasised that they intended no personal criticism or disparagement of Major Nicholson, but were nevertheless uneasy about the matter. It was reaffirmed that it had been the chief constable's right to appoint the assistant chief constable, subject to the approval of the Standing Joint Committee. This very procedure, however, ought in the interests of the service to be altered. Mr W.J. Richards proposed a motion: 'That this council is of opinion that all appointments to the higher ranks of the county police (except the chief constable) should, in future, be confined to persons of experience in the ranks of the force below that in which the appointment is to be made.' In his speech Mr Richards made the point that 'it was in the best interests of the community and the efficiency of the force that each member of it should have an opportunity for going in for a post of this character'. The public expected from the police a high standard of efficiency, integrity, and impartiality and it would be undermining those ideals if members of the force were treated with unfairness in the higher offices. From the standpoint of efficiency it seemed to Mr Richards clear that a force numbering somewhere in the neighbourhood of 500 was quite capable within itself of supplying the necessary intelligence for a post of this character, apart from the question of the men having the right to look forward to the higher posts. As the *Hampshire Chronicle* reported it: 'A man ought, after twenty or thirty years' service, to have a full knowledge of his job; therefore, if there was any chance of promotion, those who had spent their lives in studying questions of this description were the men to receive this consideration.' The resolution moved by Mr Richards was eventually put and carried, with only one vote against it. Some members present, however, did not vote.

A pleasing tribute to the ingenuity and tenderness of a Hampshire officer, Police Constable Bundy, was paid in an issue of *The Animal World* of February

1923. At Headley, a two-month-old kitten had fallen down a well over ninety feet deep. At first the constable tried to rescue the poor creature by means of a bucket but failed. 'He then put a sack over the bucket and a rabbit skin round the handle, and tied the mother cat to the handle by means of a collar fastened round her neck, and lowered her on the bucket. The mother seized the kitten and climbed back on to the sack and the cats were safely drawn to the surface. Both animals are none the worse for the adventure. Too much cannot be said in praise of Police Constable Bundy's promptitude and resource for the rescue.'

Thanks of a more customary kind were conveyed in a letter from the Provost Marshal of the Aldershot Command and the Secretary of the Military Manoeuvres Commission in appreciation of 'the excellent work done with the troops on manoeuvres by the members of the Hampshire Constabulary who were attached to various divisions, etc.' in the autumn of 1925. This willing and cheerful work under damp and uncomfortable conditions was remarked on and the Secretary of the Military Manoeuvres Commission went so far as to say '… the very satisfactory results obtained were due in a large measure to the good feeling in the area, which was shared so noticeably by the police, and which was reflected in the smooth working and the very friendly relations which were maintained throughout between the police authorities and the troops'. Throughout its history the Hampshire force has been involved in closer co-operation with the military and naval authorities than perhaps any other, and again and again the armed services have testified warmly to the constant willing and essential co-operation of the constabulary.

In April 1926 Police Constable J. Southey was highly commended for the promptness and courage he had displayed in rescuing William Gardiner from the River Meon at Droxford on 8 February that year. Gardiner had attempted to commit suicide and although it was dark at the time Southey had unhesitatingly plunged into the river eight feet deep and saved the former's life. The chief constable brought the constable's action to the notice of the Royal Humane Society and in consequence the Society's Honorary Parchment was awarded to him. In November of the same year Sergeant W. Carter was commended for his plucky action in rescuing from drowning a woman who had attempted to commit suicide at Netley. Fully dressed in uniform he had plunged into the sea for about thirty yards to a depth of five feet and succeeded in getting the woman ashore. He had then applied artificial respiration and restored her to consciousness. Unhappily however complications set in and on the following day the woman died. At the subsequent inquest the sergeant received the high approbation of the coroner.

1926 was the year of the General Strike which deeply disrupted the life of the community, aroused vehement factional passion, brought Great Britain nearer to civil strife than she had been since the Irish crises on the eve of the First World War, and above all left a legacy of rancour and suspicion which still infects the industry and politics of this country. The strike lasted from May 3rd to 12th and inevitably immense burdens were put upon the police and the large numbers of special constables raised throughout the kingdom. Observers then and since are agreed that great credit is due to all the members of the police service for the way in which they dealt with innumerable tense local situations and prevented the many sporadic incidents of unorganised violence from developing into anything like a mass uprising. The main points of strain were to be found in London and in other great cities such as Glasgow, Manchester, Newcastle, Leeds and Birmingham. On the whole Hampshire was comparatively little affected. Nevertheless, on 5 June, the chief constable announced in General Orders that it gave him 'much pleasure to publish for the information of the force the following extract from a letter which he has received from the Right Honourable Major-General Sir John B. Seely, C.B., C.M.G., D.S.O.: "I must again express, as Lord Lieutenant of the County, my high appreciation of the exceptionally valuable services rendered by the Hampshire Constabulary during the recent emergency …"

The regulations governing the marriage of Hampshire police officers changed constantly in detail. In 1923 a rent allowance was approved for those officers who could not be provided with quarters and superintendents were instructed to satisfy themselves that all payments were reasonable and that the allowance paid to constables who rented furnished apartments was not greater than the amount they would have paid if such apartments had been unfurnished. At the same time it was announced that 'In future no application for permission to marry will be considered unless the officer has five years approved service in the force or has attained the age of twenty-eight years.' For adequate housing was scarce then as now. Two years later there came a relaxation and the minimum conditions were four years' service or 26 years of age, provided that the applicant of 26 had at least two years' service. In 1927 permission to marry was brought to depend on a spell of only three years in the service, or 25 years of age. This liberalising trend, however, was not allowed to proceed too far. Later that same year a General Order 'notified for general information that any officer in the future who applies for permission to marry on the ground that his intended wife is pregnant or who marries without the chief constable's permission will be called upon to resign from the force'. And one slipshod constable was reduced two increments of pay for one year for acting in a manner likely to bring discredit on the reputation of the force, 'in being responsible for the condition of a single woman and taking no steps in the matter until she had given birth to a child'.

Towards the end of 1926 the Standing Joint Committee sanctioned the payment of an allowance of £12 per annum for the use of motor cycles for police purposes in circumstances where the chief constable considered the payment of the allowance to be justified. Such circumstances existed where large areas had to be supervised and the allowance was to be made to inspectors and sergeants in charge of such sections and at the headquarters of such divisions. In all cases the grant was to be subject to the officers concerned producing each year a satisfactory policy of insurance covering not less than third-party risks. This motor-cycle allowance was in lieu of the previous bicycle allowance and marks the steady advance of the motorised society. Another sign of the times was that in January 1927 the Farnborough Chamber of Commerce came out in support of a suggestion by the Wolverhampton Chamber of Commerce for the setting up of a subsidiary police force for traffic control only. This suggestion was supported with reasons which are essentially the same as those advanced today in the same connection and was, not unexpectedly, decried by a commentator in the *Aldershot News*.

May 1927 saw the death of former Superintendent Ernest George Hawkins, who had joined the Hampshire Constabulary in 1883 in Winchester, and soon after transferred to Bournemouth. Quite early in his service there he was commended by the local magistrates for the smart capture of a clever thief. Promotion to second-class constable had rapidly followed and after serving in the Isle of Wight he was transferred to Wickham where he obtained his first-class certificate. A sergeant in 1888, he was placed in charge of Shirley Division at Southampton and while there arrested five men single-handed. He had found them breaking into a warehouse, roped them together and taken them thus bound to the police station. In 1893 he had been inspector in charge of Alton Division and four years later, as second-class superintendent, he had been posted to Aldershot. At that time there had been a great deal of crime there, and on one occasion in 1899 there were no fewer than 54 prisoners for trial by the magistrates. In 1900 Hawkins was promoted to first-class superintendent, in which rank he remained until his retirement. At his funeral eight superintendents and a sergeant-major acted as pall bearers and thus paid tribute to this departed giant of the force.

Local government changes within the county had their effect on the organis-ation of the force. In November 1920 the parishes of Itchen and Bitterne, and parts of the parishes of North and South Stoneham were transferred to the County Borough of Southampton and in consequence the headquarters of the Southampton Division were established at Eastleigh. Shortly before, Portsmouth Borough had been extended to take in the parish of Cosham. In October 1923 the Romsey Division was amalgamated with Eastleigh Division and henceforward formed a section of the latter; thus the authorised strength of the force was reduced by one superintendent. Exactly five years later a further redistribution and reorganisation of divisions took place. At the start of October 1928 the Alton Section was absorbed by Odiham Division and the Whitehill Section by Petersfield Division. The Kingsclere Section was taken from Basingstoke Division and absorbed by Andover. Romsey Section was taken from Eastleigh Division and absorbed by the New Forest Division. Lymington and New Milton Sections were taken from New Forest Division and absorbed by Ringwood Division, while in the Winchester Division the Alresford Section was absorbed by Basingstoke Division and the Winchester Section by Eastleigh Division. At the end of the year too it was intimated that from 1 January 1929 the various divisions throughout the county were to be named and lettered as follows: Aldershot, Andover, Basingstoke, Bournemouth, Fareham, Eastleigh, New Forest, Petersfield and Ringwood were to bear the letters A, B, C, D, E, F, G, I and K respectively.

Other changes carried through at this time, all in the interests of economy, included the disbandment of the mounted establishment, consisting of one sergeant, eight constables and nine horses. Two of the horses had been hired from the Bournemouth Corporation at £150 per annum. Now the other horses were to be sold and five of the erstwhile mounted constables taken into the dismounted branch. Ten constables employed on wholetime point duty at Bournemouth were to be replaced by ten R.A.C. patrolmen. This economy gave serious concern to Bournemouth opinion and led to renewed agitation for the borough to have its own force. The *Bournemouth Daily Echo* stated that 'it does not seem to us that the Standing Joint Committee has seriously contemplated the growing police needs of the borough. Can it be said that the great and ever-increasing area of the borough is over-policed by the present force of 120 men, which works out at one man to every 900 of the population? Under the re-organisation it will be one constable to 992 of the population. … The release of police from point duty and the regulation of motor traffic has long been felt desirable in order that they may devote more time to their legitimate duty of the detection and prevention of crime. We do not suggest that this aspect of their work has been neglected in Bournemouth, but we cannot help feeling a little anxiety about the possible effect of the proposed decrease in the strength of the local force. A policeman is still a policeman even though he may be engaged specially on point duty. The knowledge that he is on duty gives a certain sense of security. He is invested with an authority which an R.A.C. patrol does not possess, though the latter may be able quite as efficiently – possibly more so – to direct and control traffic.' The *Daily Echo* went on to express its satisfaction that the proposed reduction of numbers of police might be taken as a compliment to the good behaviour of the population. 'But,' it continued, 'we are not so sure there will not be more to fear from the attentions of that undesirable class of visitor to whom places like Bournemouth are a happy hunting ground. Perhaps the telephone police boxes now being so widely adopted will minimise this danger, if and when they are brought into use locally. Meanwhile it will not escape notice that the paid police reserve is to be abolished and that reference is made to the availability of the unpaid special constables should occasion arise, which may or may not be a hint that their services will be utilised more frequently than anticipated.' The *Daily Echo* concluded resoundingly, 'On the whole the report, in so far as it relates to Bournemouth, rather strengthens the claim of the borough to manage its own police affairs and with the prospective retirement of the present chief constable for the county and the changes this will involve, opportunity should be taken to bring about the separation. Bournemouth seems chiefly likely to suffer by what the Standing Joint Committee has adopted, and the economy anticipated is so paltry as to be almost negligible.'

A few days later the *Bournemouth Daily Echo* reported further lengthy discussion in the town council upon police matters generally and especial attention was given to the suggestion that R.A.C. scouts act as pointsmen for the control of traffic. What exactly was to be their status? Councillor Game asked if they would have any authority to deal with delinquents who came along; to which Alderman Robson (a Bournemouth representative on the Standing Joint Committee) replied that they would not have the authority of the police but they would have police authority immediately behind them. The patrolmen themselves were not to be sworn in as special constables. Councillor Game persisted and asked whether these men could stop a driver and take his name and address. Alderman Robson replied that this was a point of law he could not answer. Councillor Wilkinson suggested that the scheme might easily prove one of economy before efficiency: the wages paid to the R.A.C. men and their general conditions were much lower than the police. He doubted whether the council would get a similar efficient service from the R.A.C. men as was given by the police. Indeed, the proposed change would give more work to the police. The R.A.C. men might take names and addresses, but the police would have to do the running about to verify their reports and get additional particulars. It might happen too, the councillor added darkly – he did not say it would – that an offender might belong to one of the societies of the men and there would not be the same impartiality shown as was shown by the police. All things considered there were many pitfalls and when the matter was carefully dealt with it might prove an expensive economy.

Concern for economy was constantly expressed throughout the Bournemouth Town Council's discussions. Alderman Robson stated that the first item which concerned the committee was the enormous increase in the cost of police pensions. He pointed out that when the constables' pay had been increased some years previously, after the Metropolitan Police strike, no notice had been taken of the effect that that difference in pay would have upon pensions. That was one matter that called for economy. Also to be considered was the large increase in numbers which had taken place in the Hampshire Constabulary in recent years. The pension period was now maturing and having regard to the proportion of pay received there had been a big increase in pensions in the last two or three years. As the constabulary was increased so also must the pensions increase. Alderman Robson went on to say that one of the directions in which economy had been promoted was the consolidation of the petty sessional divisions. They had been reduced by two, which had done away with two district headquarter staffs. The divisions had been absorbed into neighbouring divisions. Again, constables were able to move about the country by means of rnotor-cycles much more quickly than had been possible in days gone by. With regard to the proposed substitution of R.A.C. men for police officers, he said that it had been stated that there were ten police constables on point duty in Bournemouth. In fact there were more than that. It had been lost sight of that there had to be men for reliefs. The R.A.C. men would find their own reliefs and so the town would only have to pay for ten. Nor would it be the case that the ten police officers withdrawn would go on the pension list and thus be a cause of additional expense. No men would be dismissed. Only two would go in the ordinary course. Recruiting in Winchester had only to be stopped for a week or two and the other men would be absorbed. Alderman Robson made a telling point when he reminded his hearers that the savings to be effected had been referred to as 'a paltry £17,000'. To his mind it was not a paltry sum and as a member of the Standing Joint Committee he thought that they would have been failing in their duty if they did not explore every avenue they could to effect a saving. He pointed out that constables had not been trained for point duty; they were trained as constables for police duty.

Another civic dignitary, Alderman Luckham, struck a popular note in the course of his contribution when he averred that he was one of those who believed that if Bournemouth was to be properly looked after in the matter of police they should do it themselves. Spurred by loud cries of 'Hear, Hear,' he said that it seemed to him they were going back to the dark ages when everything in Bournemouth was controlled from Christchurch. The council had given that up and taken the governing of their own affairs to themselves. The time had arrived when they should do the same with the police. As far as the position of the R.A.C. men was concerned, he had been informed that if anything happened and they had to make a report they would not pass it on directly to the police but claimed they had to send it to their own headquarters and if the police wanted the report they had to get it from there. Again, if all possible economies had been considered, how was it that he, Alderman Luckham, had been informed that from ten to twenty men were employed in Bournemouth Police Station working and cleaning out cells and police premises. If that were so, they were paying men £3 10s. a week to wash floors that a charwoman would do for less than half the money.

Another speaker, Councillor Perty, agreed with Alderman Luckham that there should be another meeting to consider all available information. He was not happy about some of the suggestions under consideration. It seemed to him that they might be the thin end of a wedge to bring about an alteration in the conditions of employment of the police. He was not supporting any system of cheap labour and he was certainly not going to support anything that might develop into a private police force. Alderman Cartwright suggested that the Finance Committee of the Town Council should be in possession of facts as to the cost of the whole constabulary and what proportion of it was borne by Bournemouth; and also what portion of the £41,000 for police pensions that Bournemouth found. The whole discussion ended with the adoption of a proposal to refer the matter to the Finance Committee and thereafter if necessary to call a special meeting of the council. In acknowledging the tribute paid to his hard work on the Standing Joint Committee, Alderman Robson made the point that it was inevitable that the discussion would develop into the whole question of police control. If the Bournemouth Town Council were not satisfied with what the Standing Joint Committee were doing they would have to protest and ask for some separate police arrangements. So long as Bournemouth accepted the position whereby Winchester policed it, it must abide by Winchester's decisions. If Bournemouth were dissatisfied the whole position would have to be reviewed.

Other forces besides that of Hampshire were greatly exercised at this time about the whole expanding problem of the motor car and its manifold impact on society. In January 1929 the *Daily Mail* reported that all 220 men in the Buckinghamshire force were to be taught to drive cars. After that would come the introduction of motor police patrols. In addition, the members of the Buckinghamshire Constabulary were to be instructed at the Morris works in the care and maintenance of motor cars, in their construction, and in road manners, courtesy and safe driving. As the *Mail* commented, 'This is one of the most important steps yet taken by any police force in this country to deal with the growing problems of reckless driving, motor-car bandits, and traffic control.' With understandable complacency, the *Daily Mail* continued, 'This is a step that has been advocated for some time by the *Daily Mail* and should notably increase the efficiency of the police, while at the same time serving the best interests of motorists themselves. The policeman who has practical experience of the problem of safe transport from the driver's point of view will obviously have much to contribute to the solution of the difficulties of the roads. He will be able to exercise an effective discretion in the application of the letter of the law so as to use it to help instead of hindering the driver who is doing his best for safety. At the same time, he will be a more convincing witness against real offenders, who will no longer be able to escape, as they sometimes try to do, by pleading the technical ignorance of their accusers.'

The Devonshire Standing Joint Committee was also exercised over the question of traffic control and of finding the most effective persons to enforce it. The Committee could get no very clear guidance from the Home Secretary as to the desirable status of men enrolled for the express purpose of supervising traffic–the very problem which was besetting Hampshire. In Exeter itself great interest was aroused by the introduction in April 1929 of a system of electric automatic traffic control 'by means of coloured lights'. It makes curious reading today, the description of what was then so novel and is now so drearily familiar. 'The system consists of signal lights affixed at a height of ten to twelve feet on standards erected at the corners of intersecting roads on the near (left) side of approaching traffic. The signals are three vertically arranged coloured lights visible both by day and night. The top light is red denoting "stop", the centre light is amber, denoting "caution", and the bottom light is green denoting "go".' The *Express and Echo* soliloquised that the new system had come to stay and that it was now up to the public to make it work to the best possible advantage. 'Even if it does not have the desired effect of speeding up the traffic through the main streets, it will relieve constables for other work and if it reduces the number of accidents it will be a godsend.'

It has been seen how concerned various authorities were with the problem of steadily rising costs and the need to make economies wherever possible in the police service. In all the controversy which had arisen in Bournemouth, a major factor in the demand for a separate force had been alarm at the growing weight of police pensions. At a meeting of the Hampshire County Council in November 1929, it had been pointed out that in 1918 police pensions had been £8,000; in 1922 £19,650; in 1926 £30,619; and in 1927 £34,528. Captain Seward, who had drawn attention to these figures, claimed that they showed that men were going on pension in greatly increasing numbers. It had always been the practice to encourage police officers to continue serving as long as possible. This both made for economy and was essential to efficiency, in that it retained for as long as possible officers with experience and knowledge. Now, however, there was apparently a policy of encouraging officers to retire at the earliest opportunity. Captain Seward went on to say that what had really exasperated public opinion and drawn uncomplimentary remarks from various parts of the county was the recent case at Bournemouth, where an officer with a great reputation was retired at the age of 53, while the chief constable remained in his high-salaried post at the age of seventy-six. Here the captain was referring to what the press had called 'the police scandal of Hampshire'. Superintendent Garrett, an experienced and well-liked officer, had resigned from the head of the Bournemouth Divisional Police and many voices were raised to suggest that there was more behind the resignation than met the eye. What was the position of the chief constable in the matter? At a meeting of the Bournemouth Council the redoubtable Alderman Luckham put the following questions: 'Can any information as to the cause of Superintendent Garrett's resignation beyond the question of age limit be given to the council, seeing that there is considerable public opinion that the services of such an efficient officer ought not to be lost to the borough? Is the question of retirement of subordinates left in the bands of the chief constable and the retirement of the chief constable left to himself to decide? And is it not high time that the borough managed its own police?' As usual, this last question was greeted with approving cries.

Alderman Robson, the senior local member of the Standing Joint Committee, said in the course of his address, 'I think I am free to say that the resignation throughout the county, of men of the age, standing and experience of

Superintendent Garrett has raised in the minds of the committee a very grave doubt as to the wisdom of the regulations under which we are working as regards pensions. Men who are fit for many more years' service are resigning – I say resigning: I don't say why. That means that they retire on a substantial pension. The county has that to pay and we have our portion of it to pay too; and new men come up in their place – quite a good thing for them. But all the while there is that very serious financial aspect.' In the subsequent discussion sentiment for Bournemouth having its own force was very marked. Together with this went a deep concern with the powers and position of the Chief Constable of Hampshire. 'But who discharges the chief constable?' queried Alderman Luckham at one point. To this Alderman Robson rejoined, 'That goes back to an old act of parliament which could not be passed in the present day. There the act is, and he is master of the situation and until the Joint Committee tell him that he is getting too old and too uncertain in temperament, there he is. It is not your prerogative to discharge him … It is nobody's prerogative but that of the Home Office.' Nevertheless grumbles continued. It was felt that somehow or other the chief constable, himself at the advanced age of 76, must have brought pressure on Superintendent Garrett to resign at the age of fifty-three. This disparity of age rankled. The whole affair was caught up in the wider aspirations of Bournemouth towards police autonomy and was one more episode in the complex, lively, and sometimes uneasy relationship between the local authorities and the chief constable.

Major Warde's tenure of office was in fact approaching its end. In December 1928 he retired because of ill-health and that very age which had been held against him in the matter of Superintendent Garrett. He had rendered great service to the force and had guided it over years of unprecedented change and turmoil. The world of 1928 was immensely different from that of 1893 when he had assumed office. Like all men of strong personality and firm principles, Major Warde had from time to time aroused opposition. On occasion, it would seem, his enthusiasm and vigour had been marred by rashness. Yet his devotion to his duty and to the force he commanded for so long was beyond doubt or praise and his constant courtesy and consideration have been mentioned repeatedly. His final Christmas and new year's greetings to the members of the Hampshire Constabulary were of a piece with all his earlier messages. After wishing his subordinates health, happiness and prosperity then and in the future, Major Warde took 'the opportunity of bidding them farewell and of expressing my high appreciation of the support I have received from all ranks in my endeavour to maintain a high state of efficiency in the force I have had the honour and happiness to command for so many years. I have no doubt my successor, Major Ernest Radcliffe Cockburn, O.B.E., will be equally fortunate in that respect.' Less than a year later Major Warde was dead. On the evening of 1 December 1929, he passed away at a Nursing Home in Winchester. In a General Order Major

Cockburn expressed his regret, and his certainty that all members of the force would be grieved to learn of the loss of their former chief and would share with him in feelings of sympathy for the members of his family. Permission to attend the funeral at Wrotham in Kent was given to any officer so desiring and many took advantage of the opportunity thus provided. On behalf of Major Warde's relatives, Major Nicholson, the assistant chief constable and the dead man's son-in-law, sent a letter of appreciation for the messages of sympathy sent to them by Major Cockburn and the whole force. 'They were profoundly touched by your kindness in allowing so many members of the force to attend his funeral and they ask me to express to the force through you, their deepest gratitude to those who attended the funeral and also to those who wished to attend but were unable to do so owing to the exigencies of the service. No more touching tribute could have been paid to the family or to the late Major Warde himself than the spontaneous expression of regard that was made to him on behalf of the force by those who came from such a long distance to pay their last respects to their old "chief" and to support his family in their bereavement.'

Major Nicholson himself was soon to leave the Hampshire force, though in happier circumstances. With effect from 19 December 1930, he was appointed Chief Constable of Surrey. All ranks joined in congratulating him and wishing him well in his new post.

It is pleasant to turn from the bickerings over the scope of police authority and the weary clash of personalities, to note the constructive achievements of the police and the praise justly bestowed upon them. In January 1929 the Chairman of the Quarter Sessions, His Honour Judge Barnard Lailey, K.C., in his charge to the Grand Jury, congratulated them on the fact that their labours on that occasion were likely to be lighter than previously, both as regards the number of cases and the class of offence being charged. He thought that none of the cases need occupy much time or was likely to give any trouble. He mentioned one case of a man who was charged with stealing a box of apples. The case turned largely on his identification by a constable and it was suggested that a mistake had been made. His Honour remarked that a police officer was no more infallible than most of them and it was possible he had made a mistake. If, after hearing the evidence of the police officer, they did not think it warranted the man being put on his trial, they would say so; but if they had any doubt about it, he would advise them to return a true bill, so that the matter might be investigated fully. He then went on to remark that most of them had heard of late a good deal about police evidence and widely divergent views had been expressed regarding it. He himself knew little about other counties but in Hampshire he thought they were very fortunate. During some years now that he had been in the habit of having members of the county force before him in that and other courts they had made a very favourable impression on his mind. Mistakes were made, of course, but he did not remember a single case, either civil or criminal, in which he had seen the slightest reason to doubt the honesty of the police evidence. He had also never noticed any inclination or wish to take sides or anything in the nature of a struggle for a conviction. More than once he had been struck how, notably among the officers in the higher ranks, they had been careful to bring out any points in favour of the prisoner. That was as it should be and it seemed to him that a high standard had been set in Hampshire. He was glad therefore to take the opportunity of stating what his experience had been.

From June 1928 the police ceased to act as relieving officers. The chief constable had made arrangements with the boards of guardians to end the old practice of the police issuing tickets to casual wanderers for admission to certain workhouses in the county. Superintendents were instructed to see that the relevant relief ticket books were handed over in due course to the clerks to the guardians concerned. Thus one long-standing duty was lifted from the police, to balance somewhat the growing burdens thrust upon them by the post-war age. The Hampshire Constabulary had for long been accustomed to policing fairs and markets, and to coping with the manifold problems involved in military manoeuvres and such gatherings as the Aldershot Tattoo. Now they were called upon to supervise an assembly of another kind. In May 1928 the sergeant-major, four sergeants and 30 constables were ordered to parade at the aerodrome at Hamble for the Hampshire Air Pageant. Fifteen months later two inspectors, five sergeants and 60 constables were assembled at Gosport Police Station on the occasion of the Schneider Trophy Contest. Subsistence and lodgings were to be provided for all in the New Barracks, Gosport. Twelve more constables were to parade at Havant Police Station and were to be accommodated at Havant Police Station and at Hayling Island. The superintendents concerned were enjoined to use every care in selecting officers who had most knowledge of traffic control and of the locality. Furthermore officers owning motor-cycles, with or without sidecars, were encouraged to make use of them. The Hampshire Constabulary had always been concerned with the army and the navy. Now they had to deal with one of the great events in aviation in the inter-war years, and one even more important than any of the older tattoos or manoeuvres. It was to compete in the Schneider Trophy Contests that the direct ancestors of the Supermarine Spitfires were developed.

At the end of 1929 the authorised strength of the force, other than the chief constable, consisted of one assistant chief constable, ten superintendents, nine inspectors, one sergeant-major, 56 sergeants and 432 constables. In April 1931 the Home Secretary approved the strength of the force being increased to 530 officers. Further increases took place in 1936 and 1939, until at the outbreak of war the Hampshire Constabulary numbered 635 officers. In 1930 the system of promotion examinations was re-organised. It was notified in General Orders that in future 'an officer who, at his sitting the previous year, passed the examination in educational subjects or police duties, as the case may be, will not be required to sit again for the part in which he passed, e.g. an officer who passed in educational subjects and failed in police duties at his examination last year and desires to sit again this year, will only be examined in police duties and vice-versa'. Later that year the chief constable was pleased to note a general improvement, particularly in the educational papers, and expressed the hope that this would be maintained. Perhaps this compensated for the unusually heavy incidence of cases of insubordination and neglect of duty which was apparent at this time. In October no fewer than four constables were reprimanded or fined for offences of this sort. One had been insubordinate 'in word and demeanour' to a superior officer, while another, as well as 'failing to work his best in accordance with orders, in absenting himself from a traffic point without good and sufficient cause', had engaged 'in idle conversation with a tram driver' when he should have been on point duty on the above occasion. In December another constable was fined 20s. for neglecting to carry out a written order 'relative to the removal of swine from Petersfield Market'; a second was reprimanded for breach of confidence in having communicated to an unauthorised person a matter connected with the police force; while a third was fined £3 'for acting in a manner likely to bring discredit on the reputation of the force by being violent when speaking on the telephone to a member of the public at Hartley Row'.

It may be that these offences reflected a general feeling of strain on police forces throughout the country. During the twenties an unusual number of accusations was made against the police. In 1927 there was a notorious case of corruption in Liverpool and in 1928 the even more unsavoury Savidge case in London. In 1928 there was an unpleasant affair involving Sergeant Goddard of the Metropolitan Police. Public confidence had been largely restored by the report of the Royal Commission on Police Powers and Procedure. But police morale had been shaken and the effects were not restricted to London and the other great cities. Again, as the thirties went on, increasing difficulties confronted the police in many parts of the kingdom. Industrial areas were affected by unemployment, with all its attendant distress and unease; and extremist movements like Fascism waxed, focusing despair and high ambition and creating an atmosphere of violence which all too often provoked physical violence in return. Hampshire was comparatively unaffected by these disorders of the polity; nevertheless the sense of strain was there. This, together with the economic discontents, may well have been an indirect cause of those cases of insubordination noted above. In September 1931 the chief constable announced with regret that circumstances had arisen which had rendered it necessary to make special deductions from the pay of the police. The circumstances referred to, of course, were the great depression and the swingeing measures of retrenchment adopted by the government of the day to meet the consequences. Major Cockburn hoped that 'financial conditions will speedily improve so that the economy measures will not long be in operation' but meanwhile he feels sure that the members of the Hampshire Constabulary fully realise that the call upon the police was inevitable and will loyally accept the position. From 5 October 1931, sergeants and constables were to have deducted weekly from their pay 5s. 6d. and 4s. 3d. respectively. Inspectors were to lose 6s. 9d. per week and superintendents five per cent of their pay.

Evidence of the increasing mobility of crime with which the police had to contend in the thirties is provided by two elaborate national schemes for dealing with motorised criminals. These schemes were called 'Agility' and 'Express' respectively. The former provided for a system of road control for limiting as far as possible the radius of action of criminals escaping by motor vehicle; while the latter was to enable any chief constable or officer deputed to act for him to circulate important police information to all forces in any one or more districts without calling out any 'Lines' or 'Areas'. The country as a whole was divided up in rural districts by a series of 'Lines', each of which was numbered – cities, boroughs, or towns situated in a 'Line' being considered to form part of it; while in populous districts cities and boroughs were grouped together in 'Areas', each 'Area' being given the name of one of the towns in the group. Cities or boroughs with their own forces not included either on a 'Line' or in an 'Area' were considered to be 'Areas' on their own. The Metropolitan and City of London Police together were considered to be the 'Metropolitan Area', and made their own arrangements. On each 'Line' and on the borders of each 'Area' a list of 'Key Points' was compiled, comprising such places as railway crossings, road junctions and bridges. On receipt of an 'Agility' message affecting any 'Line' or 'Area' within their jurisdiction, chief constables made arrangements for the immediate posting of constables at all 'Key Points' involved. By these means it was intended to make it possible for any chief constable to call out any Line or Area which he thought might be of assistance to him in intercepting a suspected or wanted motor vehicle, or in tracing any possible witnesses who might be travelling by road and who were believed to have passed the scene of a crime within a short time either before or after its commission. It was made clear that the scheme was to be concerned with serious crime only. The actual business of the blocking of the roads and the acquisition of any appropriate apparatus, including the necessary warning lights or flags required for the purpose, was left to the discretion of each chief constable. Thus Major Cockburn in the early months of 1933 busied himself seeking advice on such matters. He considered several means of obstruction, including shock absorber elastic cord, but decided it was rather too costly. As for coils of special wire of a type introduced in the army towards the end of the war, it might well be extremely effective; it would have the effect of entangling the wheels of a car and bringing it to a halt in a very short distance; but the general opinion was that the placing of such obstructions would be far too dangerous under the law as it then stood. So Major Cockburn inclined to favour a system of red hurricane lamps together with improvised obstructions placed in an 'echelon' pattern. Other suggestions flowed in from his superintendents. Long poles on trestles, with red lamps, warning signs, and flags on either side were thought by some to be adequate. Such equipment would be fairly cheap, could be conveniently stored near the key point and could be placed in position with little loss of time by one man. 'The white pole with the red lamp would be distinct enough for any reasonably careful driver to see and if it did not actually stop a wanted car it would cause it to be distinctly marked.' Another notion was to have the lights on the road of one certain colour, to be reserved to the police, 'about thirty yards or so from the lights … a two-inch plank with chamferred sides, studded with nails, with points some one and a half inches clear of the plank and some two inches apart, be placed across the roadway or as an alternative a scaffold pole, studded or otherwise … if the lights were rushed the obstruction would then probably have the desired effect'.

The 'Express' scheme, as mentioned above, was designed to facilitate the circulation of important or urgent police information but not to activate any of the arrangements for setting up road blocks. It was a matter of passing on urgent intelligence only. Information relating to stolen motor vehicles was not to be sent out as 'Express' unless there were very special circumstances connected with the theft of the vehicle; e.g. when a serious crime had been committed in addition to the theft, and it was suspected that a vehicle had been stolen for the purpose of committing a serious crime, or when it was known or suspected that drugs or poison were aboard. Despite these injunctions, in the early days of the scheme it appears to have been used in several instances in a foolish and unjustified manner, and many senior police officers expressed doubts as to its efficiency and value.

It is interesting to compare the training of recruits in the thirties with the more sophisticated arrangements set up in later years. All such training was carried out by the sergeant-major at headquarters. This rank had a long history in the Hampshire Constabulary but was done away with shortly after the outbreak of the Second World War. It was held by a succession of formidable personalities, many of whom later attained senior rank. Thus in 1934 Sergeant-Major Liddiard was succeeded by Sergeant-Major Wright and both were subsequently to become superintendents. Wright was succeeded in February 1937 by Sergeant-Major Parker, who about a year later was followed by Sergeant-Major Durrant, the last person to hold the rank. The uniform worn by the sergeant-major was similar to that of inspectors, minus the stars, with the Royal Coat of Arms on the right sleeve. The sergeant-major trained recruits, all of whom were boarded at police headquarters and included recruits of the Winchester City and Isle of Wight forces. The recruits' day was spent as follows: from 7 a.m. until 8 a.m. they did fatigue duty and after breakfast another period of fatigue duty; from 10 a.m. until noon they were drilled on the square. The midday meal followed and then from 12.30 until 1.30 p.m. they were set to read Moriarty's *Police Law*. Then came more fatigues and from 2.30 p.m. until 4 p.m. another period of drill. Sometimes when the weather was bad some recruits, instead of drill, were given the task of pulling a large metal roller over the square and driveway at headquarters which were then of a loose pebble type surface. On Monday, Tuesday, Thursday and Friday lectures were given by the sergeant-major from 6.30 p.m. until 7.30 p.m. Thereafter the recruits were instructed to make a point outside the Winchester City boundary at 8 p.m. and were then off-duty until 10.30 p.m. by which time they had to return to headquarters.

In 1938 Major Cockburn was honoured with the award of the C.B.E., another distinction in his distinguished career. Educated at Harrow, he had entered the regular army in 1894, was a lieutenant in the Second Wiltshire Regiment in 1898 and served in the South African War, wherein he had been awarded special promotion for distinguished service in the field. Later he served with the Manchester Regiment. In 1919 he was appointed Chief Constable of Ayr, and in 1928 he was appointed to succeed Major Warde as Chief Constable of Hampshire, being selected out of a total of 130 applicants.

In 1935, another notable award was that of the King's Police Medal for gallantry to Police Constable Pirnie of Bournemouth. This distinction was gained for his bravery in tackling an armed criminal. The miscreant had been disturbed robbing a jeweller's shop during the lunch hour and escaped into the Pleasure Gardens near Westover Road closely pursued by a crowd of police and general public. Pirnie caught up with the fugitive near the Bourne stream whereupon the villain pointed an automatic pistol at the constable shouting 'Up, or I fire.' Without hesitation the policeman went in to the attack and after a violent struggle overpowered the thief. The pistol was found to have been loaded with nine rounds and to have the safety catch released.

Since 1890, it will be remembered, the Isle of Wight had been an administrative county on its own with a police force independent of that of Hampshire. Initially the island force had been 47 strong, including one inspector and seven sergeants under the command of Superintendent James Duke. Almost immediately thereafter Newport Borough Police was merged with that of the Isle of Wight and Mr Thomas Lees was appointed as the first chief constable on 10 April 1890. Ryde Borough Police continued as a separate force until April 1922 when Ryde, faced with the trebled expenditure which the post-war rates of pay and pension entailed, consented to join the Isle of Wight Constabulary. This united force continued on its own until April 1943 when it was amalgamated with the Hampshire Constabulary and the Winchester City force. Thus the police history of the Isle of Wight is intimately linked with that of Hampshire and cannot be considered apart. In its independent existence the island force was commanded by four chief constables: Mr Thomas Hastings-Lees from 1890 to 1898; Captain Harry Adams-Connor, M.V.O., D.L. from 1898 to 1935; Captain Colin Douglas Robertson from 1935 to 1938; and Lieutenant-Colonel Roy Bullen Spicer, C.M.G., M.C. from 1938 to

1943. Each of these gentlemen had a distinguished career previously and each
made a highly personal contribution to the force under their command. Mr
Hastings-Lees had formerly been the Chief Constable of Northamptonshire and
in addition was the author of *The Constables Pocket Book* and editor of *Snowden's
Police Officers' Guide*. During his nine years in office in the Isle of Wight he was
complimented more than once upon having organised one of the most efficient
and economically-administered forces in the country at that time. He resigned
owing to ill-health in 1898 and was succeeded by Captain Adams-Connor who
was to hold office for 37 years. His father had been Dean of Windsor and
Domestic Chaplain to Queen Victoria and his wife was the daughter of a high
commissioner of New Guinea. Educated at Marlborough, he served in the South
African War and had become a Captain of the Connaught Rangers. He had been
appointed Deputy Lieutenant of the Isle of Wight and held, in addition to his
M.V.O., decorations from Russia and from Spain. A strict disciplinarian with a
bent for administration, he succeeded by example and precept during his long
tenure of office in raising the force to a praiseworthy standard of efficiency.
Captain Robertson followed him in 1935, taking up his duties on 1 October in
that year. At the time of his appointment he was the Assistant Chief Constable
of the War Department Constabulary in London and was selected finally from a
total of 113 applicants. After he relinquished command of the force in 1938, he
became Chief Constable of Suffolk. The last chief constable of the independent
Isle of Wight force was Lieutenant-Colonel Spicer, who previously had been
Inspector-General of Police and Prisons in Palestine. He had been educated at
Colet Court and St Pauls, of which he had been a scholar. From 1909 to 1925
he was with the Ceylon Police except for the war years from 1915 to 1918 when
he fought and was wounded in Europe, serving with the Carabiniers. For six
years after 1925 he was Commissioner of Kenya Police. Colonel Spicer was an
enthusiastic sportsman and among his recreations he listed hunting, racing, polo,
cricket and fishing. At various times he was President of the Amateur Boxing
Association and Football Association of East Africa, Master of the Errebodde
Hunt in Ceylon, Master of the Ramleh Vale Hunt in Palestine and President of
the Automobile Club and Touring Association of Palestine. He held the King's
Police Medal and was a Commander of the Order of St John of Jerusalem.

One constable who joined the Isle of Wight Constabulary in 1913 was Mr
H.W. Luckett, who served for many years and survived both world wars. Indeed,
he held the record for the longest war service, for the First World War, of all
pre-war members of the force. He has left us many vivid recollections of his
police and military service during and after the First War. In 1914 he was on
the army reserve, was mobilised and at once was on duty at a fort at Sandown
as a range finder for the guns. He recalls firing across the bows of ships to
stop them for examination by the Royal Navy and also at what were thought
to be the enemy submarines. Later in the war he was active in bombarding the

Turks in 1916 and 1917 at the recapture of Kut-el-Amara. He saw service in Mesopotamia until Christmas 1918 and when peace was declared had marched almost to Mosul. He had attained the rank of battery sergeant-major. In the course of his long police service he had many varied experiences. Sometimes he was on duty controlling traffic outside the royal residence of Osborne House on visiting days. Again, he was on duty at Somerton Farm when the first case of foot and mouth disease had struck the island and he had the greatest difficulty in getting persons entering or leaving the premises to walk through the disinfectant provided at the gateway. On one occasion about 1930 he had just met a constable at a conference point at 3 a.m. when two men came from the direction of Osborne and Barton. One of these men, 'Big Jimmy' Willet, was known to the police and consequently the men were stopped and searched but nothing untoward was found except for a pillow slip. The next morning Sergeant Collins, who with others had been apprised of the previous night's encounter, met 'Big Jimmy' at Newport and found that he was carrying not one but two pillow slips, both full of narcissus blooms stolen from the lawn at Barton Manor. Another chance happening which led to a successful arrest took place the following year. Police Constable Batley, stationed at Carisbrooke, had a lot of rick fires on his beat. Extra police were posted for some nights to keep watch. Then one night a youth passed the spot where Batley himself was waiting muttering to himself, 'I'll fire another bloody rick tonight I will.' Forthwith he was arrested by Batley and proved to be the culprit.

It was only in 1929 that the first motor vehicle was provided for the Isle of Wight Constabulary, in the shape of a B.S.A. twin motor-cycle combination which was used on motor patrol and other duties. For eight or nine years before this the constables stationed in the countryside had relied on bicycles which, in the words of the chief constable, 'have proved to be of great assistance for efficiently patrolling the several districts and I am of the opinion that the use of bicycles should be encouraged as much as possible'. In 1920 the cycle allowance paid to police on the Isle of Wight was £2 per annum. But now the motor-cycle combination had come on the scene. The first mobile policeman on the Isle of Wight was Police Constable Francis George Rugman, who rode the new machine and for the purpose was issued with breeches and leggings, a mackintosh, a British Warm, and a peaked cap. Rugman was eventually to retire in 1955 as inspector in charge of Ryde Sub-Division, after 30 years' service. In 1931 a Ford car was provided for motor patrol and other duties. This was later replaced by a Morris and then in 1939 by a Wolseley. All of these vehicles were based at Newport and it was not until the early part of the Second World War that vehicles were provided for sub-divisional and section stations. Then seven Ariel motor-cycles were provided for use at headquarters and Quay Street police station in Newport, and at Cowes, Ryde, Shanklin, Ventnor and Yarmouth police stations.

In the thirties two competing bus companies were operating a service from Ryde to Newport and, as might have been expected, both companies were ultimately summoned for exceeding the speed limit in Binstead parish, Whippingham parish and finally in Newport borough. The police checked on the times taken by the buses over the telephone and Mr Luckett was there at Wootton to report on their passing through. The police proved their case and the companies were duly penalised.

As the decade advanced international tension increased and the threat of a new world war became more insistent. The Munich crisis of 1938 and its aftermath was a turning point; until then many people still hoped and believed that a great conflict might be avoided and the four-power Munich agreement seemed briefly to have realised their hopes. But within a few months the German occupation of Czechoslovakia impressed the overwhelming majority of British people with the certainty that war with Germany was inevitable. The whole national life was infused with this conviction and in the spring of 1939 conscription was introduced in Great Britain for the first time ever in time of peace. Already schemes of A.R.P. training had been instituted for police officers in Hampshire and elsewhere. Early in 1939 anti-gas courses were held and police officers spent many hours assembling respirators which had been issued to them in pieces. At force headquarters this work of assembly transformed more than one room into the likeness of a factory production line. A Home Office gas van was issued to the force for training purposes and during the months leading up to the outbreak of war this vehicle and its crew toured the country. Police officers were trained in the correct method of using respirators and instructed in the effects of gas. Up to and after the actual declaration of war teams of police were also engaged in filling sandbags to be used for the protection of police stations. Lorries supplied by a local firm were used in connection with this and police officers spent many hours at sandpits loading these vehicles.

In December 1938 the authorised strength of the force had been increased by six sergeants and 47 constables, bringing the total number of the Hampshire Constabulary to 635, consisting, apart from the chief constable, of ten superintendents, 16 inspectors, one sergeant-major, 59 sergeants and 548 constables. With the coming of war, however, the force was soon in need of further aid, which it was to procure from several sources. For once again many members of the Hampshire Constabulary departed to join the armed forces in their capacity as reservists. The first to leave was Police Constable Spencer on 28 September 1939, and in December 25 others followed. During the war years many others were to go, some not to return. Their places were filled by members of the First Police Reserve, which consisted of retired regular police officers, and by the newly-formed Police War Reserve. The members of this organisation were men from many different backgrounds who found themselves suddenly transported into the highly specialised world of police work, which some found strange and uncongenial and for which some were unsuited. Throughout the first years of the war more than a few fell short of the requirements of a disciplined service. In August 1940 one war reserve constable was dismissed 'for falsehood and prevarication, i.e. wilfully making false statements to senior officers in connection with the larceny of a clock and the taking of souvenirs from a crashed aeroplane at Bournemouth'. The same incident resulted in the dismissal and fining of a second war reserve constable, who had actually been 'performing duty in guarding the machine when the larceny was committed'. Another war reservist was discharged for having been found in an air-raid shelter when he should have been on duty. Other war reserve constables were permitted to resign on the respectable grounds of ill health and the services of at least one were dispensed with in the dismal certainty that he was unlikely 'to become an efficient and well-conducted constable'. The profusion of lesser offences, resulting in the infliction of fines, was matched by the steady flow of misdeeds brought home to regular officers of the force. In war as in peace there were individuals who failed to take care of clothing and equipment issued to them, or else acted in some manner or other likely to bring discredit on the constabulary. Nevertheless, it is clear that the work of the reservists was of enormous help and in the course of time several earned commendations and decorations. After the war, some of the war reservists were to remain in the force as regular officers. At first there was no organised training for them but in the summer of 1942 an instructional course was instituted for the first time.

Further assistance was of course rendered by the special constables, whose numbers had been increased shortly before the outbreak of war. At that time they had performed duty in civilian clothing, with only an armlet as a badge of office. In the early months of the war, however, they were issued with uniform and organised properly with a rank structure reflecting that of the regular force. Apparently, at first the peaked caps with which the specials were issued caused some confusion and not a little embarrassment. For the distinctive headgear was often mistaken for that worn by senior officers and saluted as such.

As in the previous great conflict war conditions imposed long hours on the police and many extra duties. One of the first of these was that of rounding up all aliens throughout the county, in particular those of German or Austrian extraction. Such individuals were brought before special tribunals whose function was to investigate the foreigners and determine the risk that each one might present to national security. In the upshot many were interned in the Isle of Man and others were sent to Australia. In March 1940 the Under Secretary of State wrote to all chief constables in the following terms: 'I am directed by the Secretary of State to say that now the work of the tribunals is completed he wishes to express his appreciation of the very valuable work done by all police forces concerned. He has been informed from many quarters that the task has been accomplished with tact and sympathy and there appears to be general recognition of the efficiency with which the examination of Germans and Austrians has been carried out. The Secretary of State would be glad if you would convey to all the officers of your force who have been concerned in this work his appreciation of the manner in which this exacting work has been performed and in particular the especially arduous work which had to be performed by the officers who acted as secretary of tribunals. He realises that in many instances considerable extra duty has been entailed and that officers with knowledge of aliens work or of foreign languages have unstintingly placed their special qualifications at the disposal of the tribunals.'

One burdensome task in the memorable summer of 1940 resulted from the massive evacuation of British and allied troops at Dunkirk. Into Hampshire came many men of the British, French, and Belgian forces and all had to be found billets of some sort. As it happened, most were accommodated at Bournemouth. All this, of course, was in addition to setting up rest centres for evacuees from areas struck by air raids and the constant preoccupation to ensure that the routes used by these unfortunates did not threaten to hinder military movements. As the war developed the whole of the south of England became to some degree 'front line' and Hampshire with its notable naval and military connections was especially affected. Unlike the fire service, the police were never nationalised during the Second World War. Nor indeed were they formally regionalised but certainly they had to adjust themselves to the regional organisation of civil defence. The prominent part played by the police in A.R.P. preparations has already been noted; in particular the police were responsible for the Wardens' Service. In the early part of the war the War Emergency or 'E' Branch was set up to deal with all aspects of police war duties and a close liaison was maintained with other civil defence organisations. For the duration of the war England and Wales were divided into 11 regions each under the control of a regional commissioner. These arrangements were designed not only to ensure the maintenance of public order and all essential services in the face of heavy aerial attack but also to plan efficiently against the contingency of invasion and occupation. A representative of the police was a member of the committees set up in each local authority area for this purpose. Every day the officer in charge of 'E' Branch reported the situation regarding bombing to the regional police staff officer at the civil defence headquarters in Reading. At the Hampshire Constabulary headquarters in Winchester an operation or 'battle' room was fitted up as a control centre in the event of invasion or a major attack in the county area. A development which was part of this whole process was the acquisition by many police stations and some police cars of radio equipment as an alternative to the telephone system if the latter failed. This medium frequency radio scheme was succeeded later by a V.H.F. scheme, the forerunner of the existing police radio network. An older and less technical means of communication was provided by carrier pigeons which were intended to act as a further channel of information between the force headquarters, the divisional stations and the civil defence headquarters in Reading. The creatures were never really needed, which perhaps was just as well, for some of them seem to have lacked a firm grasp of what was expected of them. Frequently, as opportunity arose, the birds were taken along by police officers having occasion to go to the Isle of Wight so that they might have exercise in flying back; quite often the winged messengers turned up haphazardly in parts of the county remote from their official destinations.

At the end of July 1940 it was announced in General Orders that Superintendent West had been appointed Chief Constable of Portsmouth City Police and, as Major Cockburn said, the superintendent's achievement 'reflects great credit upon himself and the Hampshire Constabulary as a whole'. Further cheerful news was that with effect from 1 July 1940, 'every constable shall be paid a supplementary allowance of 5s. per week' and in addition each constable was to be paid a war duty allowance of 3s. per week. The allowance for sergeants was to be of 4s. a week. None of these allowances was to be pensionable and furthermore 'the supplementary allowance of 5s. per week will not be paid to constables who have been granted an allowance on 12½ per cent of their pay'. By November 1940 the total strength of the force had been increased to 653 and several officers had been temporarily promoted. A few months later, indeed, the chief constable found it necessary to warn that 'appointment to temporary rank is no guarantee of promotion to substantive rank as a matter of course'. Another warning, which mirrors the hectic days of the Battle of Britain in 1940, drew attention to the fact that 'incidents have recently occurred in which the police have behaved in a manner likely to create a bad impression in the minds of the public in the matter of collecting souvenirs' from crashed enemy aircraft and their occupants. Doubtless this referred to the type of offence noted above, for which the war reserve constables had been punished. 'The chief constable desires it to be clearly understood that it is the duty of the police to guard machines and personal property of occupants until handed over to the proper authorities and strongly deprecates their acquiring any articles for themselves.' A happier order drew attention to a letter of thanks from the Chief Constable of Southampton, Mr Allen, for the services of some Hampshire officers who had been lent to the port under the Police Regional Reinforcement Scheme. After thanking Major Cockburn for his personal consideration in expediting the aid when called for, Mr Allen wrote, 'The officers of this force and myself have nothing but praise for the bearing and manner in which your personnel acquitted themselves in very difficult circumstances. It has been a real testing time for them and they all came out of it with flying colours.' The help given and the credit gained were to be repeated again and again in these years, when many of the larger cities were continually under air attack.

BOOK 5
1940-1967

Everyone who lived through these war years has his fund of anecdotes and personal experiences, very often concerned with the enemy air attacks on this country.

The Hampshire Constabulary had its ample measure of curious incidents of this kind. On one occasion in 1940 police officers observed a light on Portsdown Hill near Portsmouth. They went to investigate and were searching the area in the dark, when suddenly one of them felt something thrust into his back, and heard a menacing voice telling him to put up his hands. Uneasily he complied, and turned his head to find himself looking into the barrels of a shotgun held by a determined-looking individual in civilian clothes, wearing the armband of the Local Defence Volunteers. This body had been raised with extraordinary speed in the grim and exhilarating days following the fall of France, and soon it was to be re-named, on Churchillian initiative, the Home Guard, and to bear an honourable part in the national war effort. On another night a large bundle of leaflets which had been dropped by an enemy aircraft was found in Sparsholt churchyard. The leaflets had been scattered by the impact, and several police officers spent much time picking up every one they could find, in order to prevent the local inhabitants from being exposed to the propaganda, and perhaps corrupted by it. At last the task was done, and the police went away, only to find at daybreak that the surrounding countryside was littered as far as the eye could see with leaflets of the same kind. Again, after one air raid at Bournemouth a report was received that an unexploded bomb had landed in a garden near a hospital. A police officer went to the scene, peered into the hole, and saw the tail fins of a large bomb. Quickly he arranged for the hospital and adjoining houses to be evacuated. The Bomb Disposal unit arrived and, after cautiously inspecting what could be seen, declared it to be of a type not previously encountered. With their customary immense courage and care, the bomb disposal experts probed very warily until they could read some inscription on the metal. This legend informed them that they were looking at nothing more harmful than an electric fan. It had been blown by a bomb explosion from a nearby garage, and had embedded itself in the earth in such a way that the fan blades had been forced upwards into the likeness of the tail fins of a bomb.

An act more foolhardy than daring was that of a police officer who went to the site of an unexploded bomb in the countryside near Fareham. He found a large hole made by the bomb as it had plunged into the earth. Usually he would have retreated to a safe distance and erected the usual warning notice, but on this occasion he was tempted and lingered to pick the splendid crop of mushrooms which were growing around the crater.

On one occasion His Majesty King George VI paid a visit to an aircraft factory at Eastleigh. He arrived during an air raid when the staff had gone to ground, and the only persons in sight were a number of soldiers at drill. Appropriately enough, they were rehearsing the 'present Arms'. Despite this, the King, seeing the otherwise deserted establishment, turned to the chief constable and remarked, 'It seems we are not welcome here.' Close at hand was a naval station which was also scheduled to receive a royal visit. As soon as the authorities there knew of the King's situation, they called the officers and men from the shelters in which they had been taking refuge, and His Majesty arrived to find the sailors scrambling out from underground shelters, dusting themselves down and trying to form themselves in some sort of order. To add to the confusion a gunner in a machine gun emplacement was so excited and over-enthusiastic that inadvertently he let off a burst of fire. Fortunately no harm was done.

An alarm of another sort arose from the fear that biological warfare might be used by the enemy. An apprehensive householder at Fareham reported finding queer blue deposits on the glass of his conservatory. Police officers removed samples of the mysterious substance and sent them for analysis. It turned out to be nothing more serious than the droppings of birds which had feasted on blackberries.

The heavy air raids on southern England in 1940 and 1941 gave only too many opportunities for police officers to distinguish themselves by their alacrity and courage. In May 1941, for example, the chief constable announced with pleasure that the King had approved the award of the British Empire Medal, Civil Division, to Inspector T. McDonagh 'for his initiative in arranging mutual aid for fire fighting and entering burning buildings at considerable risk to himself, during intensive bombing, at Gosport on the night of January 10/11th, 1941. His coolness and good leadership in dangerous situations, on many occasions, have set a fine example to men under his control.' The same award was made to Police Constable W.M. Coombs 'for the resolve and courage displayed by him in extinguishing many fires caused by incendiary bombs and entering burning buildings under dangerous conditions' during the same air raid at Gosport. Another constable, by name Harwood, was commended 'for his courage and resourcefulness in dealing with an unexploded bomb at Hurn on May 10th, 1941'. The bomb, attached to a small parachute, had been foolishly picked up on the roadside by a coach driver, later fined £5, and discarded by him near houses and offices. Instances of such good service occurred throughout the war. To give but one more example, Police Constable E. Riggs, stationed at Ventnor, was in April 1943 cornmended by the chief constable 'for the prompt and skilful first aid rendered to a person whose arm had been blown off as a result of enemy action. Police Constable Riggs' action undoubtedly saved the man's life.'

The extra duties imposed on the police by war conditions naturally attract attention; but behind the exciting incidents and heroic deeds the usual work of law enforcement continued. Here too officers of the Hampshire force achieved innumerable successes. One example was the effort of Police Constable J. McMahon, who was commended for his alertness and prompt action when on duty at Lee-on-the-Solent in April 1941, which resulted in the arrest of four persons for housebreaking, and of two more for receiving stolen property. The same Constable Coombs who had been decorated for his courage under air attack, was only a few months later commended for his alertness in tracing a persistent cycle thief who had stolen 25 machines in Portsmouth and surrounding districts. In November 1941 Police War Reserve Constable A.T. Jones was praised for his alertness and promptitude in Aldershot, which resulted in the arrest of two men caught in the act of breaking open a safe in the basement of a shop. Another war reserve constable of the same name, A.W. Jones, distinguished himself by noticing that a car which he had stopped for being driven without lights contained 480 stolen tins of milk. These are only a few of a vast number of similar cases. War conditions added to, but by no means obscured, the routine struggle against crime.

At the end of May 1942 Major Cockburn retired from the office of chief constable and in a farewell order placed on record 'my keen appreciation of the constant helpfulness of my superintendents in so readily assisting me in my numerous duties and in maintaining a high standard of efficiency throughout the force, and the loyal support I have received from all ranks and auxiliary services. I naturally relinquish my position as Chief Constable of the Hampshire Constabulary, and the happy association of both Mrs Cockburn and myself with its members and their families, with much regret and extend to all our best wishes for their happiness and prosperity in the days to come.' Major Cockburn concluded by expressing his certainty that 'the splendid co-operation accorded to me will be forthcoming in like measure' to his successor, Mr R.D. Lemon. This confidence was echoed in an inaugural message from Mr Lemon early in June 1942: 'On taking over command of the Hampshire Constabulary, I would like to inform all ranks how very conscious I am of the honour which has been done to me in selecting me to command the force and to assure you that your welfare and happiness will at all times be my primary consideration. I shall look forward to meeting you all in the near future and feel sure that I may rely on your loyal and active support and co-operation in the days that lie ahead.' Mr Lemon thus became the Hampshire Constabulary's seventh chief, and his tenure of office, which was to be of 20 years, was outstripped only by the long reigns of Captain Forrest and Major Warde. Mr Lemon had been educated at Uppingham and Sandhurst, and had served in the West Yorkshire Regiment for three years. In 1934 he had been selected for the Metropolitan Police College at Hendon, and thereafter remained in the Metropolitan Police until 1937, when he had transferred to the Leicestershire Constabulary as inspector. In 1939 he had been appointed Chief Constable of the East Riding of Yorkshire. He was still a comparatively young man when he came to Hampshire, and quickly made his mark upon the force. From the start he made a point of getting to know all his men, and in this was helped by his highly developed social sense, his keen interest in sport, and his almost royal memory for individual names. Soon after he took over, the first course of instruction for Police War Reservists was held at headquarters, and Police War Reservist Penfold of the Aldershot Division gained top marks, and qualified for an Award of Merit. Thereafter similar courses of instruction were held regularly.

In November 1942 Mr Lemon created the Hampshire C.I.D. essentially in its present form. Since January 1934 there had been at headquarters a Crime Bureau and Central Detective Organisation, under the command of Detective Superintendent Osman. He had been charged with the responsibility of organising the new department and of maintaining close liaison with Scotland Yard and neighbouring forces so far as detective work was concerned, with a view to assisting the divisional superintendents in a consultative capacity. He had also been given some uniform responsibility in as much as the Winchester section of the Eastleigh Division was transferred to headquarters and placed under him. From that time records of all crimes in the county were passed to the Crime Bureau where they were kept in accordance with the report of the Departmental Committee of 1938 on detective work and procedure. Regular C.I.D. staff were to be found only in Aldershot and Bournemouth and later in 1938 Mr Osman had been posted to Bournemouth as a divisional superintendent, and the rank of detective superintendent had ceased to exist. Now Mr Lemon made sweeping changes. Officers from the existing departments at Aldershot and Bournemouth were promoted to the rank of detective sergeant and sent into those divisions where no C.I.D. had formerly been, with instructions to set up branches of the department. Many uniform officers throughout the county were made detective constables and posted to the various divisions to serve under these new sergeants. Superintendent R. Gill who was then serving at headquarters was appointed detective superintendent. He was assisted by two detective inspectors and two detective sergeants who were responsible for Special Branch enquiries, which had assumed an overriding importance in consequence of the war. Inspector Punter was in charge of the Crime Bureau and Photography. At Aldershot there were now a detective inspector, a detective sergeant and six detective constables, while at Bournemouth, in addition to a detective inspector and two detective sergeants, there were no fewer than 13 detective constables. Andover and Basingstoke had a detective sergeant and constable apiece, the New Forest had a detective sergeant and two constables, while Fareham, Eastleigh and Petersfield each had a detective sergeant and three constables.

From the war years to the present day the strength and responsibilities of the C.I.D. have steadily increased. Detective Superintendent Gill was later promoted to the rank of detective chief superintendent, and then in 1951 to that of assistant chief constable. He was succeeded as head of the C.I.D. by Detective Superintendent W.C. Jones, who in turn was later promoted to detective chief superintendent. In 1963 the strength of the C.I.D. was 81, including one detective chief superintendent, two detective-chief inspectors, one of whom acted as second-in-command at headquarters, and a detective inspector in every division except Petersfield and Basingstoke. At Fareham there was the second detective chief inspector, as well as two detective inspectors, three detective sergeants and 14 detective constables. The total strength of the C.I.D. in 1966 was 139. In the course of its history many notable cases have been investigated by officers of the department.

Another specialised branch of the Hampshire force which arose out of war conditions was the Women Police. Women established themselves so successfully in nearly every sphere of the life of Great Britain in the 20th century, they are so indispensable to the functioning of our present complex society, that it is sometimes difficult to remember how recently they have gained their political and social emancipation. Agitation for women's rights had grown in the course of the 19th century and had flared out in the extraordinary activities of the Suffragettes in the years before 1914. The war itself was the great turning-point. The women overwhelmingly proved their case, and established their right to full participation in the modern world. During the conflict the Metropolitan Police had employed some women as auxiliaries. The passing of the Sex Disqualification Act in 1919 meant the removal of the bar on women being appointed as constables. Nevertheless, such was the weight of prejudice that it was only in April 1923 that the first women police of the Metropolitan force were attested and given the power of arrest. For a comparable development, the Hampshire Constabulary had to wait until the Second World War.

For certain ancillary purposes, indeed, women had been used by the police much earlier. Thus on occasion they had been used as escorts for women prisoners, and in 1896 in Aldershot a matron was appointed to attend to female prisoners at a wage of one shilling an hour. But anything in the nature of policewomen proper belonged to later time. So far as the Isle of Wight was concerned, the first mention of policewomen is found in the minutes of the Standing Joint Committee in October 1920, when a Home Office circular letter dated 7 September 1920 was read, together with a report on the employment of women on police duties. This letter and report were considered by the Committee but no instructions were given on the matter. The issue was again raised at the

Standing Joint Committee meeting on 26 October 1925, but the Committee did not consider the circumstances and conditions in the Isle of Wight were such as to render the employment of women police necessary or desirable at that time. Again on 19 April 1926, a deputation from women's organisations in the Isle of Wight approached the Standing Joint Committee regarding the employment of women police, but failed to achieve anything. With the coming of war again in 1939, however, the situation changed. From 1942 onwards Hampshire and the Isle of Wight had an establishment of one hundred members of the Women's Auxiliary Police Corps. These ladies wore uniform, and were employed as clerks, telephonists, and drivers. Upon his appointment as chief constable in 1942, Mr Lemon was bombarded with resolutions from women's organisations throughout the county, asking for the appointment of women police. The Standing Joint Committee considered these resolutions on several occasions but decided to defer the regular appointment of women police until after the war, as it was considered essential to obtain the best possible type of recruit for this work. Nevertheless, before then several highly competent and enterprising women had succeeded in gaining entrance into, and experience of, the police world. Mrs Constance Moss joined the Winchester City Police, as it then was, as a civilian clerk typist on 16 October 1942, and has vivid recollections of her service. As well as herself there were at that time three other women employed, a senior typist to the then head constable, and two drivers. The typist apparently worked normal office hours from 9 a.m. to 5.30 p.m. but the other three worked from 6 a.m. to 2 p.m. and 2 p.m. to 10 p.m. on alternate weeks. In addition to their other duties, they acted as 'Matron' whenever required. The presence of members of the opposite sex in what had been predominantly a male world caused some awkwardness at first. Mrs Moss recalls that there was no ladies' toilet at the station, and that perforce they had to ask permission of the sergeant in charge either to make use of one owned by the Hants and Dorset Bus Company, or else if that were closed, that allocated for the use of constables. The latter course entailed the mounting of a police sentry outside, until such unorthodox occupants had vacated the place. Happily this serious lack was soon remedied, and appropriate provision made for the ladies.

Mrs Moss tells of the hectic activity of those days. She remembers the strings of telephone messages concerning escaped prisoners of war, and an occasion when some jewellery was stolen from Lord Mountbatten's home. She remembers that one of her duties was to sound the air-raid siren, and to warn hospitals first of all. When such a state of alert was on, shift work went by the board, and the women auxiliaries had to report back to the police station. Nor was she without her personal adventures. About four o'clock one morning she was pestered by an amorously-inclined individual who assured her that no respectable woman could be out at that hour, and insisted on following her through the town until she arrived at the door to the police station! Mrs Moss pays tribute to the courtesy and helpfulness of the many American service personnel stationed in Winchester, and in particular remembers with gratitude their welcome offers in the early morning of 'chow and coffee'. During the war years Winchester became a happy hunting ground for large numbers of prostitutes, both amateur and professional. On one occasion Mrs Moss had to go in a small bus to the county court with about fifteen such women, ranging in age from sixteen to sixty. In seeking advice as to how to deal with female prisoners, Mrs Moss was not always very successful. When asking how to search a woman, she was told to 'fiddle around the waist, etc., and see there wasn't anything left to hang themselves with', and nothing more. Other duties which came to her included sitting by the hospital bedside of an attempted suicide, fetching prisoners' meals from outside, and acting as a plain clothes decoy. Like all police officers, she has a kaleidoscope of memories, both grim and gay: of a coloured soldier going berserk, and a publican and his wife being shot; of a girl of 25 who was so violent that she had to be held down to be searched, and who as she struggled threw an inkpot at Mrs Moss, and shouted to her to take off her uniform, and 'let us fight it out as woman to woman'; of how the women of the office staff busied themselves in 'defleaing two constables who had been in contact with a dead old man'; and of how a girl about to give birth to a child, being rushed to hospital in a police van, caused grave alarm to the driver, who kept looking round to say, 'Don't let her have it here'. 'Above all, Mrs Moss has memories of the comradeship with some of the finest men I have known.'

In May 1944 several members of the Women's Auxiliary Air Force were allotted to the Hampshire Police. They were attested as members of the W.A.P.C., but were to be used for outside police duty. They received six weeks training in general police duties in either Birmingham or Lancashire. In July of that year the first regular policewoman was appointed to the Hampshire force. She was Miss Phyllis Yates and came as a temporary inspector from the Metropolitan Police where she had held the rank of sergeant. Unfortunately for the police, just over a year later she transferred to the probation service. In February 1946 the Home Office at last approved an establishment of one woman sergeant and ten women constables. The W.A.P.C. was disbanded at this time, and several of its members transferred to the regular force. In June that year a woman sergeant was appointed, transferred on promotion from the Sussex Police, and was posted to Bournemouth. Four months later, however, she too joined the probation service. The force was then without a woman sergeant until 1955 when Woman Sergeant Stewart transferred on promotion from Somerset. Two years later she was seconded to the British Police Unit serving in Cyprus and during her absence Sergeant Johnston was appointed, transferring on promotion from Bradford City.

In July 1958 Miss Stewart returned from Cyprus, and was promoted inspector. In the following April the number of women police was increased by four.

As so often, it proved hard to maintain full strength. Just afterwards Sergeant Johnston resigned in order to join the Northern Rhodesia Police, and her successor, appointed from Hastings Borough, left after six months in order to marry. In April 1960 the establishment of women police was increased to one inspector, three sergeants and 28 constables. Normally the three women sergeants are stationed at Winchester, Aldershot and Fareham. Of the policewomen at present serving only one is of the original ten – W.P.C. Daniels who joined the force in January 1947.

The Defence (Amalgamation of Police Forces) Regulation 1942 empowered the Home Secretary to compel police forces to amalgamate into bigger units, wherever he thought that such mergers would facilitate the movements and operations of the armed services, and of the war effort generally. It is to be remembered that by this time the United States of America had entered the war, and the south of England was destined to become a reservoir of immense armies, as the preparations burgeoned for an Allied assault on the mainland of Europe. So it was that in the course of 1943 the number of separate police forces in the south of England was reduced by twenty-one. As might be imagined, this measure of 'gleichschaltung' aroused much verbal opposition at first, and caused some heartburning. It was in consequence of this process that, with effect from 1 April 1943, the police forces of Winchester and the Isle of Wight were merged with the Hampshire Constabulary. The combined force was to be known as the Hampshire Joint Police Force, and was to be maintained by the Hampshire Standing Joint Committee – with representatives from Winchester and the Isle of Wight – as the Police Authority. Mr Lemon was appointed chief constable of the joint force, and the assistant chief constable, Mr Osman, was appointed to act as deputy chief constable. Col R.G.B. Spicer, C.M.G., M.C., previously in command of the independent Isle of Wight force, was appointed second assistant chief constable of the joint force, and was put in charge of the new Isle of Wight Division. In the same way Mr H.R. Miles was appointed superintendent in charge of the new Winchester Division, comprising what had been the Winchester City Police area together with the existing county division. Apart from the Chief Constables of the Isle of Wight and Winchester, all members of the three constituent forces were transferred in their existing temporary and substantive ranks to the joint force, and were deemed to be duly appointed as constables under the County Police Act of 1839. All standing orders, both general and specific, in operation in the respective constituent forces were to continue in force unless and until they were revoked or amended from the new joint headquarters. The ten divisions in the new force, Aldershot, Andover, Basingstoke, Bournemouth, Eastleigh, Fareham, Isle of Wight, New Forest, Petersfield and Winchester, were assigned the letters A to K respectively, with the letter I omitted. In customary style, Headquarters was to be denoted by the letters 'H.Q.'. In concluding his Order dealing with the amalgamation, Mr Lemon affirmed to all ranks his pride and pleasure at the honour conferred upon him by his selection to command the new joint force, and assured members 'that the efficiency of the joint force, together with their welfare and happiness, will always be my primary consideration, and I ask all ranks to continue loyally and zealously to discharge their duties to the best of their individual capacities, and thereby make the amalgamation to be a great success'.

In 1943 and succeeding war years many police officers were trained as incident control officers. These performed a very important function, in that they were trained to take charge of proceedings at any incident involving damage from air attack. They were responsible for co-ordinating and controlling the members of the different organisations involved, such as the A.R.P., the Fire Service, and the medical teams. It fell to the incident control officers to deploy men and vehicles as required, and in general to direct rescue work. Another sort of course held from time to time, which many police officers attended, was that concerned with bomb recognition. Such men were trained to determine the type and power of unexploded bombs by reference, if necessary, to the size and character of the holes they had made on entering the ground. Another war duty which Hampshire officers had to undertake was that of lecturing to organisations such as Civil Defence on methods of immobilising vehicles and putting such equipment as petrol pumps out of action, against the possibility of an enemy invasion of this country. In a way these talks were in character an extension of those given in relation to crime prevention; but now the neutralisation rather than the security of property was the aim. As the war progressed, the fear of invasion receded, but the need for lectures by the police if anything increased. Now the audiences were of American troops and airmen stationed in England, and the content of the lectures was an introduction to aspects of English law, and to the British way of life generally. From 1943 to 1945 the tide of the Americans into southern England reached its highest point. Everywhere they made an impact on the life of wartime Britain. When they took over the R.A.F. station at Middle Wallop, situated in the centre of the Wallop villages in Hampshire, they promptly renamed it 'Centre Punch'. In more than one district, the local constable came to be regarded as a walking encyclopedia on all things British, and to command the affection as well as the respect of the American servicemen. Very likely the Hampshire police, in their dealings with these foreign troops in their county, drew on the vast stock of experience of co-operating with the military that their force had accumulated over the previous century. Naturally, all contact with the Americans was not so amicable, nor so entirely a matter of friendly liaison. Transatlantic troops were as liable as our own to get drunk, to get rowdy, and to cause damage to property. One day a farmer near Andover noticed that some straw near a rick of baled straw had apparently been disturbed. Police were called, and after an intensive search they discovered that the interior of the rick had been converted into a room by the removal of some bales, and that an American army deserter had been living in this makeshift 'house' for some months, emerging only under cover of darkness to find food, and returning to his lair during the day.

Meantime the demands of the British armed services for more men increased. At the end of July 1942 it was reported to the Standing Joint Committee that more young policemen were being released for the services, which needed an ever greater supply of fit and intelligent young men. Thus men under twenty-five years of age were no longer reserved to the police; 131 were called up. In turn more regular duties were undertaken by special constables, and more police war reserves were appointed. Inevitably the casualties sustained by members of the Hampshire force increased. In 1942 and throughout 1943 and 1944 General Orders are marked with the sad news of the loss of police officers serving at home and abroad with each of the fighting services. Men died in action with the army in North Africa, at sea with the Royal Navy, and in the skies over Europe with the Royal Air Force. Even more than in the First World War, men of the Hampshire Constabulary played their full and worthy part in the great struggle. Some gained distinction. In September 1943 the chief constable was pleased to bring to the notice of all ranks of the force an item from the *London Gazette* dated 22 June 1943: 'The King has been graciously pleased to approve that the following be mentioned in recognition of gallant and distinguished service in the Middle East during the period May 1st, 1942 to October 2nd, 1942–W.O.2 (C.S.M.) Acting W.O.I (R.S.M.) G.A. Corney–Corps of Military Police.' This referred to Detective Constable G.A. Corney of the Bournemouth Division, and later Corney had his acting rank confirmed, and was awarded the M.B.E. He can be taken as a fit representative of all those police officers who brought honour to their force by their achievements in the armed services. Nor were all those who so served of such junior police rank. On 7 August 1943, Mr R.G.B. Spicer, assistant chief constable, Isle of Wight Division, was called up for military service, after attending a course of training under the Administrative Section of the War Office.

'D-Day' was 6 June 1944, the date of the Allied invasion of the mainland of Europe, which was the most gigantic and elaborate combined operation in the history of the world. For months beforehand immense numbers of troops and quantities of equipment were assembled in the southern part of Hampshire. The large forested areas in this part of the county provided ideal cover for such a concentration, and hardly a road in these areas was not lined with tanks, guns and troop encampments. Naturally, public co-operation with the military at this time was of the greatest importance, and senior police officers acted as liaison officers at the various military headquarters. Many minor roads were widened almost overnight to take the enormously increased traffic. One class B road north of Winchester was completely closed for some months and became a gigantic vehicle park. It was particularly suitable for this purpose because of a canopy of trees extending along it for much of the way. Over another open stretch a great arch-shaped roof was erected, creating a huge hangar-like structure. Under the protection of this roof hundreds of vehicles were modified and made waterproof in preparation for the D-Day landings. All such assembly areas became controlled zones to which access could be gained only by special pass. Together with the military, the police had the difficult task of keeping unauthorised persons away from these zones, and of prohibiting the use of cameras and binoculars. Again, routes had to be marked out for use by the invasion forces, including alternative routes in case of emergency. All this elaborate work of preparation was achieved with the help and indispensable local knowledge of the officers of the Hampshire Joint Force, assisted at times by officers from other forces moved into the area for the purpose. In December 1944 the Regional Commissioner, Southern Region, gave high praise to the Hampshire force for its help in the huge preparations for D-Day. In a letter to the chief constable he wrote, 'You have had a year of great activity, and the police force in this region played an outstanding part in the preparations for the invasion of the Continent. I should like to thank you for the co-operation of every kind I have received from the police during this vital year, and I look forward in the new year to the time when the whole Civil Defence organisation can stand down with the knowledge that its work is accomplished.'

On 1 January 1944 appeared the first number of the Hampshire Joint Police Force News Letter to Members in the Armed Forces. The assistant chief constable, Mr Osman, acted as its editor. This bulletin was instituted with the active encouragement of the chief constable and Mr Lemon indicated the purposes of the publication in a foreword to the first edition: 'Although a stranger to most of you I have felt for a long time the desirability of some means of maintaining contact with all our members who are serving in the fighting forces, of passing on items of interest concerning the force, and of their own adventures. Various difficulties have arisen, but I am glad these have now been overcome, and it gives me much pleasure to inaugurate this news letter, a copy of which is being sent to all members of the force, wherever they may be, who are serving in the armed forces. Some of you have been away now for over four years, and during this time many changes have taken place within the force of which you may be quite unaware. It is hoped that the news letter will be of interest, and bring you up to date with the main changes which have taken place, and it is then hoped to issue further news letters about every three months. Although up to now it has not been possible to communicate with all of you, everyone may rest assured he has not been forgotten. All possible steps have been taken to watch over your interests, and to ensure that when you return to the force you will be able to take up your proper position and to have every opportunity of going full steam ahead. Mrs Lemon joins me in wishing you the very best of good luck and a speedy return to the police force, when we shall take the first opportunity of meeting you all.' In this first news letter it was reported that to date 225 members of the force had joined up; 121 in the army, 28 in the navy, and 76 in the Royal Air Force. Eight were listed as having been killed in action, and three more as missing. Two others were reported to have been taken prisoners of war. Three other former constables, all in the Commandos, were noted as having been wounded but now recovered. Twenty-two members of the force were listed as having gained commissions, and Lieutenant Corney was congratulated on his Mention in Despatches and subsequent M.B.E. With regard to changes in the force itself, readers were told of Mr Lemon's succeeding Major Cockburn, and of the formation of the Hampshire Joint Police Force. Totton Section had been transferred from the New Forest Division to the Eastleigh Division, Christchurch to Bournemouth Division, and Havant from Petersfield to Fareham Division. Comment on the possibility of the wartime amalgamation proving permanent was summed up by a correspondent from the Isle of Wight in the phrase, 'Have you ever tried unscrambling scrambled eggs?' Also given were details of the arrangements for supplementation of pay, and the hope was expressed that the explanation of the complicated scheme would avoid the inundation of the Administrative Branch at headquarters with enquiries 'as with so many vacant seats in that department such queries only hinder the payment of supplementation'.

The establishment of the C.I.D. throughout the county was reported, and tribute paid to its members for 'putting up a good show against long odds' in their fight against crime. One compensation to the hard-pressed detectives was the availability of secretarial assistance from one or other cheerful member of the W.A.P.C. There were then about ninety woman auxiliaries in the Hampshire Joint Force, working as shorthand-typists, clerks, telephonists and drivers. Four had the title of leading auxiliaries and wore sergeants' stripes. The news letter commented with satisfaction that the W.A.P.C. held occasional conferences at headquarters 'on Police Federation lines when, among other things, the question of the quality of their stockings and the number of coupons to be surrendered for their uniform are said to be vigorously discussed. They also have training courses at headquarters, and the drill instructor is alleged to suffer severely from nightmares in consequence.' Nevertheless sincere compliments were paid to the help of the W.A.P.C., as well as to the special constables, the police reservists, and the police war reservists. 'The members of the police war reserve have settled down to police work very well and are of great assistance, but there is little doubt they will be only too ready to hand over the job to you on your return and to get back double quick to their own civilian occupations.' Again and again members of the force in the armed services were reassured that they would be needed more than ever once the war was over, and that all the temporary help, welcome though it was, could not compare with the quality of the regular constabulary. This reassurance was no doubt extremely timely and comforting to men uncertain of their future in an apparently rapidly-changing force. Apart from the extension of the C.I.D. to all divisions and at headquarters, as already mentioned, photographic departments had been established to cover all divisions, and considerable additions made to the photographic equipment at headquarters to provide for the publication of photographs on crime circulations. Every two months a C.I.D. conference was now held at headquarters to enable officers to discuss their problems and exchange items of interest. From time to time courses of instruction were held to enable C.I.D. officers to keep abreast of current developments. A Central Index of Convictions was about to be established when the headquarters C.I.D. staff moved in to their new quarters in the house previously occupied by the chief constable.

In subsequent numbers of the news letter much space was occupied by comment on post-war prospects, especially regarding promotion. Ordinary Seaman Toogood, formerly of the Aldershot Division, wrote to the editor of the news letter that there was a feeling that the so-called 'utility' sergeants would be promoted to substantive rank, and that the men in the armed services would come off worse. The editor's reply was, of course, non-committal, but pointed out that, when the war was over, there would be a considerable number of promotions to be made to substantive ranks, and that all the men in the armed services, as well as those officers in the force holding temporary ranks, would be considered on their merits. 'To the men in the armed forces I would say that you may rely on the chief constable for a fair and square deal, and you need have no fear of being overlooked or in any way forgotten.' Other correspondents were concerned about the possibility of sitting qualifying examinations for promotion while still in the armed services, and in the sixth news letter, dated 1 April 1945, it was announced that the examinations would be held on 19 May following. It was doubted whether it would be possible for many in the armed services to sit, but any member of the force in this country, and able to get leave, was urged to apply forthwith to the chief constable.

Naturally the news letters contained an immense amount of personal news, items concerning individual members of the force serving overseas, and also, for their information, accounts of the activities of old colleagues at work on the home front. The news submitted from each division consisted largely of such personalia, and their publication must have done much to give to far-flung members of the Hampshire Constabulary a continuing sense of comradeship and corporate loyalty. Certainly the news letter was widely admired, and both the Kent and Monmouthshire Constabularies took the Hampshire venture as model for their own 'Forces' Letters'. It is possible to trace the wartime career of some officers, as the milestones in their service experience are faithfully noted in the news letters. For example in the first number it was reported that Police Constable H.V.D. Hallett, formerly stationed at Lyndhurst, was now receiving training in flying duties somewhere in England. In the sixth issue he was one of those congratulated on receiving their commissions. Stories from many countries and many fronts flowed in. Officers undergoing flight training in North America wrote of the kindness and hospitality of the people there to British servicemen. Others wrote of the hardships endured in the fighting in the Far East, and of the campaigns in Western Europe. Police Constable W.A. White, serving in the Reconnaissance Corps in Belgium, spoke of an engagement in which some prisoners had been taken, and of his relief at not having to fill in the requisite forms for each one. Superintendent A.J. Appleton, then a major in the Civil Affairs Organisation, was at one point in charge of all the public safety problems of a French Department and at another involved in cleaning up a concentration camp full of Russian women. By way of exchange for these innumerable anecdotes of active service, the news letters told of dances, whist drives, concerts, cricket and football matches and of marriages and births. Indeed from August 1942 onwards Mr Lemon had adopted the practice of appending reports on sporting events to his General Orders, and there is no doubt that his encouragement of sport generally fostered both the *esprit de corps* of the Hampshire Joint Force, and the bonds of interest and loyalty between the force and its scattered members. Readers were kept informed of such changes in the force as the increase in number of women auxiliaries, the extension of wireless facilities, and the gradual dwindling, through age and ill-health, of the band of police reservists. It was reported to the Standing Joint Committee at the end of February 1944 that the bulk of the wireless main installation would be purchased during the current year, and that in the coming year the installation would be complete. The news letters also reflected some of the problems that were already engaging the attention of the force, and were to do so long after the end of the war. In the sixth news letter, published on 1 April 1945, there was a short notice on the housing situation. It rightly pointed out that this would be one of the most troublesome post-war problems. The chief constable had been alive to this matter for a long time and every possible step had been taken in advance. To accommodate members of the force satisfactorily 80 houses would be needed immediately, and ultimately no fewer than two hundred. In order to obtain the feeling of the people who would have to live in the houses, the chief constable arranged that all the constables and their wives in the divisions should have a meeting to discuss the type of house they would prefer, and the amenities they considered necessary. The divisions then elected one constable and his wife from each division to attend a meeting at headquarters at which the chief constable, the county architect and the borough architect of Bournemouth attended. 'A full and frank discussion took place.'

Superintendent Appleton, some of whose activities in Western Europe were reported in the news letters, had been one of the first of several police officers from Hampshire who had been drawn into the Civil Affairs Organisation, which was designed to aid the people of liberated countries in re-establishing ordered government and a stabilised society in the wake of the advancing allied armies.

He had attended a course of instruction and then been nominated for immediate appointment under the organisation with the rank of acting major. Other police officers later were appointed to AMGOT (Allied Military Government for Occupied Territory) against the time when occupied enemy territory had to be administered; some of those officers, again, were to come under the Control Commission for Germany. Inspector R.J. Walters of Winchester Division was so appointed on 12 June 1944, and in September of the same year two sergeants, F.L. Allan and T. McVicar, of Headquarters and Isle of Wight Divisions respectively, were appointed with the rank of temporary captain. At the very end of the European war, on 5 May 1945, Inspector Dore, Sergeant Maskew and Sergeant White, of the Winchester, Isle of Wight and Petersfield Divisions respectively, reported for duty with the Public Safety Branch of the Control Commission for Germany.

Several more awards and commendations were gained both at home and abroad by officers of the Hampshire force and, indeed, by members of the forces temporarily attached. Sergeant E.H. Buckley of the Sheffield Police, attached to the Fareham Division, was in June 1944 commended by the chief constable 'for his excellent work at a recent air raid in which he showed not only an entire disregard for his own safety but assisted a doctor to attend and remove two seriously injured women from a damaged house while ammunition was exploding all around them.' In September of the same year the chief constable was very pleased to bring to the notice of all ranks of the force the award of the Distinguished Flying Cross to Flying Officer A.J. McCormick, who had previously been a constable of the Isle of Wight Division. In December 1944 the chief constable in General Orders brought to the notice of all ranks of the force that His Majesty The King had been graciously pleased to give orders for the publication of the name of Police Constable W. Perfect as having received an expression of commendation for his gallant conduct on 22 June 1944, 'when, despite the danger from exploding ammunition, he searched the blazing wreckage of a plane which had crashed, to make sure that no members of the crew were still in the plane'. A similar mark of royal approval came early in 1945 to Police War Reserve Constable S. Paxton of the Fareham Division, who was awarded the B.E.M. in recognition of his gallant conduct 'when, although stunned by the force of exploding petrol, he attempted to rescue the pilot of an aircraft which has crashed and caught fire'. Flight Lieutenant D.V. Gibbs of Bournemouth also gained a D.F.C., while another Bournemouth officer, Flight Lieutenant H.D. Simmons, was awarded the American Air Medal for his achievements as a navigator with the first Allied Airborne Army at the time of the Arnhem operation.

On 17 February 1945, a first committee meeting of the Comrades' Association was held, at which Superintendent McCallum of Aldershot Division was elected Chairman, Sergeant Greenen of Headquarters Division was elected Secretary and Superintendent Chown of Fareham was elected Treasurer for the ensuing year. A meeting of a different sort was the first annual Inter-Divisional First

Aid Competition for divisional teams and individual officers, which was held at headquarters on 26 May 1945, and proved a great success. The challenge cup for this divisional competition, which had been presented by Lord Mottistone, C.B., C.M.C., D.S.O., was won by the Isle of Wight Division; while another cup for the best individual work, which had been presented by Lady Louis Mountbatten, C.B.E., was won by Sergeant A.L. Aymes also of the Isle of Wight Division. All this reflected the greatly enhanced importance of the whole subject of first aid in the context of war conditions, with their steady stream of air-raid casualties.

By then the war in Europe was over. VE-Day was 8 May 1945, and in Winchester was celebrated quietly on the whole, with little extra strain on the police. A number of streets arranged their own parties, but otherwise there was not much in the way of organised celebrations. In Petersfield, too, there was no untoward incident other than the temporary purloining of some of the allied flags on display, and their subsequent exhibition in unlikely places. Things were a little more lively in Fareham Division, where a few ricks were fired; but there too the main forms of celebration were street parties for children and returned prisoners of war, and open-air services. In Bournemouth the crowds were livelier and made some noise, but there was little rowdyism, other than the creation of a bonfire out of some deckchairs on the beach. Everywhere the mood seems to have been one of thankfulness and relief, rather than of exuberant mafficking. One exception to this, however, took place in Aldershot on the night of 4/5 July 1945, when a riot by Canadian troops caused damage amounting to £25,000. The destruction fell mainly on an amusement arcade, and on shop windows and doors. Between 400 and 500 men took part in the disturbance, and the civil and military police stationed in the town were unable to deal with the violent situation which arose. Consequently reinforcements of police from other parts of the county, and from Portsmouth, Reading, Southampton and Oxford, were called in to help. The Canadian military authorities undertook responsibility for settling all claims for damages, and refunded to the police authority half the cost of the police reinforcements, amounting to approximately £205.

In August 1945 the first police officers to be released from the armed services began to return. A General Order dated 4 August 1945 lists one sergeant and 17 constables who were due for discharge from the forces in July or August, and indicates the various stations to which they were to be posted. In September 28 more constables were notified of their new police destinations. In the same month the first 'Refresher Course' for returning officers was held at headquarters from 3 to 29 September, and was attended by the first two dozen members of the force released from the armed services. It took place in the old offices at West Hill, and the students had their meals in the County Council canteen at the Castle. The instructors were Inspector A.V. Menwood and Sergeant G.H. Griffith, and their work was supplemented by various outside lecturers. Immediately after the conclusion of the first course, the second one began, and the series was to continue until all those returned from the services had been accommodated. Commenting on this in the final news letter, Inspector Travis, the Aldershot divisional correspondent, wrote of his returning comrades 'We shall learn from them upon their return to the division how quickly the intricacies of criminal law and police duties come to the forefront of their minds again, for, with the disappearance of much of the emergency legislation, our job is fundamentally the same as in the good old days.' At this time, too, a large number of police war reservists were leaving the police service and returning to purely civilian occupations. At the end of 1945 no fewer than 119 police war reservists were discharged, as well as two first police reservists and two auxiliary police women. Throughout the war, of course, there had been a steady wastage of first police reservists on account of ill-health and advancing age, and of police women on account of marriage. It is interesting to see how the diminished numbers of the regular force had been made up by the various groups of reservists and auxiliaries. At 30 January 1939, the authorised strength of the force had been 635, which establishment was increased during the following year by six inspectors and six sergeants, and decreased by one sergeant-major, to bring the total by October 1940 to 646, including the chief constable.

In February 1945 the number of regular officers was 452, and they were aided in their work by 30 members of the first police reserve, and 372 members of the police war reserve, including women auxiliaries. In the course of the war 425 regular officers had served in the armed forces or been posted to industries such as mining. Of this total 133 were in the army, 31 in the Royal Navy, 75 in the Royal Air Force, four in the Royal Marines and two in industry. Fourteen were killed in action, ten in the Royal Air Force and four in the army. Most sad and pitiful of all was the death of Police Constable T.G. Harris, of Netley, who was killed in North West Germany by gunshot wounds on 9 September 1945, long after the end of hostilities in Europe. He was then serving as a corporal in the Westminster Dragoons, R.A.C. Two men were discharged from the army, and one from the Royal Air Force, on medical grounds, and their health did not permit their return to police duty. Fourteen were wounded, and three taken prisoners of war. Of 42 boy clerks, 13 joined the army, 12 the navy, 13 the Royal Air Force, two the Royal Marines and two the Fleet Air Arm. Four of these were killed in action.

After the war such boy clerks, who had first been appointed early in 1939, were to be replaced by police cadets. At first the cadets had no proper uniform, and worked a 48-hour week. There was no organised training for them, as such, and if they attended appropriate evening classes they did so in their own time at their own expense. In 1954, they were to be issued with uniform, and a training course devised for them. It was then arranged that technical college facilities be made available to them, and they were encouraged to attend Outward Bound courses, and to undertake activities under the Duke of Edinburgh's Award Scheme.

In addition, there was a regular camp at Brockenhurst. The advantages and disadvantages of the whole cadet scheme have been a matter of controversy in the police service: but at least it enabled the youths concerned to advance their all-round education, and to get such an insight into the police profession as would indicate to themselves and others whether they were likely in time to make successful constables.

Throughout the Second World War the police were paid a war bonus. At the end of the war, new scales of pay were introduced which resulted in some increase. The Police Federation expressed itself dissatisfied with this and pressed for more. Again, in 1946 new scales of pay were established, but still the Federation sought further increases. To arbitrate on the whole matter, the Oaksey Committee was set up. The Police Federation asked for increases ranging from 33⅓ to 54% while most police authorities recommended little or no increase. Eventually the Oaksey Committee recommended increases of from 10 to 20% for all ranks.

The war was over but life was still very straitened in Great Britain. Food and clothing were still subject to rationing, and were to remain so for some years to come. The economy, indeed the whole of society, had been strained and dislocated in the course of the war, and it was inevitable that there should be a questioning of all sorts of existing arrangements, and an urge for change and reorganisation. Thus the Police Act of 1946 opened the way to a series of post-war amalgamations of police forces. In consequence the wartime merger of the Hampshire, Isle of Wight and Winchester forces was made permanent in 1947. The new formation was named at first the Hampshire Constabulary, and later was given the title of the Hampshire and Isle of Wight Constabulary.

On 7 January 1946, the chief constable was very pleased 'to inform all ranks that His Majesty the King has awarded the King's Police Medal for distinguished service to Mr Frank Osman, assistant chief constable, and I look upon this as a great honour, not only for Mr Osman himself but on the force as a whole'. Commendations by the chief constable himself were bestowed some weeks later on Inspector T.F. Page, Police Constable W. Perfect, and Police Constable T. Trickey, for their zeal, persistence, and prompt action which resulted in the arrest of four escaped German prisoners of war. Here again is a reminder that, though the war was certainly over, things were far from being completely restored to normal. Indeed, the last German prisoners in British hands were not to be repatriated until early in 1948. Another interesting commendation from Mr Lemon went in August to Detective Constable G.R. Suter 'for his powers of observation in detecting the resemblance of N.G.C. Heath with a photograph published in the Police Gazette'. Here is a reference to one of the most notorious murderers, and most ghastly crimes, in modern British history.

Comment of a different kind attended the results of the qualifying examinations for promotion held on 18 May 1946. Twenty-two officers passed in a variety of different papers, so that now they had passed the examinations in all subjects.

Five others passed the examinations in police duty and criminal law, while 17 passed in educational subjects. With regard to the latter, the Secretary of the Union of Educational Institutions commented, 'The results seem very good. All the police sergeants have obtained an aggregate mark of at least 50%, and the general standard reached by the majority of all candidates is very satisfactory.' On the other hand, the chief constable stated drily, 'The papers on police duty and criminal law were not of a very high standard and those who have failed to pass this year should give the subjects more attention.' In the customary fashion, the attention of all officers was drawn to Police Regulation 30: 'The object of the required examination is to test the educational and theoretical knowledge of the candidate, and the fact that he has passed them shall not entitle him to promotion before another member of the force who has passed the examination at a later date.' As always, the selection of officers for promotion would depend on their ability and efficiency shown towards their duties and would not necessarily be according to seniority.

An important post-war development in the Hampshire Constabulary was the establishment of a Traffic and Communications Department at Headquarters. This was made necessary by the growing weight and complexity of motor traffic. Twentieth-century society was highly mobile and mechanical, and the police service had to adapt its methods and equipment accordingly. Throughout the previous century the only form of transport belonging to the force had been the horse and cart kept at each divisional station. This vehicle had been used by the superintendent in the course of his duties, and also for transporting single policemen and their luggage on removal to new stations. The 'Reserve Man' who normally accompanied the superintendent also used the horse when required as a member of the mounted section. Early last century pedal cycles came into use, but even then much police movement from one part of the county to another was done on foot. When longer journeys had to be made, they were accomplished by public transport where possible, and when the ensuing expense could be justified. Ex-Inspector A.J. Pragnell, who was first posted to Aldershot in 1912, remembers that prisoners were escorted between Aldershot and Winchester prison on foot, staying overnight at Alton and Alresford. As late as 1923 Superintendent W. Deacon was returning from court at Southampton to Eastleigh, when his cart collapsed ignominiously in The Avenue; fortunately no one was hurt. Only in 1925 were the carts replaced by Ford T Model 4 cars, which vehicles, like their predecessors, were reserved for the use of the superintendents. Understandably, at the same time as the carts and horses were dispensed with, the mounted section was disbanded. In 1924 the chief constable, Major Warde, already possessed a Wolseley motor car for his own use. Aldershot Division at least had a solo motor-cycle in 1926 for motor patrol duties, although it was of course under the control of the divisional superintendent. Within the next five years a divisional patrol car was also provided, and this did both motor patrol and other duties on alternate days. In 1931 motor-cycle combinations were brought into use in divisions. The first such machine in Eastleigh was a Royal Enfield. In the thirties, the divisions were equipped successively with Austin two-seater models in 1934, with Austin 12s in 1936, and in 1938 with M.G.s. There was still no traffic department as such, but the drivers of the various vehicles were recognised as traffic officers, subordinate to the divisional superintendents. The Traffic and Communications Department was set up in 1945, and was in operation the following year.

As early as June 1945 Mr Lemon had issued an appropriate directive, in which he announced that from 1 July of that year the War Emergency Department would cease to function at headquarters, and that such records as those relating to the special constabulary would be transferred to the Chief Clerk's Department. 'A Traffic and Communications Department under Superintendent Wright will be set up at headquarters on this date, and as this will be an entirely new depart-ure I would welcome the views of superintendents on the organisation and functions of Headquarters Traffic Department, which is intended to *co-ordinate* traffic problems, accident prevention, motor patrols maintenance, etc., but it is proposed that divisional superintendents shall still be responsible for the motor vehicles within their divisions and also for their traffic personnel.' The chief constable stated that the question of co-ordinating routes from one division to another might present difficulties, and that he would welcome the views of his superintendents. It was not intended that motor patrol cars should operate only in the divisions in which they were situated, and it was hoped that eventually all motor patrol vehicles would be fitted with two-way radio. The chief constable also desired superintendents to inform him how many patrol cars they each thought should be stationed in their respective divisions, and where they should be stationed in order to afford adequate supervision of the roads. Suggestions and recommendations from the superintendents flowed in, so that by the start of 1946 the nucleus of a traffic department had been formed. In January 1946 further guidance came from the Home Office, that in the opinion of the Home Secretary, police traffic departments should be responsible for the following functions:

1. Co-ordination of all road safety measures throughout the force.
2. The review and investigation of the causes of road accidents in the light of reports from the officers dealing with the accidents and all other available information.
3. The establishing of uniformity of practice throughout the force in regard to the question of prosecutions for traffic offences.
4. The maintenance of accident maps and accident statistics.
5. The organisation and supervision of the duties and training of motor patrols.

8 Senior Officers of the Constabulary, 1946. Back row: Supt V.F Stanley, Supt P.W Paddon, Supt A.J. Broomfield, Supt W.S. Cooper, Det/Supt R. Gill, Supt G. Hatcher, Supt R.E. Pascall, Supt T. Willmott; Front row: Supt A.H.W. Wright, Supt M.M. McCallum, Mr F. Osman (Assistant Chief Constable), Mr R.D. Lemon (Chief Constable), Ch/Supt S. Bennett, Supt E. Chown, Supt H.R. Miles.

6. The issue of instructions and advice to members of the force generally on methods of dealing with road accidents and measures for preventing them.
7. The periodic survey of the siting of pedestrian crossings and the stopping places of public service vehicles, and consideration of the adequacy of the provision of public parking places.
8. The establishment and maintenance of contact with the local road safety organisations, the Highway Authority and the Divisional Road Engineer of the Ministry of Transport; also with the local education authorities with regard to the instruction of school children in road safety measures.

It was the Home Office view that it would probably be convenient to combine these duties with those of the Transport and Communications Section, but, if this were done, it would be desirable that an officer, of the rank of inspector at least, should be made definitely responsible for accident prevention and road safety work. Also it was emphasised that the formation of such traffic departments 'should not be regarded as derogating in any way from the duty of all members of the force to promote road safety measures on all occasions, and to be capable of dealing with any road accident brought to their notice. The object of the traffic department, in the Secretary of State's view, is to secure that every officer in the force, and not only those specially engaged on traffic duties, shall be fully alive to his responsibilities in the matter, and shall be given the necessary instructions and advice to ensure that he can deal satisfactorily with road accident problems.' It was with this brief in mind that Mr Lemon and Superintendent Wright moulded and developed the Traffic and Communications Department of the Hampshire Constabulary.

As the first traffic superintendent, Superintendent A.H.W. Wright accomplished an immense amount of preparatory work. The number and type of vehicles in each division had to be checked, and their condition ascertained. The total mileage of first- and second-class roads in the county had to be taken into account, together with the weight of traffic and distribution of population in each area, both as it was at the end of the war, and as it was likely to be in succeeding

post-war years. Garage accommodation in each division had to be considered and made adequate, and provision made for maintenance and repair facilities. The most effective method of preventing accidents at dangerous places on the roads, by the erection of suitable warning signs and other devices, was also a matter for exhaustive discussion. In February 1946 the county surveyor wrote that his department proposed to start recording again all accidents in the county, and that for this purpose regular visits to police headquarters by one of his assistants would be necessary, in order to make extracts from the police records. He was confident that the arrangements for this co-operation would work to the mutual advantage of the police and himself. A few months later the chief constable issued a memorandum to all superintendents, stating that 'Numerous applications are being received from the county surveyor and other surveyors requesting police reports and recommendations in connection with the imposition of speed limits;

9   Traffic Division 1949 (at Peninsula Barracks, Winchester). The cars are all Wolseley 12/48s. The officer leading the parade is Superintendent Albert Henry Wright.

the extension of existing 30 m.p.h. speed limit areas; halt at major road ahead
and other similar signs; automatic traffic light signals; pedestrian crossings; bends,
etc., and other matters likely to be of benefit to road users. Very few reports of
a like nature have been initiated by the police, and it is again emphasised that it
is the duty of all members of the force to promote road safety measures on all
occasions. Superintendents will please have a survey made in connection with
the above throughout their divisions, and a report setting out any suggestions
likely to benefit road users should be forwarded to headquarters not later than
July 25th, 1946. In reports affecting speed limits a sketch of the area affected
should be submitted, together with the accident record for the past two years.
All reports relating to road signs, etc., should include the accident record of the
locality for a similar period. Superintendents should also report whether or not
they are satisfied with the location of all bus stopping places in their divisions,
and, if not, to suggest alternative sites.' Evidently the degree of co-operation
between the two sides increased, and in January 1949 a further memorandum
from the chief constable noted that from time to time he received proposals
relating to such matters as restrictions on waiting and car parking facilities from
the county surveyor, borough councils and urban district councils. These proposals
were forwarded to superintendents for their information, and where necessary

10 Triumph 498cc Speed Twins and
riders, Peninsula Barracks, Winchester
1949.

these officers, together with the traffic superintendent, attended a meeting to discuss further action. The memorandum continued: 'There may be cases when the proposals for such schemes are received by superintendents direct from local authorities; in these instances a report should be forwarded to headquarters notifying the details, and if a meeting is to be held, the time and date of same, in order that it may be decided as to whether the superintendent or inspector of the Traffic and Communications Department should attend the meeting.' Thus all such matters were brought more and more under the general supervision of the traffic department. In 1948 the strength of that department stood at one superintendent, one inspector, four sergeants and 28 constables. For purposes of supervising traffic in the county, it was divided into four areas, with a traffic sergeant at headquarters, Aldershot, Fareham and Ringwood respectively.

In the summer of 1954, the then superintendent in charge, Mr Broomfield, conducted a thorough survey of the organisation, working, and problems of the Traffic Department. To each of the traffic sergeants he sent a memorandum requesting a report on whether they found any practical difficulty, in connection with their areas of supervision, and also asking for constructive suggestions regarding the organisation of the department. The sergeants responded most conscientiously, and the matters covered in their reports ranged from the burden

11 Hampshire Constabulary Joint Branch Board, 1948. Back row: Sgt Thorne, Sgt Booth, P.C. Chislett, P.C. Kidd, P.C. Floyd, Sgt Maund, P.C. Rowe, P.C. Corney and P.C. Webb; Middle row: Sgt Allison, Inspr Bird, Sgt Brittain, Inspr Butter, Inspr Thatcher, Sgt Bond, Inspr Ellis, Inspr Cook, Sgt Longman and P.C. Mack; Front row: Inspr James, P.C. Milner, Inspr Steel (Treasurer), P.C. Truman (Secretary), Mr R.D. Lemon (Chief Constable), P.C. Day (Chairman), Mr F. Osman (Assistant Chief Constable), Inspr Crockford, Sgt Watling, Sgt McHardy and Det. Inspr Punter.

of administrative work under which they laboured, which demanded additional staff and typewriters, to the most efficient and economical method of arranging tours of duty both by day and night.

The vehicle establishment increased steadily, and in doing so kept pace with the ever-growing volume of traffic throughout the county. At the end of 1957, the force possessed a total of 105 vehicles, consisting of 31 patrol cars, 30 section vehicles, 10 C.I.D. vehicles, 11 vans and 23 motor-cycles. By December 1960 the total was 134, by December 1963 it had leaped to 177, and by 1965 it was 254, consisting of 33 patrol cars, 66 section vehicles, 37 C.I.D. cars, 24 vans and 94 motor cycles. On the eve of amalgamation the total vehicle strength was 281, and this figure included 33 patrol cars and 44 motor-cycles belonging to the Traffic Division; in addition the Hampshire and Isle of Wight Constabulary disposed of 66 section vehicles for general purposes, 26 goods vehicles, among which were some earmarked for specialist activities, 38 C.I.D. vehicles, mostly Minis, 53 light motor-cycles and 21 scooters. The force had come a long way from the superintendent's horse and cart.

An indication of the continuing shortage of food and other commodities that still existed in the post-war years is found in a commendation given by the chief constable to Sergeant H.J. Waterer for his success in detecting rationing offences by a butcher in the latter half of 1947. In June 1947 an offence more familiar to the present day was marked in the commendation given to Police Constable P.K. Townsend for his initiative and keen attention to duty, which resulted in the arrest of a man 'for larceny from and damage to a large number of telephone kiosks in Bournemouth', and in the recovery of a large quantity of post office equipment. Another commendation went to Woman Police Constable G. Stenner for her good work in locating two men in the Isle of Wight who were wanted on charges of shop-breaking and food stealing. She was one of the first regular policewomen, and her record was highly creditable; she was then still on probation, but clearly she was to have no difficulty in being confirmed a full member of the force in due course; and so it proved. Another woman constable to be commended was Woman Police Constable E.M. Daniels, who through devotion to duty had obtained useful information which resulted in the conviction of seven persons for larceny of food.

From 1 April 1948, Bournemouth had its own police force. From time to time there had been agitation on the part of the borough for independence in police matters. The Second World War caused this pressure to be set aside, and it might have been expected that, with the creation of the Hampshire joint force, and the trend towards amalgamation of forces in consequence of the 1946 Police Act, the idea would have faded away. With effect from 1 April 1947, no fewer than 45 non-county borough forces in the country had been abolished. On the contrary, however, the feeling in favour of a separate Bournemouth force was stronger than ever among the borough's residents. It was thought by many that the war experience itself had underlined the need for a police command in Bournemouth apart from that of the county. In July 1947 the Home Secretary met a deputation from the Bournemouth Corporation consisting of the mayor, an alderman, and a councillor, to discuss the matter. In a notable triumph, against the whole tide of police policy in favour of amalgamations, the Bournemouth representatives had their way. At a subsequent meeting of the council in September, it was decided by 44 votes to seven (with one abstention) to establish a separate Bournemouth Borough Police Force. On 10 November 1947, the council appointed its first Watch Committee as a step towards creating the new force. On 4 March 1948, the Watch Committee from a short list of six chose Chief Superintendent S. Bennett, of the Bournemouth Division, Hampshire Constabulary, to be Bournemouth's first chief constable. Mr Bennett had been stationed in Bournemouth since 1942. All members of the Hampshire and Isle of Wight Constabulary were given the choice of either remaining with the county, or transferring to the new force. Most officers stationed in Bournemouth chose the latter course. To quote from Sergeant R. Ford's *The History of the Bournemouth Police*: 'On the night of March 31st, 1948, a dinner was held at the Pavilion to mark the coming separation of Bournemouth from the county constabulary. Chief Superintendent Bennett presided. Representatives of the Home Office and the civil and police authorities of Bournemouth and the neighbouring counties of Hampshire and Dorset were present and that evening, in an atmosphere of warm friendship and happy memories, the curtain came down on the Hampshire Constabulary, Bournemouth. It rose again the next day on the Bournemouth Borough Police Force.'

The separation of Bournemouth from the county had an inevitable effect on the strength of the latter's police force. At the beginning of March 1948 the authorised strength of the Hampshire Constabulary was 1,016, consisting of one chief constable, one assistant chief constable, one chief superintendent, 11 superintendents, seven chief inspectors, 41 inspectors, 119 sergeants and 824 constables; also of one woman police sergeant, and ten women police constables. With effect from 1 April 1948, and on the creation of the Bournemouth Borough Police Force, that total was reduced to 842. There was now an establishment of six chief inspectors, 32 inspectors, 105 sergeants, 676 constables, and nine women police constables, together with the chief constable, the assistant chief constable, 11 superintendents and one woman police sergeant as before. The one chief superintendent's post had gone. Because of this change, five superintendents, three chief inspectors, 23 inspectors, 40 sergeants and ten detective sergeants were confirmed in their respective ranks, which hitherto they had held as temporary.

Detective Sergeant S.J.S. Bowles attained distinction in being selected to attend the first course for sergeants at the new National Police College, Ryton-on-Dunsmore, which began on 15 June and ended on 26 November 1948. Inspector R.E. Coombs, for his part, was selected to attend the first senior officers' course at the police college from 14 September to 26 November. Thereafter year by year picked officers of the Hampshire force attended one or other of the college courses. Indeed, in the years after 1945, Hampshire police officers participated in many different kinds of course, both at county headquarters and elsewhere: driving, first aid, detection, and general refresher courses became regular features, and details concerning attendance at them figure prominently in General Orders. Another change was the resignation of Brigadier F.B. Hurndall, M.C., from his position as county commandant of the special constabulary on 30 September.

In October the chief constable was pleased to bring to the notice of all ranks of the force 'that His Majesty the King has commended Sergeant J.J. McMahon, Isle of Wight Division, for his gallant conduct on March 25th, 1948, in securing and making fast a live sea-mine which was drifting in Whitecliffe Bay, Bembridge'. Another mark of royal appreciation came the following year, with the award of the M.B.E. to Superintendent M.M. McCallum, and the chief constable congratulated the superintendent most warmly on the honour 'which reflects the greatest credit on himself and is also an honour for the force as a whole'. Honour was also done to the memory of those who had fallen in the two world wars by the unveiling of the memorial plaque in the entrance hall at headquarters by Colonel J.D. Mills, Chairman of the police authority, on 23 May

1949. Representatives from each division attended, and relatives of the officers who had been killed were also present.

On 16 June 1949, the Secretary of State authorised an increase of two sergeants and five constables in the strength of the force, bringing the total establishment to 849. In 1952 the strength of the force was to increase still further to 864. The additional numbers were to allow for staff in the wireless control room, for more traffic patrol personnel, and for more men in the Havant area. Because of the pace of development a further 52 officers were authorised in March 1954, giving an establishment of 916. Again, small additions were approved in 1957, 1958 and 1959 bringing the total to 927. In February 1960, Home Office approval was given to a substantial increase to bring the establishment to a total of 1,002. The reason for this was clearly expressed by the present chief constable, Mr Osmond, in his report to the police authority in July 1963 on 'The Establishment and Organisation of the Force'. He stated, 'This increase was designed to cope to some extent with the increased population of the county and also with the reduced working week which had been introduced in 1955. Various other minor amendments were made in 1960 and 1961 to bring the total to 1,012, and in May 1961 the police authority gave careful consideration to the effect on the establishment of the force caused by the marked increase in the population of the force area. At that time the chief constable recommended an increase in the establishment of 208 men but it was felt that at that stage an increase of this size was impractical and for the time being an increase of only sixty-one was recommended to the Home Office. This was approved in June 1961, the new establishment of the force then being 1,073.' In December 1961 application was made for an increase of 15 constables for traffic purposes, and for a few senior ranks in the C.I.D. Again, in 1962, an additional sergeant was approved for crime prevention work, bringing the total of the force to 1,091. It was to argue the case for a further increase that Mr Osmond produced his formidable report in 1963, shortly after he succeeded Mr Lemon as chief constable. We shall return to this report later. It is worth noting at this point, however, that the report emphasised the individual character of Hampshire and the Isle of Wight, with its agriculture, its large residential areas, its seasonal problem in connection with holidaymakers, and above all its serious traffic problem.

The duty of policing such occasions as race-meetings, fairs and displays by one or other of the armed services, was one which never lessened, but indeed rather grew in complexity and weight with the multiplication of traffic and the ever-increasing mobility of the population. In July 1949 a letter from the chief constable of the West Sussex Constabulary thanked Mr Lemon for the services of a party of the Hampshire and Isle of Wight Constabulary at Goodwood Races. 'There was an attendance of about 140,000 and no complaints were received or crime reported. This speaks well for the work of all concerned and I would be pleased if you would convey my appreciation to your contingent.' A year later the Chief Constable of Berkshire expressed his own thanks for the help given at Ascot Races by members of the Hampshire force, and also passed on the Duke of Norfolk's thanks on behalf of the King. Further appreciation came from the Provost Marshal of the Royal Air Force, for the assistance rendered by the constabulary at the recent Farnborough Air Display. 'The success of the display was in no small measure due to the excellence of the traffic arrangements. I was particularly happy to see the close co-operation between my men and yours contributing so largely to the successful policing of the occasion.' The chief constable associated himself with those remarks, and congratulated Superintendent Chown and all police officers concerned for the efficient carrying out of their arduous duties. Again, in November 1951, General Sir Owry Roberts wrote to thank the police for their help to the army in connection with manoeuvres held the previous month. 'Your initial advice was most helpful, and the co-operation of the county police during the exercise itself was a big factor in its success.'

Congratulations on a different theme came in May 1951 from the Director of Public Prosecutions, Sir Theobald Mathew. He wrote to associate himself most warmly with the commendation given by Mr Justice Byrne at the conclusion of a trial arising out of an attempted bank robbery in Waterlooville. Mr Justice Byrne had said, 'I think that Superintendent Lee, Chief Inspector Dawes, Inspector Periman and Detective Sergeant Stevens and all other police officers ... are all worthy of the highest commendation to bring a very dangerous gang of criminals to justice. It was by their able and untiring efforts that this case was brought to light and that this trial took place.' The Director of Public Prosecutions wrote that, 'This success depended upon skilful handling of the enquiries, complete trust and co-operation between the forces concerned and, in the end, physical courage. The best tribute that I can pay is to record that all these requirements were forthcoming as a matter of course and everybody concerned is entitled to be heartily congratulated.' This was an eloquent tribute to a notable success. Praiseworthy achievements in the field of practical police work had never been rare in the history of the Hampshire Constabulary, and in the post-war years that high standard was fully maintained. Officers were commended for their alertness, thoroughness, persistence, and courage in dealing with every sort of crime and incident. In January 1950 Sergeant R.J. Sibley and Police Constable E.G. Clifford were commended for their prompt action in connection with a fire in the night at Lymington, which undoubtedly saved the life of an elderly gentleman. In July the same year at Eastleigh Police Station the chief constable presented Police Constable H.G. Bennett with a Resuscitation Certificate on behalf of the Royal Humane Society, for successfully applying artificial respiration when a man attempted to commit suicide by inhaling the exhaust gas from a motor car, while in November 1949 Police Constable R.B. Walmsley of the Traffic Department in the New Forest Division had been commended by the chief constable for his courage and fortitude after sustaining very serious injuries necessitating the amputation of one leg, and for the calm manner in which he directed operations at the scene of the accident, in which another person had been killed. These are merely random examples of a great mass of incidents in which members of the Hampshire Constabulary displayed high personal qualities and accomplished much good work.

In June 1950 certain changes took place in the composition and the authorised strength of some divisions. Kingsclere and Whitchurch Sections of Winchester Division were transferred to Basingstoke Division, while Alresford Section of Basingstoke Division was transferred to Winchester Division and, with the Winchester Rural Section, formed the Winchester Rural Sub-Division. The respective strengths of the re-arranged Basingstoke and Winchester Divisions were 50 and ninety-five. It is noteworthy that the former division also had the services of two cadet clerks, two civilian female clerks, one full-time cleaner, and three part-time cleaners: the latter division disposed of three cadet clerks, four civilian female clerks, one full-time and three part-time cleaners. The cadets were the successors of the pre-war boy clerks: while the women clerks marked the onset of 'civilianisation'. Another change in August 1951 was the transference of the headquarters of the Sandown Sub-Division of the Isle of Wight Division from Sandown to Shanklin: in future the sub-division was to be known as the Sandown/Shanklin Sub-Division.

King George VI died on 6 February 1952, and the coronation of Her Majesty Queen Elizabeth II took place on 2 June 1953. This glittering ceremony naturally required immense preparation, and involved the Metropolitan Police in a most elaborate work of planning and organisation. As was the case with many other provincial forces, a contingent of the Hampshire Constabulary performed duty in London in support of the Metropolitan Police, and were rewarded with the Coronation Medal. To celebrate the coronation, the Hampshire Constabulary held their Annual Police Sports on 30 May 1953. This sports meeting was held at Fleming Park, Eastleigh, under A.A.A., N.C.U. and W.A.A.A. rules, and was organised by the Hampshire Constabulary Athletic Club. The Honorary Organising Secretary then was Superintendent A.J. Broomfield (later assistant chief constable) and in a brief introduction to the souvenir and programme he succinctly recorded the salient points in the history of the Hampshire Constabulary Athletic Club. 'The Hampshire Constabulary Athletic Club was formed on January 1st 1929, with the object of encouraging all forms of sport, and the club now has active sections for cricket, golf, swimming, bowls, football, shooting and tennis, in addition to athletics. The first Athletic Sports Meeting organised by the club was held at the County Ground, Southampton, on August 8th, 1929. In 1930 Fleming Park, Eastleigh, first became available, and the club's athletic meeting was then held at Fleming Park annually until 1939. The meeting was resumed in 1947 and has since been held annually.' Mr Broomfield went on to express the club's appreciation of public support, without which its athletic meetings could

12   Hampshire and Isle of Wight Constabulary, Winners of P.A.A National Fooball Cup, 1959-
60. Back row: P.C. W. Ward, P.C. K. Warry, P.C. P. Kemp, P.C. M. Gordon, P.C. B. Whittington,
P.C. P. Compton, P.C. B. Ferkins, P.C. G. Theakston, P.C. M. Treleaven; Front row: Det. Insp.
R. Bowles, P.C. F. Loman, P.C. D. Randall, (Capt.), R.D. Lemon Esq. C.B.E, Chief Constable,
P.C. M. Beecham, P.C. T. Cardwell, Ch. Insp. L. Bowen.

not be financially successful, and of the facilities granted by the chief constable
for sporting activities within the club. Finally he thanked the officials of the
A.A.A. and N.C.U. and other helpers, on whose voluntary assistance the success
of the organisation of a sports meeting depended.

The expansion of the sporting activities of the Hampshire Constabulary
during and after the Second World War was certainly very striking. It was largely
the result of Mr Lemon's encouragement and, in some fields, active participation,
but he built upon sound foundations. Cricket had been played since the last
years of the 19th century, and before 1914, when leave was one day a month,
there were occasional cricket outings which were keenly anticipated by those
lucky enough to be able to attend. In 1908 a cricket cup had been presented
to the Petersfield Division by a Mr Goldsmith, to be played for annually by
the police of the division and the local tradespeople. In 1925 the Petersfield
tradesmen themselves presented a second cup, to be played for each year by
the surrounding divisions, and about the same time the Petersfield Chamber
of Commerce presented yet another cup, to be played for annually between
the police and its own members. Again, in 1927, Major Warde, himself a keen
cricketer, presented his cricket challenge cup to be competed for by the various
divisions. This cricket-playing tradition was carried on by Mr Lemon from the
time of his appointment as chief constable in 1942. All divisions of the force
fielded teams, and all entered into the various inter-force competitions; and the

force as a whole came to have an effective team. Mr Lemon himself frequently turned out to play, and was notable for his very accurate underarm bowling. He also introduced a six-a-side tournament and secured professional coaching for members of the team.

As mentioned by Mr Broomfield, a major event had been the formation on 1 January 1929 of the Athletic Club, with the object of encouraging all sports and competitions within the force. The first secretary of the Athletic Club, and the moving spirit in creating it, had been Superintendent Ernest Pragnell, who rejoiced in the appropriate nickname of 'Jumbo'. His jovial and forceful personality and immense enthusiasm had stimulated sport among the divisions, even though, at times, he had laboured with little enough support from his colleagues. Apart from cricket, the club was also concerned with football, swimming and athletics. Mr Pragnell continued to organise all sport almost single-handed in these first ten years. After Mr Lemon became chief constable in 1942, separate secretaries to organise the various sports were appointed. Angling, rifle shooting, bowls, golf and tennis all flourished from the latter years of the war. In 1955 an embryo rugby football section was formed, to take part in a seven-a-side competition in Portsmouth. Quickly the rugger players increased in number, making up in enthusiasm what they lacked at first in skill and knowledge. In 1947 Superintendent Broomfield became athletics secretary, and presided over the revival of the Annual Sports Meeting at Fleming Park. In 1954 he was succeeded by Superintendent Camfield, who held office until 1960. The events staged at the annual meetings were open, and attracted entries from a wide area in the southern counties. Many well-known athletes took part, and proceedings were supervised by A.A.A. officials. Also, certain events organised for schoolchildren received support from schools in all parts of the county. The last open meeting of this kind was held on 18 June 1960. Thereafter financial considerations, arising from a change of policy with regard to the sale of tickets to the public, led to a hiatus of several years. On 6 June 1964, the Hampshire and Isle of Wight Constabulary held its first Force Open Day at Barton Peveril Grammar School, in Eastleigh. This occasion comprehended performances by the London Irish Girl Pipers, a baby show, a water ballet and a display of aqua lung diving, as well as the conventional list of athletic events. The land sports in the afternoon were followed by water sports in the evening. Entry to all events was restricted to members of the force. The whole function was designed to provide a 'get together' for all officers and their families and to be as much a social as a sporting occasion. On 24 July 1965 was held a Families Day and Comrades Reunion, and again this was essentially a domestic gathering, combining sport and entertainments of many kinds. The different title of the meeting from that of the previous year arose from the happy fact that the members of the Comrades Association and their guests had found it possible to combine their 21st annual reunion with the Families Day activities.

13   Original County Headquarters, *c*.1956.

A royal occasion of more direct interest than usual to the police service was the Royal Review of the Police Forces of the United Kingdom by Her Majesty The Queen in 1954. This took place on 14 July, in Hyde Park, and on parade were bodies of police from every force in the country, representatives of the special constabularies maintained by the service departments, the British Transport Commission and certain other authorities, and of the training centres. No fewer than ten thousand were on parade, including regular policemen and policewomen, mounted police, special constables, police cadets, police dogs, and police vehicles. The chief constable, Mr Lemon, led the Hampshire and Isle of Wight contingent, which, together with parties from Reading, Southampton, Surrey, East Sussex and West Sussex, formed one block in the massive gathering. The great parade was undeniably impressive, and its significance was aptly summarised in the foreword to the programme for the occasion: 'Each police force has its distinctive tradition and its local pride. Each relies on the support, and if need be the active assistance, of the members of the community which it serves; and those communities in turn take a proper pride in their police. But though separate, these forces have a unity of purpose which enables them to deal with problems which transcend their boundaries. That unity in diversity is expressed in today's parade.'

Up until 1959 the Hampshire Constabulary had had no properly trained dogs of its own. The needs of the force had been adequately met by borrowing dogs and handlers from neighbouring forces, when the occasion demanded it; this had been so even with cases of escaped prisoners on the Isle of Wight. Now, however, the chief constable decided that the time had come for the Hampshire police to have their own dogs, and enquiries were made with a view to obtaining suitable dogs and handlers, and providing training for both. In July 1958 the chief constable of Surrey, who had had a Dog Section in being for a number of years and was breeding dogs both for his own use and also for sale to other forces, offered to Hampshire two puppies, and arranged for them to be trained with their handlers at the Surrey Dog Training School at Mountbrowne. At a meeting on 6 October 1958, the Hampshire Police Authority approved the purchase of these two puppies, and also determined that, subject to the approval of the Home Office, the establishment of the force should be increased by the addition of one sergeant, to be in charge of the Dog Section. By 1959 both animals had completed their training, and started operational duties. They were stationed at headquarters, which for reasons of administration seemed the most appropriate arrangement. During the year three more dogs were added to the section, and by July 1961 a further three had become operational. Besides headquarters, there were now dogs in the Isle of Wight, New Forest, Aldershot, Petersfield, Basingstoke, and Eastleigh Divisions. By 1962 each division had its own dog unit, which had the use of a small van which was in radio contact with headquarters. The divisional unit was responsible for patrols within the divisional area, and in addition was always available for calls to incidents anywhere in the county. In 1965 a more elaborate patrol system was evolved. The dog sergeant at headquarters controlled the overall allocation of duties, and dogs in adjoining divisions were paired, so that one would be on duty by day, and the other by night, each using the two divisions as one patrol area. Thus four dogs were always available for immediate use. Furthermore it was thought advisable that additional puppies should be bought and reared at headquarters until they were ready to undergo some form of training, so that replacements would always be ready to hand. The dogs have been in increasing use for many different purposes, including escort and security duties, and demonstrating road safety to schoolchildren. In 1961 dogs were called to 254 incidents and 28 arrests were effected with their aid. In 1965 they carried out nearly two thousand patrols, attended 555 incidents, and made 60 arrests; and in addition they were instrumental in recovering some 28 items of property; while during 1966 Hampshire and Isle of Wight police dogs carried out 2,051 patrols, attended 1,034 incidents, effected 96 arrests, recovered 42 items of property, and found 15 missing persons. From 1967 onwards, a compound was to be available at West Hill for all training purposes.

In June 1959 Police Constable D.S. King performed an act of bravery for which he was later awarded the British Empire Medal for Gallantry. The *London Gazette* of 9 October 1959 tells the story: 'A boat with four boys on board capsized about one mile out to sea off Hordle Cliff, Milford-on-Sea. The boys clung to the side of the up-turned boat and two of them, who had life-jackets, decided to swim ashore for help. One managed to reach the shore but the other became exhausted about 250 yards from the beach. Constable King, who had been called to the scene, stripped, swam out to the boy and brought him ashore. He was told of the other two boys clinging to the up-turned boat and, obtaining a lifejacket, immediately swam out to the boat although at the time there was a strong sea running and also a strong tide. He found the two boys clinging to the wreckage, very frightened and cold. King put his life-jacket on one of the boys and dived under the boat and found a tin can with petrol in it. He emptied the can and, after sealing it, he pushed it up the other boy's jersey, thereby giving him buoyancy. Eventually the air sea rescue helicopter arrived and picked up all three from the boat. Constable King displayed courage, presence of mind and calm efficiency in effecting the rescue of the three boys.' For his services at this same incident another constable, I.A. Handley, was awarded the Queen's Commendation for Brave Conduct. A few days later the *Southern Evening Echo* commented that the police officers at the New Milton station possessed a brilliant record of bravery, and one which was probably unique in the country. They were only eight in number, and within less than twelve months two of the officers there had been awarded the B.E.M. for Gallantry, and one had been twice awarded the Queen's Commendation. For in November 1958 Sergeant G.F. Maskew, accompanied by the same Constable Handley, had displayed great courage in arresting an armed man at Everton, near Lymington. Certainly all those officers were highly creditable to the Hampshire Constabulary.

Since 1948 the National Police College had been situated in temporary accommodation at Ryton-on-Dunsmore, near Coventry. As so often happens, the temporary had stretched out into a semblance of permanence. However, in 1960 the College was finally transferred from Ryton to Bramshill House, near Hartley Wintney. This splendid Jacobean mansion had been acquired by the Home Office, and from the beginning of 1954 had been in use as one wing or outpost of the Police College in Warwickshire. Now it took on its intended role as the centre-piece or headquarters of the new college, while alongside it a complex of new buildings was established. Inevitably the contacts between this national police institution and the Hampshire Constabulary multiplied and strengthened. For so long accommodating important military and air establishments at Aldershot and Farnborough, Hampshire was now to be the home of this national centre of the police service as well.

On 27 July 1960, the sixteenth Annual General Meeting of the Hampshire and Isle of Wight Constabulary Comrades' Association was held in the Council

Chamber of the Town Hall at Eastleigh. As President of the Association, the chief constable referred to the recently circulated news letters which had been sent to all pensioner members of the association. Three issues had now been sent out, and he understood these had been greatly appreciated. In his presidential address Mr Lemon gave a resumé of events occurring within the force during the previous year, including incidents wherein several members of the force had gained awards for brave conduct. He remarked that although the existing authorised strength of the force had increased considerably, he felt sure a much greater number would be necessary to match the growing population of the county. He gave details of housing improvements throughout the county, and said that a new police station had recently been built at Andover, and that arrangements were now being made for new stations to be built at Winchester and Totton. He also mentioned that the building of a new county headquarters on the existing site within the next few years was under discussion. Turning to another field, he informed the meeting of various sporting events which had been held, and drew attention to the proud fact that Hampshire had won the P.A.A. Football Cup for the first time ever. All sorts of other details were raised and discussed in the course of this successful meeting of the association which year by year undoubtedly did much to draw together past and present members of the force.

The Hampshire force was involved in December 1960 in the investigation of the notorious murder of Brenda Nash. She was a girl of 12 who on the evening of Friday 28 October had vanished near her home in Heston, Middlesex. Her murdered body was found on Yateley Common in Hampshire on 11 December by some young boys who were playing. Yateley Common was within the bounds of the Aldershot Division, and a team of detective officers under Detective Chief Superintendent W.C. Jones worked on the case in collaboration with officers from New Scotland Yard. At one stage they used Bramshill House as a base for their investigation. Evidence was gathered which seemed to point to the likely suspect, one Arthur Albert Jones, who lived about one mile from the home of the murdered girl. Later Jones was arraigned at the Central Criminal Court in London, was found guilty of murder, and sentenced to life imprisonment.

A spectacular road disaster occurred on 5 September 1961, at Andover. A Ford Thames articulated lorry was being driven west along the A303 road towards Andover, and started to descend Chalk Hill, about one mile east of the town. The gradient of this hill is one in ten, and about an eighth of a mile down, the brakes of the lorry failed. The enormous vehicle, weighing with its load about seventeen tons, gathered speed remorselessly. Subsequently the driver, Mr Charles Edgell, declared that he changed gear twice. 'I heard a rumbling noise. The lorry started to go faster. I put extra pressure on my brake pedal, then it went to the floor. I applied the hand brake and put the "dead man's handle" into operation. It made no difference.' At over sixty miles per hour the great lorry careered into

London Street, a narrow thoroughfare with traffic lights at the end of it. Waiting at these lights were six vehicles, four cars, a lorry, and a tractor and trailer. All these vehicles were travelling in the same direction as the runaway lorry. The lorry smashed into them, completely wrecking three, and severely damaging two others. It also demolished the fronts of five shops before coming to a stop with the front part of the lorry embedded in a safety rail. The road was completely blocked for two hours. The driver of the lorry was trapped in his cab, and had to be freed by the fire service. The firemen also sprayed the area with foam as a large amount of petrol had run out of the wrecked and damaged vehicles. Two ambulances were also on the scene to deal with the many casualties. One of them, Mrs Agnes Jones, who had been riding as a passenger in her husband's car, received fatal injuries. At the subsequent inquest, a Ministry of Transport vehicle inspector indicated a hole in a pipe which was part of the compressed air braking system, and suggested that loss of air pressure had caused the brakes to fail. The only consolation to be found lay in the fact that this appalling accident had happened on the last day of the school holidays; if it had occurred on the following day there would have been several buses full of school children in London Street at that time. As the Winchester City Coroner remarked, 'I am sure you will all agree that it was an absolute miracle that only one person died as a result of this accident.'

On 14 May 1962, Mr Douglas Osmond was appointed chief constable in succession to Mr Lemon, who left to take command of the Kent force. Previously Mr Osmond had been Chief Constable of Shropshire, and he had held that post since 1946. During the war he had served with the police in London, with the Royal Navy, and subsequently in a special police appointment with the Control Commission for Germany. He was destined to be the last Chief Constable of the Hampshire and Isle of Wight Constabulary before its amalgamation with the forces of Portsmouth and Southampton. In his report of 1963 on 'The Establishment and Organisation of the Force' he gave a clear and comprehensive picture of the Hampshire Constabulary both as it was, and as it was to become under his guidance. He made a great many cogent points. In view of the rapid development going on in Hampshire there was an urgent need for the augmentation of the force, in order to deal satisfactorily not only with existing commitments, but with those additional future ones with which the police inevitably would have to cope. Mr Osmond emphasised that already great changes had taken place in the organisation of the police service in the years since the Second World War ended. Only comparatively recently had the police tended to take full advantage of scientific and mechanical aids and the use of civilian personnel. In particular transport and communications had been considerably improved, and there were undoubtedly opportunities for the use of additional civilians. Thus it was essential not to consider the establishment of the force in isolation, but to link it with the full use of these auxiliary resources. Only if such ancillary resources were available could there be maximum economy in the number of trained police officers required, and recommendations made for limiting the number of additional police requested. Again, before further police were asked for, there had to be certainty that every serving police officer was fully and properly employed, and that his job was justified. Since 1948 there had been many additions to the establishment 'but these have mainly been grafted on to the dispositions arrived at in 1948 and no complete review has been embarked upon except in respect of one or two individual areas or functions. There has, in fact, been a tendency to thicken police cover in certain areas without ensuring that a thinning out has taken place where it would be possible.' Such a complete review the chief constable had now embarked upon, and from it he concluded that, while considerable increases were still required, economies also had been effected wherever possible.

The total strength of the force in 1963 was 1,091, consisting of one chief constable, one assistant chief constable, four chief superintendents, seven superintendents, 15 chief inspectors, 48 inspectors, 126 sergeants and 857 constables; and also of one woman police inspector, three women police sergeants and 28 women constables. In addition there was one chief inspector surplus to establishment for traffic duties in order to relieve the traffic superintendent for part-time Civil Defence duties. In making his case for a substantial increase of strength the chief constable conceded that the police authority would wish to have regard to the standards of policing elsewhere in the country, but emphasised that no two police areas were exactly alike. 'Each force has its own local problems, and the establishment for that force must be designed to cope with these problems and not with the problems existing elsewhere.' Comparisons of police areas should take account of the nature of the police commitment therein, rather than merely of respective sizes. From a comparison with other forces in the south of England, faced with roughly similar problems, it emerged that the ratio of police to population in Hampshire and the Isle of Wight was lower than in Kent, Surrey, Dorset, Devon, East or West Sussex. With a population of 894,828, there were in Hampshire 820 persons for each police officer, while in the other counties mentioned the population per policeman was always less than seven hundred and sometimes less than six hundred. These figures were not quoted in order to arrive at a 'target' establishment for Hampshire, but only to emphasise the urgent need for a sizeable increase in strength to bring standards of police cover into line with those of Hampshire's neighbours. The chief constable was to enter into an impressively detailed appraisal of the requirements of each division, but beforehand he felt it necessary to set out some of the general principles he had borne in mind in fixing the new divisional establishments. During the post-war era many factors affected police work, and added to its weight and complexity. The population of the county had increased by one-third since 1948, but the work created for the police in consequence was far greater than might have been expected. The figure of reported crime in 1963 was more than 62 per cent above that of 1955, and that spectacular increase had itself come in the wake of the post-war 'crime wave' of the late forties. Again, since 1948 the number of motor vehicles registered in Hampshire had more than trebled, and the number of road accidents and minor offences had almost doubled. Another consideration was the vast amount of visiting and through traffic, especially in the summer months. There were other ways too in which the drain in police manpower had failed to keep pace with increased commitments. There had been a great deal of new legislation, all necessitating more time to be spent on training. The inadequacy of the roads to cope with the additional traffic had resulted in police officers being required to do traffic duty to a far greater extent than the mere increase in vehicles indicated. Mr Osmond made the crucial point: 'It is not enough to provide sufficient police merely to cope with the increased work in connection with crime and traffic, for this would imply a negative attitude and an acceptance of conditions which are an affront to our society. The police service is a preventive service and the statistics quoted, deplorable as they are, must represent a challenge to any police officer worthy of his profession.'

The chief constable also urged that at least one full-time officer in each division was essential to co-ordinate all crime prevention activities. Most investigation of crime, of course, was carried out by C.I.D. officers, and in assessing the number of these to be made available, regard had to be paid to the case load of each individual officer. This burden could be eased, firstly, by having officers carry out their detective training before they were actually posted to the C.I.D.; by setting up at headquarters a small squad of operational detectives to undertake protracted enquiries all over the county; by uniformed officers, especially these on detached beats, taking over the investigation of minor crimes, and by increasing the establishment of important auxiliaries in criminal investigation, such as photographers, dog-handlers, and scenes-of-crimes officers. Hitherto all these specialists had been found from the existing strength, thereby reducing the number of men available for ordinary duties. A full-time photographer was now to be available in each division, with the rank of detective constable. Thirty-five scenes-of-crime officers, possessed of specialist training in forensic science, had previously been available part-time, but now there was to be a nucleus of full-time officers qualified in this way, which would be supplemented by part-time officers withdrawn from beats as and when necessary. The former would be classified as detective-officers.

Turning to traffic and road safety, Mr Osmond expressed the view that 'the vast increase in traffic density and in road accidents is such that it requires the same preventive attitude as that advocated by Fielding towards the prevention of crime in his day.' It was desirable to have traffic police so disposed that their mere presence was an effective deterrent to the potential offender against the traffic laws. Main roads had to be sufficiently policed so that every motorist felt that his driving was at all times under police scrutiny, 'that there is the likelihood of a police officer around the next bend'. With considerations of expense fully in mind, it seemed that an increased number of motor-cyclists was the answer. Traffic conditions were such that the police car, with its crew of two, was not only wasteful in its preventive effect, but lacked sufficient manoeuvrability to cope with traffic congestion. The motor-cycle, with its one police officer, was far more flexible in use and its deterrent effect as great. Motor-cyclists would therefore be deployed throughout the county on a local basis, although attached to the Traffic Division. Each motor-cycle officer would be wholly responsible for dealing with all traffic problems on the length of road allocated to him, and it was confidently anticipated that this responsibility and opportunity to display initiative would engender a real sense of pride. Inadequate parking facilities in towns added to the problem of traffic congestion, and occupied precious police time and effort. Thus in suitable places it was proposed to enrol a small number of traffic wardens to supervise street parking places. With the assistance of such officials it would be unnecessary in a number of places to ask for additional police as foot patrols for traffic purposes. In matters of regulating traffic, as in so many other police activities, closer contact with the public was the key to success. Already the Road Safety Committees were assisted in many ways by the police, who had a very full part to play in the traffic education of the public. Recently the education authorities in Hampshire had agreed to police officers giving road safety instruction in schools, and over 200 police officers had been trained for this work. However, this too made demands on police resources, and had to be remembered in assessing future needs.

The chief constable emphasised in his report that, notwithstanding all the progress that had been made in capitalising the intelligence and initiative of the individual officer, sufficient police on the ground remained essential to achieve a preventive effect. 'Every malefactor, in whatever field, must be made apprehensive of the probability of being discovered by a police officer.' Unfortunately, since the war police strength had been diminished by, among other things, the progressive reduction of working hours. In 1948 a sergeant or constable worked a six-day week. At the end of 1955 this was reduced to 11 days in two weeks. In addition, the amount of annual leave had risen from 12 to 17 days, together with the equivalent of six days' 'bank holiday' leave a year. Also, in each eight-hour period of continuous duty there was a three-quarter-hour break for refreshment. All these desirable men were required merely to maintain in 1963 the same intensity of patrolling as had been the case in 1948, even had there been no increase in police commitments. The point was also made that, because a beat had to be covered for 24 hours a day in three shifts of eight hours, it could not therefore be assumed that three men were all that was necessary for the task. Such an assumption took no account of absence through sickness, attendance at court, provision of escorts for prisoners, special duty at such functions as football matches, and numerous other commitments all of which entailed withdrawal of officers from beat work. Above all, the need for constant training was an increasing drain on manpower. The case for adequate reserves was overwhelming. Another factor which caused concern to the chief constable was the pressure of routine paper work on sergeants, which prevented them giving to their subordinates an adequate measure of supervision, encouragement, instruction and leadership. There was an imperative need for more sergeants. Thus provision was made for a station duty sergeant to be available on each relief in busy stations, so that other sergeants would be the better able to concentrate on more active supervision in their sections. While some police stations were excessively busy, others were not, and there was not the same necessity to keep them open for prolonged periods. In some cases the time had come for a ruthless cutting down of office hours.

With regard to the basic organisation of the force it was decided to create a new division in the Havant area, to be known as the Havant Division. Already the new police station at Havant had been designed to accommodate the divisional headquarters. The new division was formed out of part of the old Fareham Division together with a fraction of the south of the Petersfield Division, where the interests of the population inclined towards Havant and Portsmouth. The old Fareham Division had had a population of nearly a quarter of a million, and had been unwieldy in extent and configuration. The new arrangement would better correspond to existing realities. A number of minor changes in beat boundaries throughout the county were found to be necessary. Detached beat areas had been based on centuries-old parish boundaries which bore little relation to the roads and population centres of the 20th century. 'A slavish adherence to this system has resulted in cases of extraordinary over-policing as well as under-policing.' It was in the areas of rapid expansion of population that there was the greatest need for additional manpower, as it was on the housing estates that the main complaints arose of hooliganism and wilful damage by young people. For some such areas the answer lay in 'neighbourhood policing', whereby a constable was given full-time responsibility for a particular neighbourhood in the same way as a constable on a detached beat. In 1963 there were only a few places which lent themselves to such an arrangement, but the scheme had the advantage of being capable of wider adoption as new towns were developed. Little change was made in the conventional 'town beats' system, but a great deal of careful thought was given to the 'detached' beats situated in country areas and policed by a resident officer with full-time responsibility. The size of these beats and the responsibility entailed had been found to vary enormously: at one extreme one constable might be struggling with the work produced by a population of several thousand, while at the other no fewer than four constables might be policing a few hundred people. Thus recommendations with regard to the appropriate manpower were made on a basis of the real amount of work existing on each beat.

An important change in organisation already realised in 1963 was the centralisation of all emergency calls so that all of them were received in the information room at headquarters. This worked very well, but inevitably imposed a great burden on the information room staff who had to handle as many as 15,000 messages that year. The Traffic Division continued to be mainly responsible for dealing with emergency calls, but to supplement its resources each division maintained one of the divisional cars equipped with radio on constant patrol. This development too required increased manpower and more vehicles. In each divisional station a radio sub-control was instituted which enabled the divisional headquarters to communicate directly with its own vehicles, including the vehicle being used for emergency purposes. Thus pressure on the information room was relieved.

The chief constable's report also stressed the overriding importance of training, and the serious inroads it made on the availability of manpower. A more intensive scheme for the training of probationers had already been introduced, which meant that well-nigh the whole two-year period of probation was used for purposes of instruction. This in turn meant that until he had about fifteen or sixteen months' service, the young constable could only be regarded as non-operational. Thus the demands made on the training staff at headquarters were heavy, as in addition they were responsible for running refresher courses for sergeants, for training in diseases of animals work, for civil defence training, and for sundry other tasks, including the supervision and instruction of nearly sixty cadets. This last work was held to justify the employment of a full-time officer for the purpose, and provision was later made for this. A heavy additional burden on the training staff were the correspondence courses of instruction which had been started to help men study for their examinations. In 1963 no fewer than 160 officers were taking these courses. All this training activity led the chief constable to stress that there had to be both adequate training staff at headquarters and also sufficient sergeants in divisions to enable part-time divisional training officers to be effective. He proposed that provision should be made in the establishment for a 'training nucleus' of 20 constables, which would function as a small reserve of manpower for deployment as occasion arose. Summing up, Mr Osmond stated that his requirements for the future establishment of the force amounted to an increase of 303 police and 55 civilians.* Savings in existing manpower had been achieved by the abolition of unjustifiable beats and the reduction of numbers of some detached beats and sections; by the use of civilians, such as traffic wardens, in place of police; and by the use wherever possible of improved transport and communications. The proposed establishment would provide a ratio of police to resident population that compared favourably with that projected for the counties of Kent, Surrey

*Summary of Proposals (see overleaf)

Summary of Proposals

EXISTING ESTABLISHMENT

	C.C	A.C.C	Ch. Supr.	Supt. I	Supt. II	Ch. Insp.	Insp.	Sgt.	P.C.	W.P. Insp.	W.P. Sgt.	W.P.C	TOTAL	Civilians
"A" (ALDERSHOT)	-	-	1	-	-	1	7	15	101	-	1	3	129	14
"B" (BASINSTOKE)	-	-	-	-	1	-	2	8	51	-	-	2	64	5
"C" (EASTLEIGH)	-	-	-	1	-	1	6	12	90	-	-	3	113	12
"D" (FAREHAM)	-	-	1	-	-	5	11	21	163	-	1	6	208	20
"E" (ISLE OF WIGHT)	-	-	1	-	-	1	5	12	99	-	-	3	121	5
"F" (NEW FOREST)	-	-	-	1	-	2	6	11	98	-	-	3	121	15
"G" (PETERSFIELD)	-	-	-	-	1	-	2	10	61	-	-	4	78	7
"H" (WINCHESTER)	-	-	-	1	-	2	5	13	87	-	1	4	113	16
"K" (HAVANT)	-	-	-	-	-	-	-	-	-	-	-	-		-
"J" (TRAFFIC)	-	-	-	1	-	(1)	4	9	93	-	-	-	107	8
HEADQUARTERS	1	1	1	1	-	3	-	15	14	1	-	-	37	24
TOTAL	1	1	4	5	2	15 (1)	48	126	857	1	3	28	1091	126

*1 Ch. Insp. (1) surplus to establishment

PROPOSED ESTABLISHMENT

	C.C	A.C.C	Ch. Supr.	Supt. I	Supt. II	Ch. Insp.	Insp.	Sgt.	P.C.	W.P. Insp.	W.P. Sgt.	W.P.C	TOTAL	Civilians
"A" (ALDERSHOT)	-	-	1	-	-	1	8	23	109	-	1	5	148	18
"B" (BASINSTOKE)	-	-	-	-	1	-	2	11	65	-	-	2	81	10
"C" (EASTLEIGH)	-	-	-	1	-	1	6	17	120	-	-	5	150	15
"D" (FAREHAM)	-	-	1	-	-	4	8	23	132	-	1	6	175	18
"E" (ISLE OF WIGHT)	-	-	1	-	-	1	5	15	115	-	-	3	140	7
"F" (NEW FOREST)	-	-	1	-	-	5	3	19	135	-	-	4	167	19
"G" (PETERSFIELD)	-	-	-	1	-	1	2	11	69	-	-	3	87	9
"H" (WINCHESTER)	-	-	-	1	-	2	5	19	102	-	1	4	134	19
"K" (HAVANT)	-	-	-	1	-	1	5	13	101	-	-	4	125	11
"J" (TRAFFIC)	-	-	-	1	-	1	3	12	120	-	-	-	137	22
HEADQUARTERS	1	2	1	1	-	5 (1)	1	10	28	1	-	-	50	33
TOTAL	1	2	5	6	1	22 (1)	48	173	1096	1	3	36	1394	181

†1 Ch. Insp. (1) surplus to establishment

and Devon. In lengthy and graphic appendices to his report the chief constable entered into extremely detailed description of and justification for all changes in organisation and manpower. Each of the nine territorial divisions (including the new Havant one) was surveyed in turn, as well as Headquarters and the Traffic Division. Local factors and considerations of every relevant sort were set out impressively. Full account was taken of the individual character of the population in some areas, and of the peculiar traffic problems of another. Reading through the whole report, one is presented with a vivid and fascinating picture of a section of modern England seen from the viewpoint not of the geographer, the economist, the sociologist, or the politician, but of the enforcer of the law; and yet, just because the law today is so all-embracing, and touches the lives of all at innumerable points, the police perspective comprehends some elements of all these other interpretations. More and more in modern society, the police function emerges as the indispensable keystone of the whole community. Politics, industry, communications, health, welfare services, education, recreation – all these and innumerable other spheres connect and are inter-related. Twentieth-century mass society is more complicated, more mobile, more subtle, more brittle and, perhaps, more vulnerable than ever before. The police today are not only the maintainers of the Queen's peace; they are a vital cohesive force throughout the nation. Thus a survey of an English county for police purposes is no bad introduction to the nature of society in that county as a whole.

The chief constable did not imagine that the many changes in organisation and the increase in manpower that he recommended could be implemented immediately, nor indeed that such a numerical increase could be absorbed immediately into the force, even if men of the requisite standard should be available. It was highly undesirable to rush recruitment. 'I do not merely need more men, I need the best men, and I do not propose to recruit any personnel who are unlikely to conform to the highest standards of police conduct and efficiency.' But it was essential to make a start, and he looked to the full realisation of all the proposals made over a period of three years. He was ever mindful of an extract from the report of a recent royal commission on the police which he had taken as a text: 'Our conclusion is that police duties and responsibilities, although essentially unchanged, have unquestionably increased in their range and variety during the past two decades and that they are now exercised in increasingly difficult circumstances.' Mr Osmond concluded the general section of his report with the comment that 'many of the men at present in the force are working long hours and shouldering unfair responsibilities without complaint, and it says much for the traditions of the force that in spite of the clear shortage of manpower the situation regarding crime and disorder has not become completely out of hand.' The Hampshire and Isle of Wight Constabulary was one of the most important of the provincial police forces. It was not sufficient for it to lag behind other forces and improve its organisation tardily and reluctantly. Very rapidly a great deal of the increase and reorganisation was realised, and by the end of 1964 the total strength of the force had risen to 1,386.

On 1 June 1966 the new headquarters building of the Hampshire and Isle of Wight Constabulary was officially opened by Her Royal Highness The Princess Margaret, Countess of Snowdon. Plans for this magnificent construction had been laid several years earlier, but only in 1961 did they receive the approval of both the County Council and Winchester City Council. Now the buildings have at last replaced the old headquarters at West Hill. The latter had been erected in 1847 at a cost of £10,000, and the prison which was built two years later had cost £74,000, although certainly £12,000 had been realised from the sale of the old gaols. To pay for these buildings the magistrates of that time had borrowed the considerable sum of £140,000 and, after constructing the police headquarters and the prison, the balance went on building what was then the county lunatic asylum near Fareham. Amidst this rash of construction, then, was created the parent building, as it were, of the Hampshire Constabulary. Any organisation is to some extent dependent on, and affected by, the accommodation in which it is housed. The many-sided character of the Hampshire and Isle of Wight force is reflected in the diverse origins of police buildings in different parts of the county.

One of the most important places in Hampshire, with a special character deriving from its long military connections, is Aldershot. Before the army camp came to Aldershot in 1854, the total population of the place was only 875. With the coming of the soldiers, the population increased rapidly. By 1861 it was upwards of 20,000 and by 1891 had reached the figure of 25,595. It seems clear that in the very early days there was no police station, and in fact at that time the divisional headquarters were at Odiham, where the superintendent was then stationed. In 1866 a detachment of the Metropolitan Police came to Aldershot, under an Act of Parliament authorising the policing of such places as docks and garrison towns. In the next few years the existing police station was built. From the terms of the lease, dated 30 December 1867, it would appear that the station was to have been built between 29 September 1867 and 29 September 1868: but according to Lieutenant-Colonel H.N. Cole, O.B.E., T.D., in his book *The Story of Aldershot*, some latitude must have been given, as he states the police station was in fact built in 1869. Before this Colonel Cole states that 'A map of 1856 indicates a large police station at the south-east corner of the south cavalry barracks above the Rifleman public house, but the site of this police station was changed to a position on the west of the Farnborough Road, below the Royal Pavilion.' Later he says, 'On Greenhams Hill, facing the Farnborough Road, between Pavilion Road and Chetwode Terrace, stands a large building marked as Locke's Hospital. It was originally a police station, and was used as such until 1861.' In another context he says, 'The original lay-out of the camp included a police station, which was built on the west of the Farnborough Road, just below the Royal Pavilion. It was here that the first petty sessions were held on alternate Mondays. When the present-day police station court house and police quarters were built in 1869, the old police station was converted in 1861 into a lock hospital, but later became a military storehouse. The bench of magistrates who sat at the Aldershot Petty Sessions first sat at the original police station, and afterwards in the long meeting room of the Royal Hotel, until the opening of the present court house.' All these references, together with the plan of Aldershot in *A Guide to Aldershot* printed and published in 1859 by W. Sheldrake, make the site of the original police station pretty clear. Since this police station, off the Farnborough Road, appears to have been associated with the functions of the petty sessional court, it would seem to have been a civil, as opposed to military, establishment. It may well be, too, that the police who occupied that building had formerly occupied the earlier police station off Alexandra Road, at the south-east corner of the south cavalry barracks, and that this also had been a civil police station, the first one to appear in Aldershot.

According to a map of the High Street area of Aldershot, surveyed in 1871, and held in the borough surveyor's office at Aldershot, the county police station then comprised a smaller and more symmetrical building than the straggling confusion of rooms that exist today. It can be seen that the original police station was an inspector's station, there being no provision for a more senior officer. The court house was much smaller and more centrally placed than the two court rooms existing today. It is interesting to note that the structure of the present telephone room has some resemblance to a court room, and was undoubtedly the forward end of the original court room. Similarly, the original cell block can be traced; in fact, the brickwork shows traces of at least three major additions to the original building.

Odiham had been the divisional headquarters in those early days, and the police station there is considered to have been built at some time in the 17th century or possibly a little later. Before it became a police station, it was a house of correction. Vancouver's *Survey of Hampshire* states that in 1810 Odiham was the second most important town in the north of Hampshire, as regards rateable value and population. In the 17th century, there was but one house of correction for the punishment of vagrants in the county, and this was situated at Winchester. In the early 18th century there was so great an increase of vagrants in Hampshire that a second house of correction had to be established, and this was set up in Odiham. In 1746, a third house of correction was established at Gosport. Thus it would seem that Odiham Police Station was functioning as a house of correction between 1700 and 1746, but whether it was built as such then, or for some other purpose earlier, is uncertain. However, its high-walled sunken yard, and the planning of the cell block, suggest that it was at least structurally adapted as a house of correction. In the cell passage there is a bricked-up doorway which at one time led out to the north-east corner of the

14   New Headquarters, Winchester – front view – opened by H.R.H. Princess Margaret, Countess of Snowdon, on 1 June 1966.

building, where stocks and a whipping-post then stood, and remained indeed until about 1900. They have since been removed to the Bury, and roofed over for preservation and protection against the weather. Various initials and markings are scratched on the brickwork around the bricked-up doorway, including, for what it is worth, the date 1789.

When the Hampshire force was instituted, Odiham was not only the divisional station, but the only police station in the Odiham Division. This division followed the boundaries of the Odiham Petty Sessional Division, which still exists. According to William White's *History, Gazetteer and Directory of Hampshire*, a Superintendent John Callingham was resident at Odiham Police Station in 1859. He was then in charge of Odiham Police Station, and had 14 constables under his command. It is not clear when the superintendent's command was transferred from Odiham to Aldershot, but the first one to be posted to the latter place was Superintendent Stephenson. Prior to 1890, the Odiham magistrates sat in a room at the *George Hotel*, an old coaching house situated on the High Street. About 1890 the court room which is in present use was built at Odiham Police Station. The sub-divisional police stations at Farnborough and Fleet have no particular historical interest or value. On 30 May 1896, *The Aldershot News* proclaimed, 'At last, the long-denied police station has been completed. The county surveyor and architect paid a final visit to the building on Wednesday 27 May 1896, and it will probably be occupied today by the county police force. It is a neat well-proportioned building and, as a member of the force has remarked, "the prettiest little police station in the County of Southampton". Attention has been paid to convenience in designing the building, which will doubtless meet the requirements of the force for many years to come.' As for Fleet Police Station, it was first built in 1935, and in 1954 extended to its present size. The section police station at Hartley Wintney was built a few years before the First World War.

The police station at Petersfield stands in St Peter's Road and is constructed of flint and brick. It was built some time in the 1850s and is apparently the only station to have existed in the town. There is a tablet on the front wall bearing the date 1858, but on the other hand William White's *History, Gazetteer and Directory of Hampshire*, published in 1859, states that it was erected 'some years ago'. St Peter's Road was then known as New-Way and formed the drive to the mansion which Mr William Jolliffe (later Sir William) had built in 1700. This mansion had been demolished in 1760 and the police station itself stands on the site of the garden. The original cost of the police station was £1,500 and it contained accommodation for a superintendent and two constables and three cells for the temporary housing of prisoners. At the rear of the station was another flint and brick building which comprised two stables, housing for a cart, a harness room and a hay loft. Behind this again was a garden, but some years later the court house was erected there, and the only visible relic of the garden is one plum tree in the south-west corner of the site. In the 20th century the stables building was converted into two garages. In 1937 the superintendent removed himself from the station and moved to a large house in Hylton Road, and his erstwhile rooms in the station were converted into offices and stores, as were the constables' quarters. In 1956 the house in Hylton Road was vacated and sold by the police authority, and is now scheduled as an ancient building. The divisional superintendent now lives in a modern house on the north-western side of the town. In 1961 the interior of the station, except for the three cells, was completely altered and renovated, and further offices were added. Whilst this work was being carried out the station was evacuated and a new temporary one set up in a disused school in the High Street. Prior to the erection of the police station parish records refer to a market house which included a court house with some sort of cell accommodation below, which was referred to as the 'Black Hole'. This building, which was sometimes known as the town hall, stood in front of the church in the square. It had been erected in 1824 by a Colonel Jolliffe, and was demolished in 1898.

The present police station in Alton is slightly older than that at Petersfield, but was originally of a similar pattern. It was built in 1845 at a cost of £1,400, and contained a house for a superintendent, accommodation for a sergeant or single constables, and three cells for the temporary confinement of prisoners. The outbuildings consisted of stabling for two horses, a carthorse, and a harness room. Since then, of course, the station has been enlarged and improved, and in particular more modern cells have been constructed; the original ones still exist, but are no longer used. At the time of the building of the present station the petty sessions for the division were held at the *Swan Hotel* on alternate Tuesdays. Subsequently a court house was erected at the rear of the police station. It is interesting to note that long before the establishment of the Hampshire Constabulary, Alton possessed some sort of police or prison structure. An old map of Alton, dated 1666, shows the 'Caige' as standing on the north-eastern side of Normandy Hill, approximately on the site of the present assembly rooms. This 'lock-up' was in use as late as the beginning of the 19th century, and is described as a sort of shed with an old door and a window with no glass, but a wooden shutter. According to *The Town of Alton* by William Curtis, a first police station in Alton was situated at the foot of Normandy Hill, now known as Crown Hill. For many years past these premises have been used as a butcher's shop, but at the rear two cells can still be seen. For a reason unknown the police station was moved from the Normandy Hill site to a house next door to the *Red Lion Inn* in Normandy Street. Many years after this building ceased to be a police station it was a second-hand shop, and the daughter of the then proprietor remembers a room at the rear of the premises with an iron grille in it.

The first police station at Whitehill was erected in 1904, following the building of Bordon Camp, and the single-storey iron structure was in fact very similar in appearance to old army buildings which can still be seen there. The station contained an office for a sergeant, accommodation for four single constables, and four cells. For some years after its erection, a military railway ran within a few yards of it. The present police station was built in 1931 at the rear of its predecessor, and at the same time a row of three houses was constructed between the station and the Fareham-Petersfield Road. Also on the southern side of the station was built a modern court house. In 1953 five standard police houses were built on the southern side of the police station. The latter is a single-storey brick building, and originally contained an office for the sergeant, a larger office, a small room and four cells, two of which could hold up to twelve prisoners each. More recently the station has been modified and it now contains an enquiry office, three small offices, one of them for C.I.D. use, and an office for the section sergeant converted from one of the large cells.

Eastleigh Division is adjacent to Southampton Borough, and the history of police buildings in the division has been greatly affected by this fact. When the Hampshire Constabulary was formed, Eastleigh itself formed part of Woolston Division, and was very small. In 1881 the population was only about 1,000, and it can be safely assumed that there would have been but one or two police officers supervising this area. In 1890, however, the premises at 144 Southampton Road became a police station, and living quarters for married men were established in adjacent terraced houses. In 1920 the Woolston Division passed into the hands of the Southampton Borough Police, and thus there was no longer a Woolston Division of the Hampshire Constabulary. Eastleigh Sub-Division was transformed into a division, and 144 Southampton Road became the superintendent's office. The accommodation there consisted of one office with only one telephone, but three cells. In the administration of the divisional headquarters the superintendent was assisted by one clerk sergeant. The only lighting of the station was in the form of gas lamps, and these only on the ground floor. The year 1924, however, saw a big change in the Eastleigh Divisional Headquarters. Eastleigh had been elevated to being the head of a newly-formed police division of the county, and the house and grounds of Little Eastleigh, a 17th-century farm, had been acquired for the purposes of a police establishment and headquarters. The derelict farm yard, outbuildings and cottages gave place to the present block of buildings, and the old house itself became the residence of the divisional superintendent. In addition, ten other police houses were erected on the land which had belonged to the old farm. Provision was also made at that time for a court house to be built behind the police station, but these plans were never realised. The old station at 144 Southampton Road, together with the adjoining houses, continued to be used as police married quarters until 1959 when the property was sold. The site is now occupied by a bus station of the Hants and Dorset Company. During the Second World War, one member of the public, at least, found it hard to adjust to these changes. In 1943 Sergeant Maund, who was then living in what had formerly been the police station, was taking a bath in a converted cell, when he was confronted by a gentleman coming to report that his bicycle had been stolen. The fact that the police station had moved itself to Leigh Road 19 years earlier had escaped his attention. Perhaps, though, the stranger had some excuse, for an old police sign still adhered to the front of the building. Sergeant Maund understandably made haste to remove this, and brought it with him when he reported for duty later that day.

It was only in 1920, with the extension of the Southampton Borough Area to include Bitterne, South Stoneham, Sholing and Woolston, that Netley became a sergeant section station of the Eastleigh Division. In 1934 the county police station was built in New Road, Netley Abbey close to the house which had previously served the village as a station. The present building contains an enquiry office, charge room, and an office for the sergeant, whilst two constables live on the premises. There are no cells. In the early days before the absorption of Woolston by Southampton, Woolston had been a sergeant section and had covered the Netley area as far as Hamble. The original county police station was a house at 23 Woodley Road, Woolston. The sergeant in charge lived next door to the station at Number 21.

So far as Totton is concerned, a map dated 1878 shows a building named 'Amoena Villa' with the words 'Police Station' underneath in brackets. It would appear that the building was acquired from private owners, and not designed as a police station from the outset. The cell block was added at a later date. In 1962 a new police station and magistrates' court was constructed in Testwood Lane, Totton.

The present New Forest Division contains every variety of police building from the oldest to the most modern. Similarly, the character of the division comprises the extremes of rural peace and urban concentration, both of which merge into each other increasingly as the volume of traffic increases relentlessly. It would be fair to say that in periods of good weather the roads in the New Forest carry as much traffic as the rest of the divisions together. Christchurch today is overwhelmed by the great sprawl of Bournemouth, but at one time was the police headquarters for the area. The original police station there was a double-fronted house in Bargates with a thatched roof. In 1881, when the present station was erected, the old one was converted into a club; at the same time, it is said, a certain Sergeant Mathews retired on pension, and preserved his association with the old building by continuing to function there as the club's steward. When the new police station was erected it was staffed by one sergeant and five constables. It has naturally been modified in structure from time to time, but today might be considered scarcely to meet the requirements of the staff.

The police station at Fordingbridge stands in Station Road, and was erected in 1857. Over the years there have been changes in internal arrangements, but at present the building contains two offices and two cells, with accommodation for 12 prisoners. At one time Fordingbridge had its own court and its own petty sessional area, but since 1955 the accused have to appear at Ringwood. Fordingbridge today is a quiet town disturbed only by the weight of traffic passing between Bournemouth and Salisbury. A busy occasion is St Mary's Fair, which by ancient charter is held on the two weekdays nearest to St Mary's Day in September. The fair is now in the main a decorous gathering, but in years gone by it was a favourite gathering place of gypsies, with a consequent outburst of fighting, drunkenness and general uproar. Nor is Fordingbridge without other more lurid memories of the distant past. Long before the Hampshire Constabulary existed, an interesting reference to the old constable of Fordingbridge appears in the record of a notorious murder at the *Three Lyons* in the High Street. In November 1684 a wealthy traveller who had put up at the inn for the night was murdered and robbed. The constable, a magistrate and a doctor were called to the dying victim, and a 'dying declaration' was taken down, but the name of the attacker was never mentioned. The constable made enquiries and arrested the ostler at the inn, who was sentenced to death at Winchester Assizes. However, subsequent enquiries made by a government secret agent from London, Mr John Pearce, proved that the murder had in fact been committed by the landlord of the *Three Lyons*. Fortunately, the ostler had not yet been executed and the landlord in due course was himself hanged at Winchester.

The Hampshire police authority assumed responsibility for Lymington in 1853 before which the borough had been policed only by a town sergeant and possibly one constable. The office of town sergeant still exists, his duties being the control of the market stalls in the high street, and to act as superintendent of the town hall and mace bearer to the mayor. The first police station occupied in 1853 was at Buckland 'in a copse at the side of the toll house and adjacent to the Crown Inn': a convenient site, as at that time the police were also responsible for collecting tolls. In 1866 this building was considered inadequate, and the Queen Anne house in Gosport Street was purchased from the Townley family, and remained in use as the police station until 1952, when the present modern station was erected. The Queen Anne house is classified as an ancient monument, and is of great local historical interest. It has recently been converted into a restaurant. Hythe has probably undergone more change than any other part of the Hampshire police area. From a tiny watering place on the edge of Southampton Water it has become in modern times the site of an immensely large oil refinery. In consequence of all this it has become an inspector's station. The original police station (and court house) were made out of two cottages, and thus accommodation was limited. Recently, however, further alterations have been carried out and the house formerly occupied by the inspector has been converted into additional offices and a second court.

Geographically and administratively Lyndhurst is the capital of the New Forest, and the present police station was built in 1857. Before that date, the previous building had stood in a road called The Custards, which still exists. This curious name is said to be derived from 'House of Custody' which was the phrase applied by the local inhabitants to the old police station. Until just after the Second World War the police court at Lyndhurst was established in the Queen's House, a building of historic interest. Its use as a police court ceased abruptly one winter's morning when the then presiding magistrate complained vehemently of the cold. So the entire court moved to the parish hall, and the Queens House was never again used for its old purpose. However, it does still function as a sort of court in that the New Forest Verderers, who control the rights of the commoners of the New Forest, still sit there occasionally.

One of the most interesting police buildings in Hampshire was the old police station at Basingstoke, which in recent years had been used as an ordinary dwelling house. It was situated in New Street, Basingstoke, and formerly the front of the building was covered by a thick growth of ivy. When this was removed a plaque was revealed which indicates that the building was erected by the corporation in 1816. It was then used in connection with the town jail, for the minutes of the Basingstoke Borough Council of 1836 approve of the appointment of the constable as keeper of the jail, and also that the keeper's house be made into a police station. The building remained in use as a police station until 1889 when the borough force was transferred to the Hampshire Constabulary. On entering the front door one found oneself in a long passage which led to the rear of the building. Immediately above one's head, however, was a cell, access to which was presumably gained by means of a ladder. The cell was constructed of heavy timber and it abutted into an upstairs bedroom. Further down the passageway was another doorway, which led into what appears to have been a kitchen. The door here was very old and solid and had been repaired from time to time with odd pieces of timber. Past this doorway one turned right into a small courtyard off which were two cells; they, too, were of wooden construction. Photographs show the bunk or bed which ran the full width of the cell, and was an unusual height from the ground. The cell appears to have been warmed by central heating, although it cannot be said at what date this was installed. This old building was demolished in 1964, and has been replaced by a block of shops. The plaque was removed from the front wall of the old building, and is to be incorporated in the new block.

The police centre of the Isle of Wight has always been at the capital, Newport, whether the island force was part of the Hampshire Constabulary, or on its own. In May 1838 the Police Committee decided that the then Watch House was to be converted into a lock-up room for men, and a butcher's shop opposite into a lock-up room for women; also that the present town clerk's office was to be the room for the inspector of police. The first mention of a police station for the Hampshire Constabulary is found in a post office directory of 1852, which states that a building in Holyrood Street, Newport, had been converted from its previous use as a gaol into a station for the county police. In the same directory mention is made of the Newport Borough Police Station, which was also situated in Holyrood Street, and no doubt this too was a building with a past, having been a bridewell before it was acquired in 1848 for police purposes. In 1869 a house in Quay Street was bought for use as a borough police station, and completely rebuilt, with cells, at a cost of £650. This remained in use as the town police station until 1943, when the Isle of Wight force was once more merged with the Hampshire Constabulary. It is now used as a probation office. The succeeding divisional police headquarters in Fairlee Road was built in the eighties. From 1890 to 1943 it served as the office of the Chief Constable of the Isle of Wight, and since 1943 as the Isle of Wight Divisional Headquarters. At the end of 1963 a new divisional headquarters building was completed.

In Cowes the first police station was at Sun Hill, and there is a reference to this effect in the *Post Office Directory* of 1867. This station continued to be used until 1900, when a new county police station was opened, and the latter still serves as the headquarters of the Cowes Sub-Division. The first police station in Ryde was situated in Newport Road, and was used by the county constabulary. The present station is in Station Street, and was formerly used by the Ryde Borough

15   Lymington Police Station, built 1952.

Police and the Isle of Wight Constabulary. In 1890 the site for Sandown Police Station was purchased for £210, and in the following year the Isle of Wight County Council approved a tender of £1,065 for the erection of the present police station in St John's Road. In December 1892 the Chief Constable of the Isle of Wight reported to the Standing Joint Committee that he had taken possession of this station. Ventnor gained a new police station in 1861 for the use of the Hampshire Constabulary, and in 1884 additions costing £363 8s. were made to it: a dormitory for the constables, a guard room, cleaning room, pantry and privy were among the facilities provided. In 1940 this station was destroyed by enemy action. A temporary station was set up in St Catherine's House in Ventnor, and later this building was purchased by the police authorities and is still used as the police station today. Shanklin gained its first proper police station only in September 1951. On the 28th of that month a new building was opened by Mr Acheson Webb, the Chairman of the Isle of Wight County Council, and since then has been the headquarters of the Shanklin Sub-Division. In earlier days there had been no police station as such, and police business had been carried on at the house of the resident constable or sergeant. The station at Yarmouth, again, is very new. It was occupied in September 1966, and incorporates a sergeant's office, an enquiry office, an interview room, a detention room, and a flat for the resident constable. This building replaces the old station dating from before 1890 which was demolished in 1965.

16   Modern Division Headquarters, Havant, 1964.

One of the newest police stations in the county is that at Andover, which was officially opened on 30 September 1959 by Colonel J.B. Scott, Chairman of the Hampshire and Isle of Wight Police Authority. The ceremony was attended by senior police officers and county and civic dignitaries, including Sir William Johnson, C.M.G., C.B.E., one of Her Majesty's Inspectors of Constabulary, Mr R.D. Lemon, C.B.E., the chief constable, Mr A.J. Broomfield, the assistant chief constable, and Mr Alan Lubbock, Chairman of the Hampshire County Council. In his address Colonel Scott recalled the history of the police in Andover which went back before 1846, when there had taken place a consolidation between the Andover Borough Police Force, consisting of one sergeant and four constables, and the county force. He referred also to the old police station in Andover, which had been taken over as such in 1857. Before that date, it had been the town gaol: in this the history of the Andover police buildings falls into a familiar pattern.

An interesting old building with a strong police connection, as indicated by its name, is The Old Police House at Kimpton. It was built in 1610 of brick and flintstones, and has a thatched roof. The wood used in its construction is old ship's timbers. This house, along with many others in the village, was at one time owned by the local squire, a Colonel Randolph, who lived in Kimpton Manor. Before the early sixties there were no policemen stationed in the village;

because of the rowdyism of troops stationed near by, Colonel Randolph sold the house to the police authority so that there should be a constable in the village. Three constables in turn occupied the house, and then in July 1910 a mounted man, P.C. Swash, was transferred there. He kept his horse in the stables of the *New Inn*, close at hand. Swash retired from the force in 1920 but continued to live at the Old Police House, which he at first rented, and then in 1925 bought from the police authority. His married daughter, Mrs Marchant, still lives there. In 1966 a new police cottage was provided.

The Hampshire and Isle of Wight Constabulary of the last third of the 20th century, on the eve of amalgamation into an even bigger police unit, may well seem a far cry from the Hampshire force of earlier days. In an elaborate organisation, equipped with all sorts of technical apparatus, and increasingly involved in many of the problems of an extremely complex and mobile society, there might seem little place for the individual eccentricities which were so rich a feature of the Hampshire Police in the Victorian era. We seem a world away from such incidents as that which used to be an annual event at the village of Selborne when, on one Sunday during the hop-picking season, the gypsies would gather together and fight the local inhabitants. Everyone participated joyfully. On one occasion the village constable, carried away by excitement, joined in, and ultimately had to be rescued by some powerful villagers, but not before he had sustained such injuries that he had subsequently to be invalided out of the force. Another vivid and masterful member of the force last century was a Police Constable Pope, who was stationed at Alton. During the hop-picking season, again, he had his own method of dealing with the gypsies. He was a very strong individual, and would advance upon the *Three Horse Shoes* at Worldham, arming himself on the

17   Modern Police House, 1967.

way with a stick cut from the hedge. Choosing his moment, he would then beat the gypsies out of the inn with his stick, finish up their beer, and return to Alton in a very happy mood. All such anecdotes of these days reflect the life of a society still centred overwhelmingly on the villages, each one possessing its own strong sense of identity. A new constable having been stationed at East Meon, he was accepted as a member of the community only after he had been baptised in the stream, while another policeman made himself unpopular at Bishop's Waltham, and was thrown into the pond. The local parson objected to this action, and was promptly thrown in too. A file of the Hampshire Regiment had to be sent from Winchester to calm things down. About all these episodes there hangs the same air of rustic horseplay. Before the amalgamation of the Romsey Borough Force with the Hampshire Constabulary in 1876, the Head Constable of Romsey and the officer in charge of the Hampshire Constabulary in Romsey Hundred took great delight in locking each other up when drunk on the other's territory.

Less rumbustious recollections of the life of the police at the end of the last century have been furnished by Mrs A. Pink, an old lady who is the daughter of that Superintendent Julius Sillence who served in the Hampshire Constabulary from 1871 to 1906, and who from 1895 until the end of his service was deputy chief constable. From 1881 Mrs Pink lived with her father in Winchester. At Westhill she was close to the prison, and she remembers that when murderers were executed a bell was tolled, and that on one given day the bell sounded three times. It was the superintendent's duty to attend executions and when he removed the rope from one man's neck he was startled when the corpse gave a great exhalation of breath, and for a moment the police officer thought that the man was not dead.

The superintendent kept two or three horses at Westhill and was responsible for buying all the horses for the constabulary. Periodically, too, weights and measures were checked at Westhill, and Mrs Pink remembers that at such times the yard and nearby roads were often packed with the horse-drawn vehicles of tradesmen bringing their scales for checking. The quality of food and petroleum was also periodically tested. Her mother, Mrs Sillence, was apparently held in great esteem, and constables with problems would come to her for advice, and sometimes for her intercession with her husband, the superintendent. In this they were not always successful. One of Mrs Sillence's tasks was to search female prisoners. On the other hand, one of her more pleasant activities was to organise outings for constables and their families to places of interest in the county, and these journeys were always undertaken in a procession of carts, crowded with everyone who could possibly attend. As a child, Mrs Pink was often taken by her mother to visit constables' cottages. The whole picture is of a leisurely and even-paced way of life, in which individuals depended on themselves and each other for entertainment and assistance. Then, as always, the members of the force relied immensely on their wives and families for comfort and support. At times, too, the wives of police officers gave direct help to their husbands' colleagues, in work of a kind which in later years might have fallen to women police. About 1906 a Mrs Moody and another officer's wife were sent to a house in Bournemouth, which was a suspected brothel, to find evidence of any disorderly conduct. In this respect they failed, and merely succeeded in having their fortunes told by a rather doubtful character, who among other revelations foretold that Mrs Moody would marry a seafaring man. At this time Mrs Moody was not only married to Police Constable Moody, but was expecting her first child!

Mr Sillence himself, who had a distinguished police career, and had been the central figure in many dramatic episodes in the 19th century, made some interesting observations in 1906 about the changes in uniform that had come about in his time. 'When I joined we wore a curious hat something like a shako with a shiny top and two shiny bands, one on each side. We wore long tunics. In 1872 we were served out with helmets, and with them short tunics with white piping. With the long tunic we used to wear heavy overcoats with collars which nearly enveloped one's head when they were turned up and which when turned down sat in a stiff thick fold over the shoulders. Now we have a decided improvement of that pattern. The uniform is now much neater than it was then. Another alteration is the serving out of serge tunics for the summer.' By the time of the First World War helmets were worn during the winter months from 1 October until 9 May, and in the summer period a pill-box type peak cap was worn which had a knob in the centre, with a white cover which was removed in inclement weather. In wet weather gaiters were worn with the trousers overlapping the top of the gaiters, which were laced up; for those officers that used cycles, serge was worn with breast pockets, and, in wet weather, puttees. Greatcoats were of the closed neck type. Officers on foot duty wore dress type serge with no breast pockets, but instead two pockets just below the belt at the back. The belt worn had a rose and crown buckle with the words 'County of So'ton', and a sling was worn on the side of the belt for carrying the cape. The numerals on the epaulettes were in white piping. The badge on the helmet was in the form of a rose and crown with the letters 'H.C.C.' in the centre. The dress type serge ceased by 1923, but the serge with white piping and numerals continued in use for some years thereafter.

The uniform of the Hampshire Constabulary may indeed have altered over the years, and the nature of the community which the force serves may have changed profoundly, at least in certain areas and in some respects. We have seen the long process whereby, over more than a century and a quarter, the Hampshire police evolved under the leadership of a series of remarkable men to become one of the largest and most distinguished county forces in the kingdom. We have seen too how, since the Second World War, the hitherto undifferentiated organisation of the force has developed a number of specialist departments, such as the Traffic Division, the C.I.D., women police and cadets. Above all, we have seen how the whole pace of life has quickened, and how varied, unremitting and unrelenting have become the demands on the police service. But the essential work of policing continues without pause. Now as always this work has hinged on the character of the individual police officer, who has so often brought to his activities high qualities of good humour and humanity. Of this last there are innumerable examples. In several cases of emergency police constables have acted successfully as midwives. In January 1929 one officer was on night duty in Bournemouth, in bitterly cold weather, when he was informed that a man clad only in a shirt was sitting out on a flat roof, with his legs hanging over the edge. The unfortunate individual turned out to be suffering from delirium tremens. With patience and skill the policeman spoke to him, and got him back to bed, and ultimately he recovered. Another characteristic humanitarian act occurred a few years earlier. A police constable, suffering from a heavy cold, was on his way to Droxford to report sick. As he was passing a farm near the River Meon, he was called by farm labourers to the river where a man was trying to drown himself. Notwithstanding his own illness, the constable immediately plunged into the water, fully dressed, and eventually succeeded in saving the would-be suicide. Soaked to the skin, the policeman returned home, but was pleasantly surprised the next day to find his cold had completely gone. Such gallant efforts have been far from rare; also, as we have seen, the annals of the Hampshire Constabulary are rich with humour, which has so often lubricated the necessary discipline of the service. Such anecdotes as we have noted could be matched with countless others, which are told and retold by members of the force. They play their part in creating tradition and maintaining *esprit de corps*. They serve also to remind us that while the Hampshire Constabulary is greater than any of the individuals who have served in it, it is the admirable character of these same individuals which has enabled the force to operate over the years with both humanity and efficiency, and thus secure the respect of the community. Perhaps ex-Sergeant J.B. Woodley, who joined the Hampshire Constabulary in 1898, speaks for all members of the force in saying: 'It was a hard life, but we were contented and proud of our job, as we were much respected by the public as a whole.'

On 1 April 1967, the Hampshire and Isle of Wight Constabulary was to end its separate existence, on amalgamation with the forces of Portsmouth and Southampton. The roots of English police are indeed local. Now the size and nature of the locality may be changing, and the claims of a wider loyalty becoming imperative. But the need for an intimate understanding of its own territory on the part of the force concerned, and for co-operation between police and public, remains as vital as ever. Only thus can the Queen's Peace be maintained. In the ceaseless struggle to uphold and strengthen the rule of law in England, the Hampshire Constabulary has played a long, a proud, and an historic part.

Index